# THE SINGING CREEK
# WHERE THE
# WILLOWS GROW

Opal Whiteley

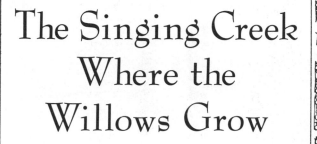

# The Singing Creek Where the Willows Grow

### THE REDISCOVERED DIARY OF
### OPAL WHITELEY

presented by
## BENJAMIN HOFF

TICKNOR & FIELDS
NEW YORK
1986

Library of Congress Cataloging-in-Publication Data

Whiteley, Opal Stanley.
The singing creek where the willows grow.

"The portion of Opal Whiteley's diary printed herein was originally published in 1920 under the title The story of Opal" — Verso t.p.
Bibliography: p.
1. Whiteley, Opal Stanley — Diaries.   2. Authors, American — 20th century — Diaries.   3. Children's writings, American — Oregon.   4. Oregon — Social life and customs.
I. Hoff, Benjamin, 1946-     .   II. Whiteley, Opal Stanley.   Story of Opal.   III. Title.
PS3545.H625Z47   1986      818'.5203 [B]      86-5915
ISBN 0-89919-444-3

Printed in the United States of America

S  10  9  8  7  6  5  4  3  2  1

The portion of Opal Whiteley's diary printed herein was originally published in 1920 under the title *The Story of Opal*. Punctuation, paragraph division, and chapter titles in this edition are Benjamin Hoff's.

The author is grateful for permission to quote from the following works:

*Fabulous Opal Whiteley* by Elbert Bede. Binford & Mort Publishing, 1954. Reprinted by permission of the publisher.

*Opal Whiteley: The Unsolved Mystery* by E. S. Bradburne. Reprinted by permission of The Bodley Head, Ltd., for and on behalf of Putnam and Company.

"I Shall Come Back," from *Shoes of the Wind* by Hilda Conkling. Frederick A. Stokes Company, 1922. Reprinted by permission of the author.

"Stopping by Woods on a Snowy Evening," from *The Poetry of Robert Frost* edited by Edward Connery Lathem. Copyright 1923, © 1969 by Holt, Rinehart and Winston. Copyright 1951 by Robert Frost. Reprinted by permission of Henry Holt and Company.

"Mysterious Oregon Author Stirred 1920 Literary World" by Lorna Larson, from *Old Oregon* (June 1949); and "Opal Whiteley: A Princess in Fairyland" by Inez Fortt, from *Old Oregon* (May-June 1969).

For Sadie McKibben,
    Dear Love & Her Husband,
and The Man Who Wears Gray Neckties
    And Is Kind To Mice

B. H.

I shall be coming back to you
From seas, rivers, sunny meadows,
   glens that hold secrets:
I shall come back with my hands full
Of light and flowers . . .
I shall bring back things I have picked up,
Traveling this road or the other,
Things found by the sea or in the pinewood.
There will be a pine-cone in my pocket,
Grains of pink sand between my fingers.
I shall tell you of a golden pheasant's
   feather . . .
Will you know me?

from
"I Shall Come Back"
Hilda Conkling (age ten), 1922

# CONTENTS

# MAGICAL
## OPAL
## WHITELEY

ONE SUMMER MORNING IN 1983, I was looking for a book on a shelf of the local public library. I was about to reach for it when I noticed the one next to it, and pulled that out, instead — an old, worn volume entitled *The Story of Opal: The Journal of an Understanding Heart.*

As the introduction explained, it concerned a little girl named Opal Whiteley, who had lived in Oregon around the turn of the century. It seemed to consist of part of a diary she had written. I glanced through the book. It looked appealing. It had a haunting, time-arresting quality, like the sound of a music box. And it seemed to have something more. I checked *The Story of Opal* out and took it home.

A few days later, at ten o'clock in the morning, I began to read it. At two-thirty the next morning, I finished the last page, closed the book, and looked out at the trees in the moonlight for a long time. For over sixteen hours, I had been following in the footsteps of a communicative genius, the likes of whom I had never before encountered. And now that the experience was over, it seemed much too short. I didn't want it to end. I decided that I was going to find out more about Opal Whiteley and learn why her book, an American classic if there ever was one, had apparently been forgotten.

As I was soon to discover, *The Story of Opal* had been an immediate success on its publication in 1920. But one year later, it was out of print. The public had come to suspect literary fraud. Opal's diary referred to her "angel parents" — her original parents, she said, who had died when she was about four years old. But Opal Whiteley was

3

not an orphan. Her family had proof enough of that. The diary contained many French names for flowers, animals, birds, and geographic features (her Angel Father was, she claimed, a French naturalist). But she apparently hadn't studied French as a child. It also included names of mythological and historic figures. But at the time that Opal was supposed to have written the diary, she was a little girl in an Oregon logging settlement. In some passages, Latin liturgical phrases were mentioned. But she was not a Catholic.

The public was even less inclined to believe what Opal claimed to have written as a child when it became apparent that no one in her own family seemed to believe or understand her. As her grandmother put it in a newspaper interview in 1920:

> She was always a queer girl — a great hand to ask questions. She nearly worried Lizzie, her mother, to death asking questions about all sorts of things at all sorts of times. . . . When she wasn't chattering or asking questions, or reading or writing, she would be looking at nothing with big eyes, in what some people call a brown study, but what I call inattention and absentmindedness. . . . She used to have such queer fancies about the wind and the trees and the stars talking to her. . . .
>
> I never did understand her, and switching didn't seem to make her any different. She would climb up in a big evergreen over the pigpen, and get to studying about something, and drop out of the tree into the mud. Lizzie would spank her or switch her, or if Lizzie wasn't feeling up to it, I would. I would talk to her, and she would look right at me, as solemn as an owl; and then, when I was all through, I would say, "Will you remember what I have said?" She would say, "I was thinking of something else. What did you say?" And I would have to spank her all over again. She certainly was a trial.

Considering these difficulties, and the passage of almost eighty years since she had supposedly begun the diary printed in *The Story of Opal*, how could *I* expect to discover whether or not it really was her childhood diary — and, if so, why she had written what she did? But I was determined to do just that.

The more I examined the enormous amount of material written about Opal Whiteley, the more I realized how unknown she had been, in spite of — and *because* of — her once great notoriety. The more I learned about her from people associated with her past, the more I felt impelled to write about her fascinating life. I soon realized that, although the research methods I had once used as an investigative reporter would provide the facts necessary for such a presentation, the facts by themselves were not going to bring me to an understanding of Opal's enigmatic character. So as I worked, I immersed myself in an atmosphere created from whatever I could find that related to her, including letters, photographs, and even particular pieces of music. In the process, I became acquainted with someone very special. And bit by bit, facts that had seemed confused and contradictory at first began to arrange themselves in a clear pattern, and an extraordinary story began to emerge.

Opal Irene Whiteley was born on December 11, 1897, in Colton, Washington. Shortly before her fifth birthday, the family moved to Wendling, Oregon. A year later, they moved to Walden, a logging community near the rapidly growing mill town of Cottage Grove, in the southern end of Oregon's Willamette Valley. There, in the latter half of her sixth year, Opal began to write a diary, which she kept in a hollow log in the nearby forest. In it she described her

*Opal, around* 1902
(University of Oregon Library)

home, her animal friends, her cathedral area among the trees, and "the singing creek where the willows grow."

Using her own phonetic form of spelling, she printed with crayons on pieces of scrap paper a neighbor woman brought her. The crayons were left for her in a secret place in the woods, where she would leave notes asking the fairies for more "color pencils" to write with. To make the most of each piece of paper, she used both sides, printing to the edge of the page, carrying unfinished words over to the next line. Her diary began:

TODATHEFOA
KSRGONAW
AFRUMTHEH
OWSEWEDO
LIVINTHARG
ONALITULWAA
WATOTHERAN
CHHOWSEWH

Today the folks are gone away from the house we do live in. They are gone a little way away, to the ranch house where the grandpa does live. I sit on our steps, and I do print. I like it, this house we do live in, being at the edge of the near woods. So many little people do live in the near woods. I do have conversations with them.

According to Opal's family, she was able to form words from primers at the age of three. At five, she entered school, the youngest child in the community to do so. She passed two grade levels her first year at Walden. Her father and friends said that she was "always writing."

Now teacher is looking very straight looks at me. She says, "Opal, put that away." I so do.

*"The mamma and the papa,"*
*Ed and Lizzie Whiteley, around 1900*
(University of Oregon Library)

*"The ranch house where the grandpa does live"*
(University of Oregon Library)

Instructors and classmates remembered her for her small size, her modest, quiet nature, her ability to observe and reason from her observations, her shining eyes, her eagerness to learn, and her tendency to daydream.

I was quite late to school. Teacher made me stand in the corner, to get my lesson with my face to the wall. I didn't mind that at all. There was a window in that part of the wall. It was near the corner. I looked looks at my book, sometimes. Most of the times, I looked looks out the window. I had seeing of little plant folks just peeping out of the earth to see what they could see. I did have thinks it would be nice to be one of them, and then grow up and have a flower, and bees a-coming, and seed-children at falltime. I have thinks this is a very interest world to live in. There is so much to see out the window when teacher does have one to stand in the corner to study one's lessons.

The teacher at Walden's one-room schoolhouse would read aloud to her second-year class from Greek mythology. Then her students would write down what they could remember. After she had corrected their errors, they would print the stories into their composition books. This early exposure to legendary heroes seems to have provided the foundation for Opal's interest in classical names, which she applied to her favorite animals and trees, much to the amazement of people around her.

Her curiosity appeared insatiable. As a friend put it, "She overflowed with energy and enthusiasm, particularly to be learning something new all the time. She absorbed knowledge like a sponge." She read every book in the house, and every book the neighbors had. A younger sister recalled Opal reading to her as a child, from one of Opal's favorite books. From it, she said, Opal took many of the names for her companions. The book was Thomas Babington Macaulay's *Lays of Ancient Rome*:

Lars Porsena of Clusium
  By the Nine Gods he swore
That the great house of Tarquin
  Should suffer wrong no more.

. . . . . . . . . . . . . . . . . .

Alone stood brave Horatius,
  But constant still in mind;
Thrice thirty thousand foes before,
  And the broad flood behind.


In addition to reading as though each opportunity were her last, Opal questioned family members, friends, and everyone she met. According to her father, she would sit up until late at night, asking about one subject after another. She carefully listened and observed. Acquaintances remembered that by the time she was six, she talked like a grownup. Her few human friends tended to be young adults, such as those she called "Dear Love and her husband," a newly married couple; "the girl who has no seeing," a blind girl who lived down the road; and "the man who wears gray neckties and is kind to mice," a worker at the nearby lumber mill. Her usual companions, though, were Thomas Chatterton Jupiter Zeus, "that most dear velvety wood-rat"; Lars Porsena of Clusium, "that very wise crow"; and Brave Horatius, "such a lovely dog."

Whatever time Opal could spare from her chores was spent on long walks through the woods. There, she made friends wherever she went. Her father claimed that she could tame any creature in the forest. A childhood companion recalled that "the birds and butterflies came to her, and sat in her hand."

Although she associated mostly with animals and adults, she was very fond of younger children. They, in turn, were fascinated by her. They gathered around her, and followed her as she walked. A woman who had spent her summers near the Whiteleys starting when she was about six, and Opal twelve, recalled:

It was pure joy to be with Opal. I have never forgotten my summers with her. To her I owe my love of nature. Through her I learned to see beauty in everything.

When she was a little girl, Opal dreamed of someday writing books for children about the inhabitants of the field and forest. As she grew older, the dream became a driving force, powered by her observation that juvenile scientific publications of the time tended to be either dry or condescending and provided little inspiration for the majority of their readers — and without inspiration, the knowledge they offered was not willingly absorbed. She often expressed the desire to learn as much as she could of what she saw around her, in order to better communicate its value to others. To that end, she applied ever increasingly refined methods of gathering, organizing, and memorizing information.

Coinciding with her love for the natural world was her love of religion, which had been in evidence since the beginning of her school days. Accounts were given of Opal and her younger sister Pearl sitting quietly in Sunday School at the Cottage Grove Christian Church, their legs dangling from the pew. When called upon, little Opal would stand up, walk to the front of the church, recite passage after passage of the Scriptures from memory, then return to her place and sit down, leaving the rest of the children awestruck. Some Cottage Grove residents claimed that she had memorized the Bible from cover to cover at an early age. Her familiarity with the language of the King James Version is reflected in much of the wording of her diary.

When she was eight, Opal joined the local chapter of Junior Christian Endeavor, a fundamentalist religious organization concerned with encouraging social growth and spiritual awareness among young people in isolated areas. At the time, the Whiteleys were living at Star, a logging community in the hills east of Cottage Grove. It was there, in behalf of the Junior Endeavor program, that Opal's organized teaching efforts began, at the age of thirteen. In an interview in 1920, the man who had been president of the parent organization, Oregon Christian Endeavor, recalled:

> I met Opal first at a Christian Endeavor convention at Cottage Grove in 1911. During my address, I noticed a dark-haired little girl, not over twelve or thirteen years old, whose big black eyes never left mine. . . . I could not help but notice her rapt expression. I spoke to the young people about the great need of developing the junior societies. I compared the children with flowers that God had planted in the great outdoors. At the close of the meeting, this little black-eyed girl, with her mother, came up to see me. She told me of her love for nature. She seemed preternaturally bright and precocious. Her interest was so great that I at once picked her out as a future C.E. worker. I told her to gather the children together in her neighborhood of Star, Oregon, and teach them about nature.

Opal soon gained a reputation as a teacher of the forest and its ways. Parents from the nearby logging camps brought their children to listen to her. The then editor of the Cottage Grove *Sentinel* later described a talk Opal gave when she was about thirteen, in a two-room makeshift museum of natural history. Specimens covered the walls of both rooms, he wrote, as well as a number of tables. Opal described the butterflies, moths, and rocks in the collection, giving their names in Latin as well as in English, without a glance at the labels. She told about their physical characteristics, their personalities, and the lessons they were able to teach to those who studied them.

In spite of Opal's Junior Endeavor affiliation, her personal form of religion seemed to have more in common with that practiced by Saint Francis of Assisi than with the usual small-town fundamentalism — or, for that matter, with any other known variety of Christianity. She expressed no desire to preach the gospel to anyone. Instead, she wanted to interest children in the spiritual power at work in the world around them, and in the messages it passed along to those who watched and listened. "God made the out-of-doors," she replied to an inquirer. "You learn to love Him when you understand His handiwork and His creatures."

On Sundays, and sometimes during the week in the twilight hour, Opal took the logging-camp children to her cathedral in the forest. There, moss carpeted the ground, delicate wildflowers lined the aisles, and huge trees towered protectingly above. More flowers grew on the altar, which was formed from earth and stones. The children sat on moss-covered logs and listened to the singing of birds in the treetops. "We sometimes did not talk at all," said Opal.

A woman who had been involved in Junior Endeavor work recalled:

> She didn't just read the Bible, as the other leaders did, and then have [the children] sing and recite verses. She told stories. I remember one time the lesson was about the Resurrection, and she told us all about how, just as a person is buried, a seed is buried, and how from the seed there comes later a beautiful flower, and how death is not really death but being born into a new environment. Then she told about the caterpillars she had gathered, and how they went to sleep in their cocoons and were reborn as butterflies. She always taught by stories and illustrations like that, and the children wouldn't stir, they were so interested.

Another woman described Opal's talk at a regional Junior Endeavor conference in Portland: "Her voice filled the room . . . as she spoke about God being everywhere, and how every little creature, plant, and tree in the woods bore testimony to His presence. The audience was spellbound."

The same witness described Opal's contrasting personality prior to the meeting: "At dinner, Opal contributed nothing to the conversation. She answered in mono-syllables, and she sat very quietly, her eyes on her plate."

It seems that from an early age, Opal exhibited signs of what would now be known as schizophrenic behavior. Her frequently strange conduct was apparently intensified by her tendency to eat poorly, deny herself food, or simply forget about meals — all of which she tended to do more and more as she grew older. People called her "a loner" — "shy" — "withdrawn" — "different." They also called her "a charmer" — "warm" — "very affectionate" — "the first to offer help." Both sets of descriptions fit her fluctuating personality. Today, orthomolecular treatment of schizophrenia is attaining impressive results, through approaching the illness as a biochemical malfunction and nutritional imbalance, rather than as a purely mental condition. But at the time, no such therapy existed.

This day — it was a lonely day. I did have longings all its hours, for Angel Mother and Angel Father. In-between times all day at school, I did print messages for them on gray leaves I did gather on the way to school. I did tell on the leaves the longings I was having.

One of the strangest manifestations of Opal's schizophrenia was her intermittently stated claim that she was not, in fact, Opal Whiteley. Beginning in her grammar school days, Opal expressed to several people her belief that she was an adopted child, and that her real parents were of different nationality from the Whiteleys. They used to take her on walks, she said, and teach her to observe what was around her. She said her mother encouraged her to write down what she saw, and told her stories from history; her father talked to her of animals and plants, and showed her how to compare the appearances of things. Opal eventually claimed that when she was about four years old, her father died on an expedition in a faraway country, and her mother drowned in a boating accident. After that, she said, she was taken on a long journey and substituted for the original Opal, who had just died. She declared the substitution had been made as Mrs. Whiteley and her first two daughters, Opal and Pearl, were traveling to Wendling (preceding Mr. Whiteley, who was concluding his business in Colton).

Her story seems to have had several variations, each of which changed in detail as the years went by. In one version, she maintained that the two girls had been exchanged in the hospital shortly after the original Opal was born.

According to Opal, her real name was Françoise, and her real father was the naturalist Henri d'Orléans, a prince of the French royal family of Bourbon. Although the woman she claimed as her real mother was a rather shadowy figure in her earliest accounts, in time she was able to describe her as Prince Henri's cousin, Princess Marie — who, said Opal, had been married to the prince in a secret ceremony. Later still, Opal was to claim that her angel mother was an Austrian archduchess, and that she had not drowned, after all.

Fantasy though it was, her angel parent story had a historic foundation. In August 1901, when Opal would have been nearly four, Henri d'Orléans died at the end of an expedition through India and Indochina. Opal somehow learned of the incident, and began an infatuation with the naturalist's life and the land he had explored and loved. In an account of her childhood printed in the Cottage Grove *Sentinel* in 1915, she wrote:

One of my pet hobbies . . . was to be a missionary to India. I thought much of this, and often told my school mates that when I should become grown up, I was going away over to India. Everything I could find out about India was either clipped out of the papers and pasted in a little book I kept especially for that purpose, or was copied in this book.

No one in the community seems to have placed much faith in Opal's tale of adoption. She bore an obvious resemblance to the other Whiteleys; she looked exactly like the Opal in photographs taken before the alleged substitution; she remembered people, animals, events, and objects from the town of Colton; and she spoke no French, which she would have, if she had been raised as she claimed.

Some people from outside the community wondered about her story, though, for she was intellectually unlike the rest of her family, and was the only one of the Whiteleys with a strong love of the natural world. One or two of these people claimed to have heard Mrs. Whiteley say that Opal was not her daughter — something she was recorded as having said from time to time about her other children as well, when in an irritable mood, but something that her other children apparently did not take seriously.

At least to a certain extent, Opal appears to have based the characters of her angel parents on what she saw as the positive side of her real parents, primarily her father, whom she knew best. And she appears to have based the diary's shallow Mr. and Mrs. Whiteley ("the papa" and "the mamma") on what she saw as their *negative* side — which may explain why "the papa" is hardly mentioned, for Opal was known to have adored her father from her earliest childhood. It may also help to explain the many unpleasant references to "the mamma," considering that Opal as a child seems to have seen her mother primarily as the family disciplinarian.

Today in the morning, when the mamma was in the other room, I did take down from its hook the papa's big coat. I did put it onto me, and it did trail away out behind. I like to wear the papa's big coat. Jenny Strong, who comes to visit us, says the reason I like to wear the papa's big coat is because it makes me more grown-up. She's wrong. The reason I like to wear the papa's big coat is because it has pockets in it — *big* ones — nice ones to put toads and mice and caterpillars and beetles in. *That's* why I like to wear the papa's coat. Why, when I go walking in the papa's big coat, nearly the whole nursery can go along!

This morning, just as I was making a start out the door to the nursery, the mamma came into the kitchen. She did hurry to the door, and I did hurry out — but she caught me by the end of the coat. She did get that coat off of me in a quick way. She hung it back on its nail. When it was hung on its nail in the proper way, she gave to me a shoulder-shake. And I did go to feed the chickens.

Opal's father, Charles Edward ("Ed") Whiteley, worked in the woods around Cottage Grove as logger and foreman for various lumber companies. His French Canadian lineage included some North American Indian ancestry, which was reflected in Opal's facial features and dark complexion. He was said to have been a gentle, quiet man with a flair for telling stories. Although, like his wife, he displayed little interest in wildlife, he was very fond of Opal and provided space for her studies and collections, which at one time filled two rooms of the house.

Opal's mother, Mary Elizabeth Scott Whiteley, spent much time reading to her children from collections of poetry and fairy tales. "Lizzie" Whiteley was known as a kind, sensitive woman who encouraged Opal's love of art, music, writing, history, and drama. Apparently, Opal was not close to her mother in her early years, but gradually became so. The only point of disagreement between them seems to have been Opal's devotion to natural science, which Mrs. Whiteley considered excessive, and which she allegedly opposed as contrary to her plans for Opal's future as a home-maker.

Another possible source for the characters of Opal's angel parents was her uncle, Henry Pearson, a miner and self-taught naturalist who entertained his young niece whenever he came visiting with accounts of the animals and birds he had tamed and rescued, as well as with imaginary stories about their lives. In addition to mentioning him in her diary, Opal seems to have included him in a semiautobiographical short story she wrote at nineteen, in which a girl is introduced to wildflowers and birds by her uncle, who instead of attending social functions, "preferred to roam over the hills and through the meadows."

When Opal was about thirteen years old, two of her acquaintances were visiting a mutual friend, when she came running to the house with a large hatbox in her arms and tears streaming down her face. Her younger sister Faye had found her diary and had torn it to pieces, she told them. (According to several witnesses, including one of Opal's teachers, this sister habitually destroyed things belonging to Opal, in particular her books and wildlife illustrations.) Her friends examined the torn pages. They later described what they had seen: childish printing on pieces of wrapping paper, grocery bags, and envelopes. It was at this friend's house that Opal stored the mutilated pages of the diary that for seven years had been her closest companion.

In 1915, when Opal was seventeen, a Christian Endeavor field secretary visited her community of Star on an inspection trip. While there, he observed Opal's work among children and the elderly. Astounded by what he saw, he returned to the organization's headquarters and delivered a glowing report. Soon after, the president of Oregon Christian Endeavor invited Opal to speak at the annual state convention in Eugene, twenty miles north of Cottage Grove. In his words, "She was a knockout. She captured the convention. Every delegate . . . sat up and took notice of this little mountain girl who had such perfect self-possession and who was so absolutely at ease in her talk."

At the convention, she was elected chairman of the committee on resolutions. Then, impressed by her enthusiasm, eloquence, and organizational skills, the delegates elected her state superintendent of Junior Christian Endeavor.

The position as she redefined and recreated it required continual travel and speechmaking, and eventually involved supervision of the programs of 3,400 young people. By all accounts, she excelled at it. Prior to her election, Junior Endeavor had fifteen societies, or chapters, in Oregon. In two years of her leadership, the number of societies had risen to one hundred, with a gain of over three thousand members.

After the convention, Opal stayed with an aunt in Eugene for a week. Due to a deficiency of credits caused by her many activities, she had not yet graduated from high school, in spite of her early progress. But she decided to visit the University of Oregon while she was in the city, to examine the school's natural history collections and ask the professors some questions. The Eugene *Daily Guard* described the reaction:

> Tutored by nature, a tiny seventeen-year-old mountain girl, her hair down her back, has opened the eyes of the Eugene teaching profession and left it gasping for breath. Educated by herself in the forests of the Cascade Mountains, she has made a college education appear artificial and insignificant, university officials admit. In three days, she became the talk of the faculty of three educational institutions. Entrance rules have been cast aside; scholarships are proposed; a home was found for her in Eugene — everything has been done to keep her here.
>
> "This experience happens to a university but once in a generation," declared Warren D. Smith, head of the university geological department. "She knows more about geology than do many students that have graduated from my department. She may become one of the greatest minds Oregon ever has produced. She will be an investment for the university."
>
> "She is a travesty on our educational system," explained A. B. Sweetser, head of the botany department. "Is all our great system wasted, is it hindering normal development?"

Despite the faculty's initial optimism, however, entrance rules remained inflexible and only a small scholarship was approved. During the spring and summer of 1915, Opal worked to earn money for her education, and took correspondence courses from the university. The following school year, she finished high school in Eugene, commuting from the family's new home in nearby Springfield. In the fall of 1916, she enrolled as a freshman at the University of Oregon.

In addition to attending an initial twelve credit hours of classes — in which she earned two "Honor" grades, one "Superior," and two "Mediums" — she spent her spare moments studying in the university museum and library. "Every moment on this earth is too precious to waste," she remarked to someone at the time. She was said to have borrowed more books than anyone in the history of the school. She read them while she ate, pacing restlessly back and forth; she read them as she walked — or ran — to class; she read them while perched in trees. As she had since her early school days, she acquired other publications from teachers, acquaintances, and various organizations.

Professors and classmates remembered her as a shy but friendly, refreshingly feminine young woman who liked ruffles and full dresses, but who had a disconcerting tendency to dash out of the classroom in pursuit of butterflies. The university president's wife once came upon Opal on her knees, singing. In front of her, apparently enjoying the attention, was an earthworm.

In the spring of 1917, Opal was chosen to represent Oregon at the national Christian Endeavor convention in New York City in July. She sent away for travel folders, and made detailed preparations for the trip. But it was never taken. Late in May, following a long illness with cancer, her mother died. At nearly the same time, Leonidas Scott, Opal's grandfather, died. When she returned from the services in Washington, Opal showed little interest in the planned convention trip. She also showed little interest in maintaining contact with the rest of her family.

*Superintendent of
Oregon Junior Endeavor,
1917*
(University of
Oregon Library)

*A dramatic pose for
Hollywood, 1918*
(Massachusetts
Historical Society)

Apparently, the attitude was mutual. The Whiteleys had been shocked by her seeming lack of grief over her mother's death. On Mrs. Whiteley's last day, Opal's grandmother had asked Opal to stay home to say goodbye to her mother. "No, I must go to school," she sadly replied, and resolutely walked out the door. She later expressed her sorrow in letters to friends, and often carried flowers to her mother's grave, a few miles south of Eugene. According to a Christian Endeavor couple with whom Opal sometimes stayed on her travels, she would awaken night after night, calling out to her mother. But the family avoided her more and more.

Distracted from her schoolwork during the spring semester by her tremendous efforts in behalf of the Junior Endeavor program, and then by the death of her mother and grandfather, Opal had accumulated five "incompletes," thereby losing her eligibility for a scholarship. During the summer of 1917, she traveled throughout Oregon, giving lectures to finance her second year at the university. Posters pictured her in an angelic white dress, holding some butterflies, with her dark, loosely braided hair hanging down below her waist. Her lecture titles included "In the Woods," "In the Fields," and (her favorite) "Nearer to the Heart of Nature." In order to allow people of limited means to attend her talks, she insisted that the admission charge be no more than ten cents, regardless of where she was speaking. In July, as a one-day participant in the Chautauqua adult education program, she spoke on the birds and flowers of the Pacific Northwest before an audience of three thousand at Gladstone.

Opal began her second college year in the fall and attended for six months, until the money she had earned from odd jobs and lecturing ran out. She lived by herself in a small house on the edge of the campus, which she quickly filled with an estimated sixteen thousand specimens of natural history. A new interest in genealogy prompted her to change her middle name from Irene to Stanley when she discovered a titled ancestor in the Stanley branch of her

# OUT OF DOORS

Do you want to know more of the life of the woods and fields?
Would you like to find joy in the everyday things around you?
Hear this Nature Lecture by Miss Opal Whiteley.

Topic _____

Date_____ Time_____

Place _____

**Admission 10 Cents**

family. She attended a series of lectures on mental power given by the well-known mind analyst Jean Morris Ellis, whom she had met a couple of years before. Mrs. Ellis gave Opal a character reading, and declared her to have a remarkable capacity for achievement in the areas of literature, art, and science. Later, Mrs. Ellis was to describe herself as "haunted" by Opal's genius, and by her "utter unlikeness to any child I had ever known."

During her second college year, Opal founded the Phusis Philoi ("Nature Lovers") Club for young women interested in science, art, and music. Under her plan, the club members were to become teachers of children in their home communities, using principles and methods she had found effective. In addition, they would serve as directors of a proposed children's museum. A press release from Eugene in February 1918 described the goal:

Like a true "Sunshine Fairy," the name by which she has been known since a child, Opal Whiteley, a sophomore at the University, is bringing her nature study work, carried on since early childhood, into practical everyday use for the children of the state.

A children's museum of natural history, made for and by children, is her latest plan for helping the boys and girls get the key to the fairyland of the out-of-doors.

"The museum, which will be established on a small scale in Eugene next fall," says Miss Whiteley, "will represent work of the boys and girls of the state. It will be their museum." Among other things, it will contain specimens of minerals, fossils, flowers, butterflies, and other insects of Oregon, carefully selected and prepared by the children, sketches of their observations of nature, life histories of the birds and butterflies, interesting homes from the fields and woods, and photographs and snapshots of children becoming acquainted with the things of the out-of-doors. . . .

When the museum has become established after its start in Eugene and has grown to sufficient proportions, the dream of its founder is to have a real children's museum in some centrally located town of the state. Around the building will be a garden of the wildflowers of Oregon. At the museum will gather once every year children interested in the wonders of the out-of-doors, who will come from different parts of the state to talk over what they have been learning, and ways in which they can find out other things.

After the museum is established, the Phusis Philoi

*"The Sunshine Fairy,"* 1916
(Binford & Mort Publishing)

plans to issue a monthly bulletin to the children all over the state, telling them of the nature life of Oregon, what the children have done, and about the progress of the museum.

A few days after the announcement, Opal left Oregon for Southern California, to earn money to finance her educational and literary plans. She took with her all her possessions — including her entire collection of natural history specimens — many of which she subsequently deposited in a Los Angeles department store warehouse owned by the father of a friend. She also took with her a number of photographs of herself attired in various costumes. With these dramatically posed pictures, she visited Hollywood film agencies and studios, hoping to find a part in the movies. Every morning, she set out, filled with hope; every evening, she returned to her lodgings, disappointed. After six weeks of trying, she gave up.

Although the motion picture industry failed to recognize Opal's magnetism, the audience for her lectures and classes quickly grew, attracted by titles such as "Music and Musicians of the Out-of-Doors," "Along the Road," and "The Relationship Between Nature and Art." She reported teaching children of twenty-one nationalities. (Those who could not afford to pay for lessons were charged nothing.) Encouraged by enthusiastic parents, she decided to develop one set of talks, "The Fairyland Around Us," into a book of the same title — the first of her long-planned series of books on the natural world written especially for children. She sent a description of the proposed contents to some of the most affluent families of America and Europe, and by obtaining loans, contributions, and advance payments from them, raised $9,400 to pay for its printing. She planned a deluxe, suede-bound edition for wealthy subscribers, and a less expensive version to be sold in bookstores.

After schools closed in June and children scattered for the summer, Opal cut back her teaching to one day each week and made the most of the opportunity to write. In approximately three months of exhausting work, she turned her lecture notes and previously collected material into the rough manuscript of *The Fairyland Around Us*. When printed in December 1918, the book contained 274 pages, of which 126 consisted of text, 15 were devoted to photographs of her students and animal friends, and 91 were reserved for illustrations of wildlife — in color, to aid identification.

*The Fairyland Around Us* was a blend of Opal's storytelling, observations of plant and animal life, accounts of her classes, passages from her childhood notebooks and the later, undamaged years of her diary, and quotations from the major poets. Like her other writings, it balanced seriousness with humor, scientific scrutiny with mysticism, and information with emotion. To that extent, it could be compared with Henry David Thoreau's *Walden*. Yet it was unlike anything else in print. In it, Opal wrote of such things as the magic of twilight:

> To the Birds belongs the morning hour; but to us, to you and me, and some of our little brothers of the field and forest, this [twilight] hour belongs. It is the hour when we think about the things that are yet to be. We dream and we listen — listen to the lullaby songs of the Trees, to the twilight chorus of the Frogs, to the Vesper Sparrow, to all Mother Nature's evening music we listen and dream — and in the midst of our dreaming stop to ask Mother or Father about things, where things come from and what they are here for. And some things seem so far away, and some things seem so near in this the twilight hour.

In another passage, she conveyed the mysterious enchantment of night:

> Last night I went into the Forest. Moonbeam fairies brightened the path that leads towards the Cathedral and into the woods beyond. I went softly — and listened — and I heard the patter, patter of hurrying

27

little feet scurrying over the woodland floor. Now and then I stopped very still and kept so for a few minutes — and saw these little folks who made those faint patterings and rustlings as they went this way and that. A Wood-rat scampered across my path. Farther along a Skunk moved from one log to another. . . . Seven trees and two logs distant I came upon the Flying Squirrel fairies. Down the path fifty paces and two stumps to the right were four dear Wood Mice. The night [was] wonderful. Over my head the tall Fir trees reached upward to the sky. Through their branches Moonbeam fairies came and glorified the tiny mosses and vines. Upon the harp-strings of these forest trees the wind musicians played sweet lullabies.

As the work of the typesetters progressed, Opal made many changes in the wording. Finally, with a few hundred copies' worth of unbound pages completed, including thirty-five of the color illustrations, the printers demanded an additional $600, to cover the cost of the alterations. Opal could not provide any more money. So they dumped the type and destroyed the plates for the rest of the illustrations. In doing so, they nearly destroyed Opal Whiteley. She lost her energy and hope, and for a time had no will to live.

After a while, Opal managed to earn enough money to pay for the binding of two to three hundred copies of the book. In place of the missing color illustrations, she pasted in appropriate reproductions from postcards, study guides, and magazines, and added the captions by hand. The process was strenuous and time-consuming, but eventually most of the bound books were completed and sent to subscribers. In return, Opal received glowing letters of appreciation from such eminent figures as Theodore Roosevelt, William Howard Taft, Kate Douglas Wiggin, and Mary Roberts Rinehart. P. P. Claxton, U.S. Commissioner of Education, wrote: "I have read your book with interest and delight. I should be glad indeed if copies of it could be put in all of the schools of the United States."

Following the recovery of her health, friends urged Opal to take *The Fairyland Around Us* to the East Coast, and show it to publishers. She borrowed money for the trip, and left California in July 1919.

Late one September afternoon, her money almost gone, she entered the office of the prestigious *Atlantic Monthly*, in Boston. The magazine had recently begun to publish books under its own imprint, and someone had suggested to Opal that she talk to its editor.

The editor was Ellery Sedgwick, one of the most respected men in publishing history. He glanced through the book. Finding little in it to interest him, he told Opal that he must decline. But then, intrigued by her personality, he questioned her about her background. As she talked, his interest increased. He asked if she had kept a diary. She said she had. He said he wanted to see it. Opal, nearly at her breaking point, began to cry. She told him it had been torn to pieces. He asked if she had kept the pieces. She had, but they were stored in Los Angeles. He told her to send for them without delay. They soon arrived — "crammed in a hatbox," he was later to recall.

Opal remained in the Boston area to reassemble her diary. At Ellery Sedgwick's insistence, she moved into the spacious Brookline home of his mother-in-law, Mrs. Walter Cabot. There, she was supervised in her work by various members of the household. According to Ellery Sedgwick, the scraps of paper, when spread out, covered a substantial portion of the floor of a very large bedroom of the house. A year later, in his introduction to the published portion of the diary, he described the process of putting the pieces together:

We telegraphed for them, and they came — hundreds, thousands, one might almost say millions of them. Some few were large as a half-sheet of notepaper; more, scarce big enough to hold a letter of the alphabet. The paper was of all shades, sorts, and sizes: butchers' bags pressed and sliced in two, wrapping-paper, the backs of envelopes — anything and everything that could hold writing. The early years of the diary are printed in letters so close that, when the sheets are fitted, not another letter can be squeezed in. In later passages the characters are written with childish clumsiness, and later still one sees the gradually forming adult hand.

The labor of piecing the diary together may fairly be described as enormous. For nine months almost continuously the diarist has labored, piecing it together sheet by sheet, each page a kind of picture-puzzle, lettered, for frugality (the store was precious), on both sides of the paper.

The entire diary, of which this volume covers but the two opening years, must comprise a total of a quarter of a million words. Upwards of seventy thousand — all that is contained in this volume — can be ascribed with more than reasonable definiteness to the end of Opal's sixth and to her seventh year. During all these months Opal Whiteley has been a frequent visitor in the *Atlantic's* office. With friendliness came confidence, and little by little, very gradually, an incident here, another there, her story came to be told. She was at first eager only for the future and for the opportunity to write and teach children of the world which she loved best. But as the thread of the diary was unraveled, she felt a growing interest in what her past had been, and in what lay behind her earliest recollections and the opening chapters of her printed record.

Her methods were nothing if not methodical. First, the framework of a sheet would be fitted and the outer edges squared. Here the adornment of borders in childish patterns, and the fortunate fact that the writer had employed a variety of colored crayons, using each color until it was exhausted, lent an unhoped-for aid. Then, odd sheets were fitted together; later, fragments of episodes. Whenever one was completed, it was typed by an assistant on a card, and in this way there came into

*"The labor of piecing the diary together may fairly
be described as enormous."*
(Massachusetts Historical Society)

being a card-system that would do credit to a scientific
museum of modest proportions. Finally the cards were
filed in sequence, the manuscript then typed off and
printed just as at first written, with no change whatever other than omissions, the adoption of reasonable
rules of capitalization (the manuscript for many years
has nothing but capitals), and the addition of punctuation, of which the manuscript is entirely innocent. The
spelling — with the exception of occasional character-
istic examples of the diarist's individual style — has,

in the reader's interest, been widely amended. [In addition, the names of some minor characters were changed by Opal shortly before publication in order to avoid embarrassment to them.]

Beginning in March 1920, the material in the diary's first two years was serialized in the *Atlantic*, resulting in a phenomenal number of new subscriptions. In September, the Atlantic Monthly Press released it as a book, under the title *The Story of Opal: The Journal of an Understanding Heart*.

It caused a sensation. Wearied and disillusioned by the recent war in Europe, the American public eagerly turned to what the *Atlantic* labeled "a revelation of the spirit of childhood." According to an advertisement in the December issue of that magazine, "The variety of interest in this Diary is amazing; parents are ordering it for their children, friends for each other. There seems to be no age limit to its appeal." Within a few weeks after its publication, *The Story of Opal* had become the most talked-about book of its time.

And nowhere was it talked about more than in Cottage Grove, Oregon, thanks to Opal's angel parent story, which she included as her introduction to the book and serialization of the diary:

Of the days before I was taken to the lumber camps, there is little I remember. As piece by piece the journal comes together, some things come back. There are references here and there in the journal to things I saw or heard or learned in those days before I came to the lumber camps.

There were walks in the fields and woods. When on these walks, Mother would tell me to listen to what the flowers and trees and birds were saying. We listened together. And on the way, she told me poems and other lovely things, some of which she wrote in the two books [she made for me], and also in others which I had not with me in the lumber camps. On the walks, and after we came back, she had me to print what I had seen and what I had heard. After that, she told me of different people and their wonderful work on earth. Then she would have me tell again to her what she had told me. After I came to the lumber camp, I told these things to the trees and the brooks and the flowers.

There were five words my mother said to me over and over again, as she had me to print what I had seen and what I had heard. These words were: What, Where, When, How, Why. They had a very great influence over all my observations, and the recording of those observations during all the days of my childhood. And my mother having put such strong emphasis on these five words accounts for much of the detailed descriptions that are throughout my diary.

No children I knew. There were only Mother and the kind woman who taught me and looked after me and dressed me, and the young girl who fed me. And there was Father, in those few days when he was home from the far lands. Those were wonderful days, his home-coming days. Then he would take me on his knee, and ride me on his shoulder, and tell me of the animals and birds of the far lands. And we went for many walks, and he would talk to me about the things along the way. It was then he taught me [the observation game of] *comparer*.

There was one day when I went with Mother in a boat. It was a little way on the sea. It was a happy day. Then something happened, and we were all in the water. Afterward, when I called for Mother, they said the sea waves had taken her, and she was gone to heaven. I remember the day because I never saw my mother again.

The time was not long after that day with Mother in the boat, when one day the kind woman who taught me and took care of me did tell me gently that Father too had gone to heaven, while he was away in the far lands. She said she was going to take me to my grand-mother and grandfather, the mother and father of my father.

We started. But I never got to see my dear grand-mother and grandfather, whom I had never seen. Something happened on the way, and I was all alone. And I didn't feel happy. There were strange people that I had never seen before, and I was afraid of them. They made me to keep very still, and we went for no walks in the field. But we traveled a long, long way.

Then it was they put me with Mrs. Whiteley. The day they put me with her was a rainy day, and I thought she was a little afraid of them, too. She took me on the train and in a stage-coach to the lumber camp. She called me Opal Whiteley, the same name as that of another little girl who was the same size as I was when her mother lost her. She took me into the camp as her own child, and so called me as we lived in the different lumber camps and in the mill town.

With me, I took into camp a little box. In a slide drawer in the bottom of this box were two books which my own mother and father, the Angel Father and Mother I always speak of in my diary, had written in. I do not think the people who put me with Mrs. Whiteley knew about the books in the lower part of the box, for they took everything out of the top part of the box and tossed it aside. I picked it up and kept it with me, and, being as I was more quiet with it in my arms, they allowed me to keep it, thinking it was empty. These two books I kept always with me, until one day I shall always remember, when I was about twelve years old, they were taken from the box I kept then hid in the woods. Day by day, I spelled over and over the many words that were written in them. From them, I selected names for my pets. And it was the many little things recorded there that helped me to remember what my mother and father had already told me of different great lives and their work; and these books with these records made me very eager to be learning more and more of what was recorded in them. These two books I studied much more than I did my books at school. Their influence upon my life has been great.

Shortly before the preceding words appeared in the *Atlantic*, a series of strange, crudely typed, anonymous letters that attempted to substantiate Opal's adoption claim began to arrive at Cottage Grove. They failed miserably in the attempt, however, for they were soon shown to have been typed by Opal herself in Boston. Mr. Whiteley, convinced that his daughter was in some kind of trouble, wrote urgent letters inquiring about her health. The reply he received from Opal was hardly reassuring:

You ask what in the world is the matter with me. Nothing is. I am not having vagaries of mind. And as to what you say about who has been telling me all [about being adopted], no one has. You ask if I can't change that, or have I sold it. Sold or unsold, it couldn't be changed — it's the diary as it is, just as I printed it when I was a very little girl. As the diary goes on there are many things in it which my own mother and own father taught me. . . .

It was kind of you to say . . . for me to tell you about my troubles. It is the first time you have ever said it in my life. . . .

You said that my diary is causing you a lot of trouble. I am sorry, and I regret the annoyance the reporters have caused you. But really the most trouble isn't yours — it is mine, because I would like so much to know more about my own mother and father. I want so very much to have again the two books that they wrote in.

In the meantime, accounts of Opal's alleged adoption had been circulating in the nation's press, and a rapidly growing number of reporters had begun to appear in Cottage Grove. In the increasing confusion, no one seems to have noticed the uncanny resemblance between Opal's angel parents and Ed and Lizzie Whiteley. What Opal's family and neighbors *did* notice was that her diary's portrayal of Mrs. Whiteley as "the mamma" was one-sided, at best. "She has sold her birthright and slandered the name of her good mother," Opal's grandmother angrily declared. The Whiteleys waited for Opal to "come to her senses." But when she instead proceeded to deny any familial connection with them, they responded by disowning her.

Hurt and embarrassed by ceaseless publicity over the diary's adoption claim and its unflattering depiction of Mrs. Whiteley, harassed beyond endurance by reporters, Opal's younger brother and three sisters eventually changed their names and moved away, after giving relatives strict instructions not to reveal their names or their locations. Their attempts to deal reasonably with the press had brought them nothing but trouble.

In March 1920, for example, one newspaper presented an interview with Opal's widowed grandmother, Achsah Scott, who was taking care of the four remaining Whiteley children in her little house in Saginaw, Oregon, while their father worked. In spite of the fact that Mrs. Scott clearly had her hands full taking care of the family, and in spite of the fact that, as the article acknowledged, "They are so bewildered that they preferred not to talk . . . at all when seen today in their rural home," the reporter persisted — and even listed the address of the Scott home: "the second house on the road to the right, beyond the little white church on the hill."

A later news article mistakenly identified Opal's sister Pearl as the destroyer of the diary; stated that "there is intimation that should Pearl decide to talk or let her guardians talk for her, much that is now mysterious would be revealed"; gave the name and address of the family with whom Pearl was staying while attending business college in Portland; gave the name of the school; gave the name Pearl had registered under; and described an attempted interview at her guardian family's home, with Pearl calling to the head of the household to "please stop talking!" The reporter, who had tried to argue her way in after deception failed, wrote, "Pearl Whiteley's advent in Portland and her studiously preserved silence only tend to deepen the mystery." As a result of this and other articles, Pearl Whiteley was followed by reporters wherever she went.

Across America, doubt of the diary's authenticity began to grow, fed by reports from the Cottage Grove area that indicated the adoption tale was false. If the angel parent story was a fantasy, speculators reasoned, the rest of the diary was probably untrue as well — and, in all likelihood, so were the claims regarding the age of its author. The question of age became the most hotly argued of all. But in the growing controversy, a great many people seemed to ignore what Opal's writing was largely concerned with — the world around her, the world that no one seemed to notice:

This woods is gray in winter, when come cold days. And gray shadows walk among the trees. They touch one's face with velvet fingers, when one goes walking there. . . .
Lichen folks talk in gray tones. I think they do talk more when come winter days. . . . Most grownups don't hear them at all. I see them walk right by in a hurry, sometimes. And all the time, the lichen folks are saying things; and the things they say are their thoughts about the gladness of a winter day.

The diary described the small things Opal saw, and the greatness she found within them:

Today the grandpa dug potatoes in the field. Too, the chore boy did dig potatoes in the field. I followed along after. My work was to pick up the potatoes they got out of the ground. I picked them up, and piled them in piles. Some of them were very plump. Some of them were not big. All of them wore brown dresses. . . .

And all the times I was picking up potatoes, I did have conversations with them. Too, I did have thinks of all their growing days there in the ground, and all the things they did hear. Earth-voices are glad voices, and earth-songs come up from the ground through the plants; and in their flowering, and in the days before these days are come, they do tell the earth-songs to the wind. And the wind in her goings does whisper them to folks to print for other folks, so other folks do have knowing of earth's songs. When I grow up, I am going to write for children — and grownups that haven't grown up too much — all the earth-songs I now do hear.

I have thinks these potatoes growing here did have knowings of star-songs. I have kept watch in the field at night, and I have seen the stars look kindness down upon them. And I have walked between the rows of potatoes, and I have watched the star-gleams on their leaves.

Skeptics called the diary a hoax. No little girl could have written it, they said. Some of them theorized that during her residence in Los Angeles, Opal either wrote all of her alleged childhood diary or made extensive additions to pages written when she was younger. Their assertions were based on the following discoveries:

At a Los Angeles home Opal stayed in for six months, she allegedly borrowed two French language-instruction books and a Roman Catholic manual. She was said to have spent over twelve hours a day writing in her room, and to have studied at the public library every other day until dinner, after which she would work far into the night. In a 1920 letter describing these matters to the editor of the Cottage Grove *Sentinel* — who promptly reported them to the nation's press — Opal's hostess wrote that she had seen "sheets of big printing" spread out on Opal's bed. She added that some of these pages were left behind when Opal moved, but were destroyed unread.

According to the doubters, this information explained the diary's inclusion of French words and Latin phrases; the references to "borning days" and "going-away days" of historic figures; the use of classical names for favorite animals and trees; and the sophisticated, often philosophical tone of Opal's writing.

As further apparent evidence of trickery, a paragraph in *The Story of Opal* describing how she fed a family of wasps was found to have, as one critic put it, "exactly the same wording, exactly the same sentences, exactly the same punctuation" as a paragraph in *The Fairyland Around Us*. Opal's detractors asserted that she must have taken the passage from the latter and printed it into her diary. After all, they reasoned, she would not have been able to copy it from the alleged childhood diary into *The Fairyland Around Us* if her diary pages had been torn up as she claimed they had been.

The skeptics became even more skeptical on the discovery of several French royal family names hidden in the diary's occasional groupings of French words. For example, at one point, Opal wrote:

> I did sing . . . *le chant de fleurs* that Angel Father did teach me to sing, of *hyacinthe, éclaire, nenufar, rose, iris, et dauphinelle, et oléandre, et romarin, lis, églantier, anemone, narcisse, et souci.*

The first letters of the names of the flowers add up to form *Henri d'Orléans*. Critics claimed that this sort of activity was much too sophisticated for a little girl from Oregon to have carried on.

But there was more to the situation than they were willing to see.

To begin with, it didn't seem to occur to them that a little girl of Opal's intellectual caliber might be able to make philosophical observations, play word games, or copy such things as French botanical names or Latin phrases at six or seven, as others less gifted might do later on in life. Applying the standards by which they measured the age of the diary's author — those determined by what normal children her age were considered to be capable of and likely to do — one would have to conclude that, among many possible examples, Wolfgang Amadeus Mozart did not begin to compose music at six after all (after becoming a keyboard virtuoso at five), and that Yehudi Menuhin did not make his orchestral debut on the violin at the age of seven. If the critics had approached Opal as a possible child prodigy, had made investigations to determine the level of her childhood abilities and her access to information, and had then applied appropriate standards of judgment, they might have revealed something of substance. Unfortunately, they did nothing of the kind.

A possible explanation for the presence of the paragraph found in *The Fairyland Around Us* can be easily arrived at. As a child, Opal often wrote autobiographical accounts in her school notebooks, and then copied them into her diary. Considering that she saved her old notebooks, and that she used some of their contents in writing *The Fairyland Around Us*, it is hardly surprising that the passage appeared in both that book and her diary. Moreover, the paragraphs are not word-for-word identical as the critics claimed they were. In *The Fairyland Around Us*, the description in question contains five differences in wording from that in *The Story of Opal*, and an additional sentence — improvements such as might be made when rewriting something written at an earlier age. (It also contains seven differences in punctuation, which — though of lesser importance, since punctuation in *The Story of Opal* was added to the diary pages, anyway — can serve to show how poorly the critics examined what they were criticizing.) Furthermore, one might

40

reasonably assume that if Opal had been cunning enough to fabricate a childhood diary, printing and all, she would have been cunning enough to refrain from including a paragraph from another book of hers — one that a number of people had already read.

A great deal of evidence in support of child authorship can be found in a careful reading of the diary, for its detailed descriptions of events are such as could only have been recorded by someone seeing and experiencing them at the time. To a greater extent than might be explained by the unusual empathy of a twenty-year-old writer, they are given from the physical, mental, and emotional viewpoint of a child, telling what things were heavy, difficult to unfasten, too high to reach, hard to make sense of, frightening, irritating, or comforting. They reflect a child's nondifferentiation between what older people consider important or unimportant, and are communicated with an intense, unselfconscious simplicity that no adult could have forged.

The two published years of Opal's diary recorded, in eyewitness detail, incidents proved to have taken place when she was six and seven years old. Before serializing the diary in the *Atlantic*, Ellery Sedgwick had painstakingly attained verification of its descriptions of people and events, and their approximate dates. These were reverified before the book's publication, as he wrote in his introduction to *The Story of Opal*:

Month after month, while chapters of the diary were appearing in the *Atlantic*, snatches of the same history, together with descriptions of many unrecorded episodes, came in the editor's mail; and though the weaving is of very different texture, the pattern is unmistakably the pattern of the diary. Dates and names, peregrinations and marriages, births, deaths, and adventures less solemn and less apt to be accurately recollected, occurred just as the diary tells them. The existence of the diary itself was well remembered, though for many years Opal had never spoken of it; a friend recalled the calamitous day when the abundant chronicle of six years was destroyed; and a cloud of witnesses bore testimony to the multitudinous family of pets, and some even to the multi-colored names they bore.

According to Ellery Sedgwick, the diary was unquestionably the work of a child, and by nature precluded undetectable alterations of any kind. In addition, he said, the alleged age of the paper it was printed on had been confirmed by several scientists who had examined it at his request. In a letter to the *Oregonian* in 1920, he wrote:

> It is too much to hope, of course, that all people will believe in the authenticity of the diary. I suppose nearly half of those who read [*The Young Visitors*, by] Daisy Ashford still think it a fraud subtly perpetrated by Sir James Barrie. That Opal's is a far more remarkable case, involving creative effort and not a mere reflection of an environment, intensifies the difficulties of believing. With these difficulties I for one heartily sympathize, but I have come to believe myself in the authenticity of the manuscript because of the overwhelming testimony which confronts all of us who have worked with it.

Twenty-six years later, he wrote in his autobiography:

> Of the rightness and honesty of the manuscript as the *Atlantic* printed it, I am utterly convinced; more certain am I than of the authorship of many another famous diary, for I have watched the original copy reborn and subjected it to the closest scrutiny.

In 1960, his opinion was given substantial support by the findings of a professional examiner of questioned documents, who microscopically analyzed some of the diary pages. According to his report, the paper was of a kind manufactured only before World War I. Its fibers showed the results of exposure to damp weather, such as would be expected of paper stored outdoors. The marks on it were made with crayons of unusually high quality, which would have been available during the time of prosperity preceding 1914, and not in the closing war year of 1918, when Opal was staying in Los Angeles.

It might be noted that those who disputed the authenticity of the diary never examined any of its pages, and that those who *have* examined some of them — including this author — have come away convinced that no adult could possibly have printed them.

If the diary pages had not been torn up years before their submission to the *Atlantic*, as Opal claimed they had been, it might somehow have been possible for her to have added to them such things as the French names and phrases. But since these words are spread throughout the text, it would have been extremely difficult for her to have inserted them without rewriting the entire diary — considering that both sides of every sheet were filled with closely spaced letters, and that any additional material would therefore have overflowed the page. If the pages *had* been torn up — and there were witnesses to support that claim, but none to support the alternative — it would have been impossible for her to have made additions convincingly fit the previous writing, both in content and appearance.

Interestingly, the one possible opportunity for Opal to have added something to her diary seems to have been overlooked for the most part by her detractors. The occasional French phrases seemingly unnecessary to the narrative, such as the long list of flower names in the previously quoted "chant de fleurs," could have been added as the original hand-printed words were transcribed into the typed manuscript in Boston. According to a 1920 letter from Ellery Sedgwick describing the diary reconstruction process to an English publisher, after Opal had reassembled each page,

43

she would place it in an envelope and write its words on the outside, as well as on a separate piece of paper. Then a trusted *Atlantic* secretary would type the passage on a card, to be placed by Opal in its proper part of the sequence. As this work went on, the French phrases could conceivably have been written on the envelopes or sheets of paper, and thereby incorporated into the text. It is a matter of record that Ellery Sedgwick omitted from *The Story of Opal* a number of sentences containing French references because, as he explained on numerous occasions, "they would strain public credulity." His *Atlantic* files contain a typed record of all the omitted material, which includes names of people and places mentioned in the books of Henri d'Orléans (not passages from these books, as critics claimed) and very brief descriptions of four royal family heirlooms described in the memoirs of the Duchess of Orleans — English translations of which had been published in 1859 and 1860. However, there are at least three weaknesses to the preceding conjecture. First, Ellery Sedgwick's assertions would seem to rule out the likelihood of alterations to the transcribed text. In the letter describing the diary's reconstruction, he wrote, "During this process [the secretary] spent a great deal of time working with Opal over the manuscript. She, as well as I and many other friends and witnesses, followed the whole performance carefully." In the previously quoted letter to the *Oregonian*, he wrote that "Whenever a passage has struck me as . . . over-mature, I have looked it up in the original, and have in every case been entirely convinced." Second, until the appropriate diary pages are located — only a few pages are known to exist today, none or which pertain to the passages mentioned — there can be no way of proving that anything was added to the transcriptions. Third, by their nature the phrases in question are not vital to the narrative; therefore their insertion, if proved, would hardly invalidate the major portion of the diary.

The theory that Opal's knowledge of the French language was gained in adulthood is clearly invalidated by the fact that her diction tends to be French in character throughout *The Story of Opal*. Unlike isolated names and phrases, the odd syntax is too extensive to have been appended at a later date:

I have wonders — where is Brave Horatius? He comes not at my calling. Two days he is now gone. For him I go on searches. . . . But I have no seeing of my Brave Horatius.

The more closely the skeptics looked into the technical problems involved, the less certain they became that Opal could have added anything to pages written in childhood. They decided that she must have written *the entire diary* during her months in California — the only period in her post-Endeavor, post-college life in which she would have had any time to do such a thing. If they had studied the circumstances more closely, however, they would have seen that the time available was insufficient.

Opal spent her first six months in Los Angeles in the previously mentioned home. For the first month and a half, she was occupied with trying to find a part in the movies. After that, she was busy promoting, organizing, and conducting her classes and lectures. During the final three months of the period, she was writing *The Fairyland Around Us* — which would explain her trips to the library and the hours of writing in her room.

As nearly as can now be determined, Opal seems to have spent the four months remaining between the end of her initial six-month residence and the end of the year in refining the manuscript of *The Fairyland Around Us*, typing and mailing a prospectus on the proposed book to American and European patrons of the arts, collecting money for its printing, negotiating with the printers, correcting proofs of the printed pages (a difficult job, because of the numerous quotations and scientific names included), rewriting portions of the text, and continuing her research and teaching efforts. According to notes later discovered among her possessions, as well as to references made in an interview, she may also have been working at the time on something she referred to as her "bird book." She claimed to have shown this manuscript, or partial manuscript, to Ellery Sedgwick at the same time she showed him *The Fairyland Around Us* — and, in fact, a reference to it was printed in the postscript to *The Story of Opal*. However, no trace of it has yet been found.

If Opal had written her childhood diary in Los Angeles, it would have to have been during the seven-month interval between the end of 1918 and her trip to the East Coast to find a publisher for *The Fairyland Around Us*. But within that amount of time, minus what she spent on her other activities, she would have had to laboriously print an estimated quarter of a million words describing from perfect photographic recall the events of nearly six and a half years of her childhood, gradually changing her grammar, spelling, and style of printing as the material progressed. Before doing so, she would somehow have had to find a sufficient quantity of properly aged envelopes, grocery bags, and wrapping paper upon which to write her diary. After completing it, she would have had to tear it, page by page, into thousands of pieces — a rather unlikely thing to do to her writing if she wanted to have it published. And she would have had to carry out these actions so meticulously that the results would fool everyone who examined the diary and subsequently expressed an opinion on it. All of this would have had to follow her exhausting work on *The Fairyland Around Us*, and the collapse of her health caused by the destruction of its plates.

By all appearances, Opal's last several months in Los Angeles were hardly conducive to diary-forging. An attempted assault resulted in severe spinal problems, which caused her so much pain that friends took her to a hospital. There, she underwent an operation in which pieces of steel were implanted in her spine. (These were later removed in Boston under the direction of Ellery Sedgwick's physician, who prescribed for her a program of back-strengthening exercises.) She apparently survived on small amounts of poor-quality food, and often ate nothing at all. She was continually moving, because of difficulties allegedly caused by people who tried to take advantage of her in various ways. At this time, she began to be bothered by a debilitating fatigue — a common symptom in cases of schizophrenia — which was to grow worse as years went by.

According to the woman with whom she was residing around May of 1919, Opal had been spending most of her time cutting out wildlife illustrations and pasting them into copies of *The Fairyland Around Us*. She had previously been staying in a bare attic room without even a bed to sleep on, had very little strength, and appeared half starved. The completion of the two hundred or more copies of *The Fairyland Around Us* must have taken her a considerable amount of time. Each finished book had a minimum of fifty-six added color illustrations, each of which was carefully centered on an otherwise blank page. Several of the books contained additional small pictures pasted into spaces in the text. The illustrations had to be cut out, labeled by hand, and then pasted in. Except for some initial help from a friend, Opal seems to have done the work by herself.

These details, conclusive though they may seem, were not the only ones overlooked by those eager to prove that Opal wrote her diary at the age of twenty.

An examination of the *entire* letter written by her hostess of six months is very illuminating. Its author writes that she and her daughter had given a visiting friend basic Spanish lessons at dinner, to prepare her for residence at a ranch where the language was used. The daughter of the house remarked on similarities between words in Spanish and French, after which names for objects were given in French as well. "After Miss Kafka left for Fresno," the letter states, "the lessons were dropped, as Opal lacked all facility for foreign languages. Therefore, it surprised me when she asked me for a French dictionary." It might not have surprised other people, considering the language lessons that occurred before it. But they were not mentioned in printed accounts at the time.

In the same correspondence, Opal's hostess specifies that the "sheets of big printing" she allegedly saw in Opal's room were "on white typing paper." It is open to question whether she saw printing as in Opal's childhood diary, or instead saw printing such as Opal used at the age of twenty to inscribe poems on some of the illustrations in *The Fairyland Around Us* — both very strange, crowded forms of "big printing," but each very different from the other. No one will ever know now, for Opal's hostess allegedly destroyed the pages Opal left behind, without reading them. (Anyone investigating her testimony might have wondered why she *didn't* read them, considering that she seems to have pried into practically everything else Opal did, even to the extent of examining the contents of her wastebasket.) Just as noteworthy as the insubstantial nature of this woman's evidence regarding the style of printing she supposedly saw, or its content, is the fact that her letter's crucial words, *"on white typing paper,"* were not included in the majority of articles describing what she wrote. As a result, many readers were left with the impression that pieces of scrap paper such as had been used in the diary had been found with large, childish letters printed on them, when in reality no such discovery had been made.

As a result of the "revelations" of the diary discreditors, more and more people came to support the adult-author theory as reasonable and likely. Gossip was added to gossip, conjecture to conjecture. Readers were made to feel cheated, ashamed to have believed Opal's claim of child authorship, and embarrassed even to have a copy of *The Story of Opal* on their bookshelves.

At one point, it seems, someone at a Boston social gathering began a rumor that Opal had confessed to writing her diary in adulthood. Soon the story was reported as fact in a leading society magazine, after which newspapers spread it across the country. No sooner did Ellery Sedgwick look into the possibility of taking legal action against the offending publications than rumors surfaced alleging that *he* had admitted that the diary was a fabrication. After "news" of this sort had circulated for a while, the *Atlantic* began to receive letters from indignant mothers who had, they said, returned their recently purchased copies of *The Story of Opal* to bookstores, having informed their children that the author and publishers of the book were not to be trusted.

In the meantime, reporters sent to investigate the authenticity of the diary seemed more concerned with stirring up controversy than with providing information to settle the dispute, as the records of their many news articles demonstrate. They garbled dates; they distorted facts; they fabricated evidence to support their speculations. People sympathetic toward Opal became increasingly reluctant to share what they knew with members of the press. The few people who came forward in her defense were ridiculed or dismissed as gullible and ignorant.

One of these was Oregon City attorney G. Evert Baker, who, as president of Oregon Christian Endeavor, had recognized the abilities of thirteen-year-old Opal Whiteley and had encouraged her to teach children. By the time *The Story of Opal* was published, he had known its author for nine years, and had communicated regularly with her during her months in Los Angeles. He said:

> Because Opal Whiteley is not cast in the same mould that the rest of us are, and because we love uniformity, she is being bitterly assailed as an imposter. . . .
>
> Opal lived with us for months. We became deeply attached to her. She is a sweet, lovely, refined girl. I cannot in my mind associate Opal with fraud and trickery. She was truthful, though she saw many things in nature and her surroundings that I, myself, could not see. . . .
>
> You will find plenty of people to tell you that Opal is a persistent publicity seeker, that she is frivolous and insincere; but I believe that is the jealousy of those who resent what they do not understand. I will always

believe that Opal is a genius, and my one regret is that I was unable to have Opal meet Theodore Roosevelt, for he was big enough to appreciate her.

Such words went unheeded. Hounded by critics, besieged by letters from angry readers, caught between them and various people representing the interests of Opal Whiteley, Ellery Sedgwick removed his introduction from later printings of *The Story of Opal* and sold the publication rights to the American branch of the English house of Putnam and Company, publishers of the British edition of the book. *The Story of Opal* was never rereleased, however, by Putnam's or anyone else. For within less than a year after its publication, interest in it had died.

And so, just when the door to recognition had begun to open for Opal Whiteley, it was slammed shut in her face. Her discredited book was thrown into the cellar of literary obscurity. But over the years, in spite of the efforts of the skeptical, it would speak out for her with its small voice, helping to ensure that its author would not be completely forgotten.

In 1923, Opal published and distributed a small collection of her poems and stories, entitled *The Flower of Stars*. In it was the following poem, "The Little Room." It is doubtful that she intended it as a comment on what had happened to her writing, but it might well be used as such; it describes the situation perfectly:

> In Man's heart is a little room.
> He has named it
> Oblivion.
> And things are ranged along its walls
> That he does not wish
> To think about.
> Every time that he pushes something
>   in there,
> He closes the door very tightly.

But in hours when he is weary,
In the hours that walk around
    some midnights,
When high fires have burned
To a low flicker,
Then the little door swings on its
    hinges
And no thing
Will make it stay closed
All of the time.

When he is near death,
All the velvet-footed wanderers
    in there
Join the throng around his bed.
"We will not die," they whisper
To one another,
While Beauty waits with drawn lips,
And dry eyes.

But there is heard
The patter of a little sad rain
In her heart's garden,
Where some little flower buds
That were once thinking of the sun
Will never open,
Because Man keeps a little room
Of oblivion in his soul.

After publication of *The Story of Opal*, Opal began to
be followed, flattered, and harassed by people of dubious
character, some of whom were seen making inquiries in the
Cottage Grove area. They seemed to fall into two categories.
The first believed that she had psychic powers. There appears to have been a possible basis in fact for their belief.
Some of Opal's students claimed that she would sometimes
go into a trance and levitate while sitting in the branches

of trees. A woman Opal met in California overheard her and a well-known clairvoyant of the time discussing the "wood nymphs" that they saw around them as they walked. But Opal apparently considered such abilities to be of small importance, and did nothing to publicize or capitalize on them. Her other group of followers were said to have been after the money they believed she would eventually inherit, rightfully or not, from the estate of Henri d'Orléans. Some of them encouraged her increasingly paranoid suspicions of the staff of the *Atlantic* and other people around her.

Owing to real and imagined persecution, conditions in the Boston area became unendurable for Opal. She moved to New York, and then to Washington, D.C. In 1923, she left America for England, sponsored by Edward Grey, Viscount of Fallodon, the renowned English naturalist and former foreign secretary. In 1919, while serving as ambassador to the United States, Lord Grey had read the *Atlantic's* serialization of the diary. "Charmed by Opal's intimacy with bird life," Ellery Sedgwick wrote, "he arranged a visit, and during the thirty years I guided the *Atlantic* I have never watched two more delighted and understanding friends." A few months after the meeting, Lord Grey wrote the introduction to *The Diary of Opal Whiteley*, the British edition of *The Story of Opal*. Tremendously impressed with its author's knowledge, abilities, and character, he remained to the end of his life her strongest supporter.

No doubt because of her worsening schizophrenia, Opal's life more than ever came to resemble a fairy tale. Soon after arriving in England, she left for France, where she visited the mother of Henri d'Orléans — Françoise Marie Amélie d'Orléans, the widow of Robert, Duke of Chartres. According to a copy of a letter from Opal to the duchess — in which, contrary to rumors of the time, she makes no claim to be the daughter of Henri d'Orléans — Opal intended to compile a book about Prince Henri. His mother, it seems, was curious about the circumstances surrounding his death. Apparently to satisfy her curiosity, she provided Opal with financial support for an investigative voyage to India. She died in 1925, before Opal returned from her journey.

Following in the footsteps of her Angel Father, Opal traveled nearly nine thousand miles across India by train, camel, ox cart, horse, and elephant. Along the way, she collected legends and geographical information, and photographed almost everything she saw.

For ten months, beginning in September 1924, Opal lived in the guest house at the palace of the maharana of Udaipur, ranking prince of Rajputana — a cluster of princely states in northwestern India (all of which were later absorbed by the state of Rajasthan). Henri d'Orléans had been fascinated by Udaipur, one of the oldest territories in the country. His fascination was evidently shared by Opal, who presented herself at the maharana's court under the assumed name of Françoise d'Orlé.

A correspondent for the *Oregonian*, in India a few years later on a fruitless quest to find Opal, sent back the following description of her surroundings at Udaipur:

Udaipur is high up in the hills of Rajputana, and is surrounded by a country as parched and barren as the drier parts of eastern Oregon. The capital city, however, is beautifully situated amidst three artificial lakes, and on all sides are beautiful trees. The main palace is located on the edge of a large lake, and the summer palaces are on small islands in the lake. Their white walls come down to the water's edge everywhere, except where gardens lead down to the marble steps that serve as landing places for the boats. The trees in the interior courts hang over the walls and almost dip their branches into the water. Many of the rooms and courts are all of sculptured marble, and particularly beautiful are the delicately sculptured marble screens behind which the ladies of the palace sit and watch what may be going on in the court below. They thus can observe without being observed.

For pure romantic situation, there is nothing finer in all India. It fits in perfectly with our dreams of oriental splendor. . . . The city is justly known as the Venice of India, but is strictly an Indian Venice. In fact, it is old India, for there seems to be very little evidence of foreign influence.

While in India, Opal wrote of her experiences. According to an Indian civil service official with whom she had been in constant touch at Udaipur, "She worked for months [under] intense pressure, sometimes sixteen hours a day, at recording from the lips of Indians details of the manners and customs of the Rajputs. I know that she penetrated to corners to which no European had ever before found his way, and witnessed rites and ceremonies to which no European had hitherto been admitted."

She later sent to the *Atlantic* a photo-illustrated manuscript for a book about the maharana and his court, entitled *The Sun King and His Kingdom of Mystery in Unknown India.* (According to legend, the maharana's ancestors were descended from the sun.) Both the *Atlantic* and Putnam's expressed interest, but disagreements arose over contract terms and over what information was to be printed regarding Opal's alleged French ancestry. As a result, the planned book never appeared. Beginning in 1929, however, it — or part of it — was serialized in a fashionable London magazine, *The Queen,* under the title *The Story of Unknown India.*

In the final installment, "Farewell to Udaipur," Opal wrote of the visit of Prince and Princess Arthur of Connaught:

It is a special privilege to be at Udaipur during a royal visit because of the illumination of the lake palaces, as well as of those along the shore. Everything is outlined in tiny flames from oil in miniature clay saucers. The little lights dance like tongues of flame upon the water, and the ripples vary their length. There could

54

be no magic scene more beautiful in all the *Arabian Nights*, and it suits the austerity and simplicity of the Maharana's habits and character that the great palace, which so easily might be over-decorated, has only a single line of lights, barely outlining its massive grandeur.

After the pageantry of many-starred fireworks, the aged Maharana stood in his white robes as [might] some king from an ancient Celtic fairy-tale, and garlanded each one of us with the honour-garland of Udaipur, which is of golden threads.

And so amid the twinkling lights everywhere . . . we went home to rest from all the ceremonies of the day, but never to forget the pageantry of Udaipur alight.

In 1925, Opal left Udaipur to return to England. When she said goodbye to the maharana's daughter, she wrote, the princess gave her a bracelet for eternal friendship, and asked her to stay in Udaipur "for always."

In 1926, she traveled from England to Rome, and then to Vienna, where she spent two years in an imperial convent. Following her return to England in 1928, she lived for a few years in London, moved to Oxford, then returned to London in 1935. According to progressively incoherent notes and partial manuscripts later found among her possessions, she worked sporadically on her memoirs, her revised book on India, and one or two books on religious themes. Rejected as an imposter by her alleged French family, unable to maintain a job, she lived as a ward of the city. With her small allowance, she purchased books instead of food. London used-book sellers remembered her as a strange, lonely woman who searched obsessively for volumes on the French royal family and other subjects, paying a few pence for each. During the second world war, she was often seen scavenging for books in the rubble of bombed buildings.

As Opal's health declined, her communications grew increasingly paranoid and despondent. In 1941, for example, she wrote to the chairman of Putnam's:

Dear Mr. Huntington:

Please will you lend me money to buy books I need in my work? I shall be able to pay you back in about six months. I am very careful in my work and I need the books to complete the work. I am able to buy them at second hand shops and Farringdon Road, but I haven't the money. I will call for the answer because someone is getting the letters and all help sent. All the beautiful illustrations for my books sent to me have been unjustly taken. . . .

In 1948, authorities found her starving in a dead-end section of the London suburb of Hampstead. Her squalid basement bed-sitting flat was filled from floor to ceiling with wooden boxes holding an estimated total of ten to fifteen thousand books, many of which were said to contain underlined passages and notes in Opal's handwriting. Judged incapable of taking care of herself, she was placed in Napsbury Hospital, an aged, rambling public institution several miles north of London. She has been there ever since, for the past several years occupying a room on the third floor of the farthest building of the hospital complex. Her many boxes of possessions were stored in a warehouse, under authority of the Court of Protection.

In 1949, a project was organized to improve her situation. As *Old Oregon*, the University of Oregon Alumni Association magazine, announced:

A few remaining friends in England have decided to try to collect a small fund to move Opal from the public institution where she is receiving no beneficial treatment to a private mental hospital they have located that will assure personal treatment and privacy.

In America, the fund raising was coordinated by the then retired Ellery Sedgwick through the *Atlantic Monthly*. Few people seemed interested. News articles mentioning the appeal typically included accounts of Opal's alleged trickery — hardly the sort of thing to provide incentive for contributing money toward her support. To many readers old enough to recall the scandal surrounding publication of *The Story of Opal*, Opal Whiteley was an embarrassment and a fraud. To a large number of those too young to remember, she appeared the perpetrator of an old hoax, the author of a falsified piece of writing they had not read. The campaign failed to raise enough money to move Opal from Napsbury.

In 1958, the English writer Elizabeth Bradburne arranged a radio program on Opal Whiteley for the British Broadcasting Corporation. After the broadcast, a listener wrote:

Thank you very much for your advice about obtaining *The Diary of Opal Whiteley*. Your information about her life convinces me that she is the little person we knew in Hampstead as "The Little Princess." So I'll tell you what I know of her.

An Irish friend of mine once met a sad little lady in the Catholic chapel on the way to Camden Town, and took her home to dinner. The little lady ate sandwiches in a way that showed she was very hungry, and spoke only a little, in a soft, cultured voice. She was very grateful, and of course was asked to come again. Thus began a series of weekly visits which continued over some years. She told my friend that she was a princess of the House of Orleans, and that her name was Françoise Marie de Bourbon-Orléans.

My friend made inquiries and learned from the parish priest that she was in fact an American subject who had suffered a head injury during the blitz. Her relationship to the royal house of Orleans was an unfortunate delusion, which caused her to spend her meagre allowance on . . . books of French history which she couldn't afford.

She talked a lot to my friend, and took her to her room in, I think, South Hill Road, off Haverstock Hill. It was stacked from floor to ceiling with books and magazines; one moved up and down the lanes between books. And there, my friend told me, she saw a thing which shook her — an article in *The Queen* written by "Princess Françoise Marie de Bourbon-Orléans," and above it, a photograph of the "Little Princess" herself. . . .

I met her once only. She wanted to see my baby girl. I felt at home with her at once. I remember a small, graceful, and gracious hand, an air of quiet dignity in a small round person, and brown eyes with an expression at once child-like, appealing, sad, and wise. She asked in a gentle way if she might hold the child. I remember handing over the baby rather doubtfully, then felt a pang of envy to see how expertly those little hands soothed it, and the soft voice calmed it. I believe that she was a trusted baby-sitter at that time. There is no doubt that she must have found contentment in that sort of work.

In his autobiography, *The Happy Profession*, Ellery Sedgwick wrote:

To tell the full story of Opal Whiteley would require a documented volume, illustrated by photographs, of the masses of material still in the *Atlantic*'s possession, and to complete it, strange adventures of my own should be added, tales of espionage, flights and pilgrimages, still difficult to understand, to say nothing of people of note who slipped in and out of the story.

No one seems to have been interested in writing such a story. It can never be adequately written now. Ellery Sedgwick died in 1960. Lord Grey died in 1933. Many others who had once known Opal are now gone. For the most part, the *Atlantic*'s Opal Whiteley file consists today of inquiries from curious readers, old news clippings and book reviews, and letters from Opal to Ellery Sedgwick and his wife.

The diary manuscript is gone, taken by Opal when she left Boston. No one seems to know where it is, or if it still exists.

In 1977, because of rising storage costs, Opal's books were sold. No list was made of the titles. At that time, several letters, photographs, and notes were discovered among her possessions and were given to interested parties. (Other such material had been given away in the late 1950s, including a few surviving pages from the earliest years of the diary.) The remaining items were disposed of.

According to people who have visited Opal at Napsbury over the past several years, she seems to have had little to do except fantasize to the flickering images of the ward's television set. Her conversation, as reported by visitors, has tended to consist of rational answers to questions, interspersed with paranoiac statements about staff members and wistful remarks about friends who have died. Over the years, she has grown fat on hospital food. Now failing in health at eighty-nine, she has little chance of recovery.

In the meantime, *The Fairyland Around Us*, the first of her doomed series of books for children, has never been released by a publisher. The few remaining copies of it are almost impossible to find . . .

How sweet is eventime along the road — the music of the breeze, the prayer whispers of the Earth-folk — the twilight chorus, and now I hear the Vesper Sparrow sing.

The only published segment of her diary has been out of print for over sixty years . . .

I set the pail on a little stump. Brave Horatius stayed to guard it, and I did go the way that leads to the hill-top. I did have longings to dance. Most every day, I do dance. I dance with the leaves and the grass. I feel

thrills from my toes to my curls. I feel like a bird, sometimes. Then I spread my arms for wings, and I go my
way from stump to stump, and on adown the hill.
Sometimes I am a demoiselle, flitting near unto the
water. Then I nod unto the willows, and they nod
unto me. They wave their arms, and I wave mine.
They wiggle their toes in the water a bit, and I do so,
too. And every time we wiggle our toes, we do drink
into our souls the song of the brook — the glad song it
is always singing. And the joy-song does sing on in our
hearts. So did it today.

And so, her childhood diary discredited, her other writings ignored and lost, Opal Whiteley ends her life, forgotten
and far from home. When she is gone, what will remain of
who she was? Perhaps it will be as she wrote in *The Flower
of Stars*:

> "She is dead," they said,
> And they gathered up the things
> Of her days —
> Life's little spindle,
> Her gentle ways. . . .
>
> The hopes of her pleasing,
> Her little vigil hours,
> The chest of her maiden dreams,
> The flowers of a gladder faith,
> The lavender of old tears. . . .
>
> Afterwards, in one old chest
> In the room she had slept in,
> They found the gentle joys
> Of her waiting years. . . .

Opal's greatest desire in life was to earn her living by
writing. But that was never to be.

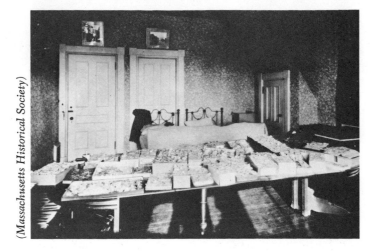

Every now and then, a news item about Opal Whiteley appears. Invariably, it is accompanied or soon followed by statements describing her diary as a fabrication. The following is typical:

> After publication, investigation showed that the diary was not actually written when Opal was a child, but was cleverly composed at a later age. Worn reference books and plagiarized passages were discovered.

Those articles which do not attribute Opal's downfall to willful dishonesty ascribe it to a deteriorating mind. But there was more to the situation than that. For Opal's mental condition was at least in part the result of a long series of health-breaking incidents caused by hostile people, such as the printers who melted down the plates for *The Fairyland*

*Around Us* and the skeptics who attacked her secret childhood diary as a hoax. Moreover, the mental state of Opal Whiteley, and the angel-parent fantasy it produced, was not what stopped dead the phenomenal sales of *The Story of Opal* in approximately ten months. If anything, it *increased* public interest in the book. Instead, it was the charges of adult authorship that turned the published portion of her diary into an object of contempt. At best, her "exposers" were guilty of inexcusable bungling. At worst, they were guilty of deliberate falsification of evidence. Whatever their motives, whatever the extent of their awareness, they were responsible for the defamation of a highly sensitive woman who was incapable of defending herself, and for the encouragement and intensification of a tragedy.

If the alleged proof that Opal had written her diary as a young woman had been presented in a court of law, it would have quickly been revealed for what it was. Unfortunately, it did not appear in court. Instead, it appeared in newspapers, magazines, and books, across the nation. And the reputation of an author dedicated to the enlightenment of children was wrecked. With it was destroyed the credibility of her entire diary. Today nothing to anyone's knowledge remains of it but a few faded scraps of paper.

Ironically, the true story of Opal Whiteley is far more interesting than any of the falsehoods her critics created and endorsed. But in their rush to incriminate her, they seem to have overlooked it. Opal's was the story of a uniquely gifted communicator who told of two still largely unknown realms — that of the natural world, and that of childhood. And from its beginning, it was the story of a *writer*. Far from being a literary fraud, Opal Whiteley was an embodiment of literary expression, who lived her love for writing in everything she did.

My favorite assessment of Opal's writing was made by Constant Huntington, chairman of the English publishing house of Putnam. "Miss Whiteley's books are not a matter of a season's interest," he wrote in 1921. "I regard the Diary as a very remarkable work of genius, ranking with the great works of all time." Certainly no other book has appealed to me as strongly — as though it had been written especially for me — as has the diary of seven-year-old Opal Whiteley. No other book has done as much to deepen my awareness and appreciation of what it means to be *alive*. In addition, I cannot think of any literary work that more intimately reflects the personality of its author.

Opal's writing is, as she was, an extraordinary combination of what are often seen as opposites — humor and seriousness, intellect and emotion. Her humor is as light as fairy dust and elfish laughter; her seriousness is as substantial as stone. Her intellect does not condescend to readers, nor put them at a distance, but instead enables them to draw nearer to her, and to an understanding of life. Her emotional expression reaches airy heights and the darkest depths, yet seems completely effortless and unselfconscious.

Despite her diary's sometimes wordy approximation of French syntax ("I do have thinks," "I did wait waits") — which in itself is a remarkable creation — she writes with a masterly simplicity such as few authors achieve even after many years of practice. Yet behind that economy of expression, a seemingly endless variety of phrasing can be found. Each time I read a chapter of her diary, the words seem new, changing, different, like water bubbling up from a hidden spring. And once again I'm amazed at the vitality behind them.

The most haunting quality of her writing, though, is its unique intensity of vision. Opal Whiteley did not merely *care* for the world; she was *in love* with it. It told her many of its secrets, and she did her best to pass them on to others. She was able not only to understand, but to communicate that understanding, with a spiritual and emotional power unequaled, in my opinion, by any other American writer.

Marjorie Fleming, Scotland's famed child writer, was championed by Sir Walter Scott, the literary giant of his time. He encouraged her, took her for walks, featured her at banquets, and introduced her to other members of literary society. When "Pet Marjorie" died in 1811 at the age of eight years and eleven months, her letters, copybooks, and journals were carefully preserved. Her home in Kirkcaldy was later made a museum in her honor. Mark Twain was said to have been captivated by her writings, and to have spent the last few weeks of his life studying them. Other authors called her "the youngest immortal in the world of letters," and declared her compositions "more wonderful than the pyramids." Yet her creations, skillful and charming though they are, seem pale when compared with those of Opal Whiteley. Opal surpassed her in prolific output as well, owing to her amazing energy, which lasted far longer than that of most child prodigies. Today, however, most of what she wrote is gone. Whatever it might have said, and whatever value it might have had for readers, has been lost forever. What little is left remains unappreciated. So does she. In its annual "Bohemia Days" festival, Opal's home town of Cottage Grove celebrates its past. But throughout the festivities, hardly a word is spoken of the local girl who for a brief time became the most famous author in the history of Oregon.

Why is there no Opal Whiteley museum somewhere, filled with records of her writing, her teaching, and her life? Why is there no study of her manuscripts, her notebooks, her teaching principles and methods, and her amazingly effective ways of gathering, organizing, and memorizing information? Why is there today practically no interest in her at all? Because many years ago, the literary world claimed to have been cheated. Perhaps it is time to look a little closer at what is being thrown away, and to reconsider who cheated whom. For it seems to me that the literary world cheated Opal Whiteley, rather than the other way around — and by doing so, deprived her of her rightful place in literary history.

Instead of pitying her for her schizophrenia, and the

many problems it created, we can appreciate what it allowed her to do — to enchantingly express herself in writing at an earlier age than would normally have been possible. For ordinarily, young children of even the highest intelligence have a hard time separating themselves from what they are doing, seeing, or thinking, in order to write about it. In Opal's case, I believe, schizophrenia may have provided the necessary detachment. But as it unlocked the door to literary skills abnormally early in her life, so it prematurely locked the door again as it worsened, before she reached her middle years. And her quality of expression, which might have been expected to grow richer with passing time, faded away instead.

While she was young, though, Opal Whiteley made the most of her abilities and time, and wrote, and wrote, and wrote. And because she did, we can see the neglected beauty of the world as she saw it, and be reminded of its importance by the enlightening eloquence of a magical child.

That is why, to me, the much discussed angel-parent story is not the most vital element of the diary. Instead, it is the profound, thankful happiness of the little girl who watched and listened to, and energetically participated in, the world around her. "There is so much joy in the woods," Opal wrote. That joy flows through the pages of her book from beginning to end, like the singing waters of the creek she loved. It is unmistakably real. No fantasy can compare with it — neither that of seven-year-old Opal Whiteley nor those of today's Industrial Man. It is timeless, yet extremely timely. For never before has it been so urgently needed.

As Opal demonstrated, the natural world has a great deal to teach inquirers who approach it with respect. But only incomplete answers will be obtained by those who try to force its secrets from it. It is clear by now that the uncaring application of superficial scientific knowledge is endangering the functional integrity of our planet and threatening the existence of the human race. At the same time, the social and spiritual symptoms of humanity's growing alienation from the earth could hardly be more obvious. Yet their cause is largely ignored. And in the current atmosphere of increasing materialism, conservatism, and apathy, popular attention is turning ever further from natural laws.

For years the public has been inundated with clinically detached reports on the value of the natural world, made by clinically detached writers. These presentations have had little significant effect. Few people learn to love the earth by reading them, for they neither contain nor communicate any such emotion.

Perhaps it is time for another kind of report, written by another kind of writer. Perhaps it is now time to hear from a little girl named Opal Whiteley. I believe that sooner or later she will accomplish what other writers have failed to do. And I predict that, although she may be forgotten and unknown at present, one day she will be honored as a very special teacher, and followed in spirit as she once was followed in the woods of Oregon — the shy, secretive dreamer, the charismatic charmer, the woodland fairy, the dancer on the hilltop, the friend of every form of life on earth. She will live on, as young and fresh as ever, in her words of long ago — for anyone to see, and know, and love.

# The
# Singing Creek Where
# the Willows Grow

# Chapters

# Names in the Narrative

*Agamemnon Menelaus Dindon*: A pet turkey.
*Adamnan of Iona*: A sheep.
*Alan of Bretagne*: A fir tree.
*Aidan of Iona come from Lindisfarne*: The shepherd.
*Albéric de Briançon*: A sheep.
*Alcuin*: A sheep.
*Alfric of Canterbury*: A sheep.
*Anacreon Herodotus*: A lamb a little more little than the other little lamb.
*Andromeda*: Sister hen of Clementine.
*Anthonya Mundy*: Solomon Grundy's little pig sister that has not got as much curl in her tail as has Solomon Grundy.
*Aphrodite*: The mother pig.
*Aristotle*: A pet bat who died of eating too many mosquitoes.

*Bébé Blanche, Bébé William*: Two little trees by Edward III.
*Bede of Jarrow*: A sheep.
*Ben Jonson*: One of Minerva's baby chickens.
*Brave Horatius*: The shepherd dog.
*Byron*: A fir tree in the lane.

*Cassiopée*: A neighbor's pig.

*Cardinal Richelieu*: One of Minerva's baby chickens.

*Charlemagne*: The most tall tree of all the trees growing in the lane.

*Clementine*: A Plymouth Rock hen.

*Cynewulf*: A sheep.

*Dallan Forgaill*: A sheep.

*Dear Love and her Young Husband*: Neighbors and dear friends.

*Edmund Spenser*: One of Minerva's baby chickens.

*Edward III*: A fir tree near the singing creek where the willows grow.

*Edward, Prince of Wales*: A younger tree growing near unto Edward III.

*Edwin of Diera*: A sheep.

*Elidor*: A sheep.

*Elizabeth Barrett Browning*: A pet cow with poetry in her tracks.

*Elsie and her Young Husband*: Neighbors and interesting friends.

*Epicurus Pythagoras*: A lamb.

*Étienne of Blois*: A fir tree in the woods.

*Felix Mendelssohn*: A very dear pet mouse.

*Felix of Croyland*: A sheep.

*Francis Beaumont*: One of Minerva's baby chickens.

*Geoffroi Chaucer*: A little squirrel that was hurt by the black cat.

*Godefroi of Bouillon*: A fir tree in the woods.
*Good King Edward I*: A fir tree growing in the lane.
*Good King Louis VI*: A grand fir tree in the woods.
*Grandpère*: The father of Angel Father.
*Guy de Cavaillon*: A sheep.
*Gwian*: A sheep.

*Homer Archimedes Chilon*: A little lamb more big than all the other lambs.
*Hugh Capet*: A fir tree growing in the lane.

*Isaiah*: A plain dog.

*Jean de la Fontaine*: One of Minerva's baby chickens.
*Jean Molière*: One of Minerva's baby chickens.
*Jean Racine*: One of Minerva's baby chickens.
*Jenny Strong*: A visitor with an interesting bonnet.
*John of Gaunt, Duke of Lancaster*: A tree growing near unto Edward III.
*John Fletcher*: One of Minerva's baby chickens.

*Keats*: An oak tree in the lane.

*Lars Porsena of Clusium*: A pet crow with a fondness for collecting things.
*Lionel, Duke of Clarence*: A tree growing near unto Edward III.
*Lola*: A little girl in school, who had wants for a white silk dress.
*Louis II, le Grand Condé*: A wood-mouse with likes to ride in the sleeve of my red dress.
*Lucian Horace Ovid Virgil*: A toad.

*"The Mamma"*: Mrs. Whiteley.

*Marcus Aurelius*: A lamb.

*Mathilde Plantagenet*: The baby calf of the gentle Jersey cow, that came on the night of the coming of Elsie's baby.

*Menander Euripides Theocritus Thucydides*: A most dear lamb that had needs to be mothered.

*Michael Angelo Sanzio Raphael*: A grand fir tree with an understanding soul.

*Nannerl Mozart*: A very shy mouse.

*Napoleon*: The Rhode Island Red rooster.

*Nicholas Boileau*: One of Minerva's baby chickens.

*Oliver Goldsmith*: One of Minerva's baby chickens.

*Orderic*: A sheep.

*"The Papa"*: Mr. Whiteley.

*Peace*: A mother hen that has got all her children grown up.

*Periander Pindar*: A lamb.

*Peter Paul Rubens*: A very dear pet pig.

*Pius VII*: One of Minerva's baby chickens.

*Plato, Pliny*: Twin bats.

*Plutarch Demosthenes*: A lamb.

*Queen Eleanor of Castile*: A fir tree in the lane growing by Edward III.

*Queen Philippa of Hainault*: A fir tree growing by Edward III.

*Raoul de Houdenc*: A sheep.
*Raymond of Toulouse*: A fir tree in the woods.

*Sadie McKibben*: A comforter in time of trouble.
*Saint Louis*: A fir tree growing in the lane.
*Samuel Taylor Coleridge*: One of Minerva's baby chickens.
*Savonarola*: A sorrel horse.
*Shelley*: A fir tree growing in the lane.
*Sir Francis Bacon*: One of Minerva's baby chickens.
*Sir Philip Sidney*: One of Minerva's baby chickens.
*Sir Walter Raleigh*: One of Minerva's baby chickens.
*Solomon Grundy*: A very dear baby pig.
*Solon Thales*: A lamb.
*Sophocles Diogenes*: A lamb with a short tail and a question-look in his eyes.

*Theodore Roosevelt*: A fir tree in the lane.
*Thomas Chatterton Jupiter Zeus*: A most dear velvety wood-rat.
*Tibullus Theognis*: A fuzzy lamb with very long legs.

*William Makepeace Thackeray*: A little bird that was hurt.
*William Shakespeare*: An old gray horse with an understanding soul.
*William Wordsworth*: An oak tree in the lane.

*The first page of Opal's diary*

# One

# The Road beyond the Singing Creek, and the Railroad Track with Shining Rails

Today the folks are gone away from the house we do live in. They are gone a little way away, to the ranch house where the grandpa does live. I sit on our steps, and I do print. I like it, this house we do live in, being at the edge of the near woods. So many little people do live in the near woods. I do have conversations with them. I found the near woods first day I did go explores. That was the next day after we were come here.

All the way from the other logging camp in the beautiful mountains, we came in a wagon. Two horses were in front of us — they walked in front of us all the way. When first we were come, we did live with some other people, in the ranch house that wasn't all builded yet. After that, we lived in a tent. And often when it did rain, many raindrops came right through the tent — they did fall in patters on the stove, and on the floor, and on the table. Too, they did make the quilts on the beds some damp; but that didn't matter much, because

they soon got dried, hanging around the stove. By-and-
by, we were come from the tent to this lumber shanty.
It has got a divide in it. One room we do have sleeps in.
In the other room, we do have breakfast and supper.

Back of the house are some nice wood-rats. The most
lovely of them all is Thomas Chatterton Jupiter Zeus.
By the wood-shed is a brook. It goes singing on. Its joy-
song does sing in my heart. Under the house live some
mice. I give them bread-scraps to eat. Under the steps
lives a toad. He and I, we are friends. I have named him
— I call him Lucian Horace Ovid Virgil.

Between the ranch house and the house we live in is
the singing creek where the willows grow. We have conversations. And there I do dabble my toes beside the
willows. I feel the feels of gladness they do feel.

And often it is I go from the willows to the meeting
of the road. That is just in front of the ranch house.
There the road does have divides. It goes three ways.

One way, the road does go to the house of Sadie McKibben. It doesn't stop when it gets to her house, but mostly I do. The road just goes on to the mill town, a little way away. In its going, it goes over a hill. Sometimes, the times Sadie McKibben isn't at home, I do go with Brave Horatius to the top of the hill. We look looks down upon the mill town. Then we do face about, and come again home. Always we make stops at the house of Sadie McKibben. Her house, it is close to the mill by the far woods. That mill makes a lot of noise. It can do two things at once: it makes the noises, and also it does saw the logs into boards. About the mill do live some people, mostly men-folks. There does live the good man that wears gray neckties and is kind to mice.

Another way, the road does go the way I go when I go to the schoolhouse where I go to school. When it is come there, it does go right on — on to the house of the girl who has no seeing. When it gets to her house, it does make a bend, and it does go its way to the blue hills. As it goes, its way is near unto the way of the *rivière* [river] that sings as it comes from the blue hills. There are singing brooks that come, going to the rivière. These brooks, they and I, we are friends. I call them Orne and Loing and Yonne and Rille and Essonne.

Near unto the road, long ways between the brooks, are ranch houses. I have not knowing of the people that do dwell in them; but I do know some of their cows and horses and pigs. They are friendly folk. Around the ranch houses are fields. Woods used to grow, where now grows grain. When the mowers cut down the grain, they also do cut down the cornflowers that grow in the fields. I follow along after, and I do pick them up. Of some of them, I make a *guirlande* [garland]. When the guirlande is made, I do put it around the neck of William Shakespeare. He does have appreciations. As we go walking down the lane, I do talk with him about the one he is named for, and he does have understanding. He is such a beautiful gray horse, and his ways are ways of gentleness. Too, he does have likings, like the likings I have, for the hills that are beyond the fields — for the hills where are trails and tall fir trees, like the wonderful ones that do grow by the road.

So go two of the roads. The other road does lead to the upper logging camps. It goes only a little way from the ranch house, and it comes to a rivière. Long time ago, this road did have a longing to go across the rivière. Some wise people did have understandings, and they did build it a bridge to go across on. It went across the bridge, and it goes on and on between the hills — the hills where dwell the talking fir trees.

By its side goes the railroad track. Its appears are not so nice as are the appears of the road, and it has got only a squeaky voice. But this railroad track does have shining rails — they stretch away and away, like a silver ribbon that came from the moon in the night. I go a-walking on these rails. I get off when I do hear the approaches of the dinkey-engine. On this track on every day, excepting Sunday, comes and goes the logging train. It goes to the camps, and it does bring back cars of logs, and cars of lumber. These it does take to the mill town. There, engines more big do take the cars of lumber to towns more big.

Thomas Chatterton Jupiter Zeus has been waiting in my sun-bonnet a long time. He wants to go on explores. Too, Brave Horatius and Isaiah are having longings in their eyes. And I hear Peter Paul Rubens squealing in the pig-pen. Now I go — we go on explores.

# Two

## The Habits of Lars Porsena of Clusium, the Comforts of Michael Angelo Sanzio Raphael, and the Freckles of Sadie McKibben

Today was a warm, hot day. It was warm in the morning, and hot at noon. Before noon and after noon and after that, I carried water to the hired men in the field, in a jug. I got the water out of the pump to put into the jug. I had to put water in the pump before any would come out. The men were glad to have that water in the jug.

While I was taking the water in the jug to the men in the field, from her sewing-basket Lars Porsena of Clusium took the mamma's thimble, and she didn't have it and she couldn't find it. She sent me to watch out for it, in the house and in the yard and everywhere. I know how Lars Porsena of Clusium has a fondness for collecting things of bright colors, like unto my fondness for collecting rocks; so I ran to his hiding-place in the old oak tree. There I found the mamma's thimble. But she said the pet crow's having taken it was as though *I* had taken it, because he was my property — so I got a spanking with the hazel switches that grow near unto our back steps. Inside me, I couldn't help feeling she ought to have given me thanks for finding the thimble.

Afterwards, I made little vases out of clay. I put them in the oven to bake. The mamma found my vases of clay. She threw them out the window. When I went to pick them up, they were broken. I felt sad inside. I went to talk things over with my chum, Michael Angelo Sanzio Raphael. He is that most tall fir tree that grows just back of the barn.

I scooted up the barn door. From there, I climbed onto the lower part of the barn roof. I walked up a ways. Up there, I took a long look at the world about. One gets such a good wide view of the world from a barn roof. After, I looked looks in four straight ways, and four corner ways. I said a little prayer. I always say a little prayer before I jump off the barn into the arms of Michael Angelo Sanzio Raphael, because that jump is quite a long jump, and if I did not land in the arms of Michael Angelo Sanzio Raphael, I might get my leg or neck broken. That would mean I'd have to keep still a long time. Now I think that would be the most awful thing that could happen, for I do so love to be active. So I always say a little prayer, and do that jump in a careful way. Today when I did jump, I did land right proper in that fir tree. It is such a comfort to nestle up to Michael Angelo Sanzio Raphael when one is in trouble. He is such a grand tree. He has an understanding soul.

After I talked with him and listened unto his voice, I slipped down out of his arms. I intended to slip into the barn corral, but I slid off the wrong limb, in the wrong way. I landed in the pig-pen, on top of Aphrodite, the mother pig. She gave a peculiar grunt — it was not like those grunts she gives when she is comfortable.

I felt I ought to do something to make up to her for having come into her home out of the arms of Michael Angelo Sanzio Raphael, instead of calling on her in the proper way. I decided a good way to make it up to her would be to pull down the rail fence in that place where the pig-pen is weak, and take her for a walk.

I went to the wood-shed. I got a piece of clothes-line rope. While I was making a halter for the mother pig, I took my Sunday-best hair-ribbon, the blue ribbon the Uncle Henry gave to me. I made a bow on that halter. I put the bow just over her ears. That gave her the proper look. When the mamma saw us go walking by, she took the bow from off the pig. She put that bow in the trunk. Me, she put under the bed.

By-and-by, some time long it was, she took me from under the bed and gave me a spanking. She did not have time to give me a spanking when she put me under the bed; she left me there until she *did* have time. After she did it, she sent me to the ranch house, to get milk for the baby.

I walked slow through the oak grove, looking for caterpillars. I found nine. Then I went to the pig-pen. The chore boy was fixing back the rails I had pulled down. His temper was quite warm. He was saying prayer words in a very quick way. I went not near unto him. I slipped around near Michael Angelo Sanzio Raphael. I peeked in between the fence-rails. Aphrodite was again in the pig-pen. She was snoozing, so I tiptoed over to the rain-barrel by the barn. I raise mosquitoes in the rain-barrel for my pet bats. Aristotle eats more mosquitoes than Plato and Pliny eat.

On my way to the house, I met Clementine, the Plymouth Rock hen, with her family. She only has twelve baby chickens now. The grandpa says the other one she did have died of new monia, because I gave it too many baths for its health.

When I came to the house, one of the cats — a black one — was sitting on the doorstep. I have not friendly feelings for that big black cat. Day before the day that was yesterday, I saw him kill the mother hummingbird. He knocked her with his paw, when she came to the nasturtiums. I didn't even speak to him.

Just as I was going to knock on the back door for the milk, I heard a voice on the front porch — it was the voice of a person who has an understanding soul. I hurried around to the front porch. There was Sadie McKibben, with a basket on her arm! She beamed a smile at me. I went over and nestled up against her blue gingham apron with cross-stitches on it.

The freckles on Sadie McKibben's wrinkled face are as many as are the stars in the Milky Way, and she is awful old — going on forty. Her hands are all brown and cracked, like the dried-up mud-puddles by the roadside in July. And she has an understanding soul. She always has bandages ready in her pantry when some of my pets get hurt. There are cookies in her cookie-jar when I don't get home for meals. And she allows me to stake out earthworm claims in her back yard.

She walked along beside me when I took the milk home. When she came near the lane, she took from her basket wrapping-papers, and gave them to me to print upon. Then she kissed me good-bye upon the cheek, and went her way to her home. I went my way to the house we live in.

After the mamma had switched me for not getting

back sooner with the milk, she told me to fix the milk for the baby. (The baby's bottle used to be a brandy bottle, but it evoluted into a milk bottle when they put a nipple on it.)

I sit here on the doorstep, printing this on the wrapping-paper Sadie McKibben gave me. The baby is in bed, asleep. The mamma and the rest of the folks is gone to the ranch house. When they went away, she said for me to stay in the doorway, to see that nothing comes to carry the baby away. By the step is Brave Horatius. At my feet is Thomas Chatterton Jupiter Zeus. I hear songs — lullaby songs of the trees. The back part of me feels a little bit sore, but I am happy, listening to the twilight music of God's good world. I'm real glad I'm alive.

# Three

# The Many Things that Opal sees when she is sent Straight for the Milk

The colic had the baby today, and there was no Castoria for the pains. There was none because yesterday Pearl and I climbed upon a chair and then upon the dresser, and drank up the new bottle of Castoria. But the bottle had an ache in it, and we swallowed the ache with the Castoria. That gave us queer feels. Pearl lay down on the bed. I did rub her head. But she said it wasn't her head, it was her *back* that hurt. Then she said it was her *leg* that ached. The mamma came in the house then, and she did take Pearl in a quick way to the ranch house.

It was a good time for me to go away exploring. But I didn't feel like going on an exploration trip. I just sat on the doorstep. I did sit there and hold my chin in my hand. I did have no longings to print. I only did have longings not to have those queer feels.

Brave Horatius came walking by. He did make a stop at the doorstep. He wagged his tail. That meant he wanted to go on an exploration trip. Lars Porsena of

Clusium came from the oak tree. He did perch on the back of Brave Horatius. He gave two caws. That meant he wanted to go on an exploration trip. Thomas Chatterton Jupiter Zeus came from under the house. He just crawled into my lap. I gave him pats, and he cuddled his nose up under my curls. Peter Paul Rubens did squeal out in the pig-pen. He squealed the squeals he does squeal when he wants to go on an exploration trip. Brave Horatius did wait and wait, but still those queer feels wouldn't go away. Pretty soon, I got awful sick.

By-and-by, I did have better feels. And today my feels are all right, and the mamma is gone a-visiting, and I am going on an exploration trip. Brave Horatius and Lars Porsena of Clusium and Thomas Chatterton Jupiter Zeus and Peter Paul Rubens are waiting while I do print this. And now we are going the way that does lead to the blue hills.

Sometimes I share my bread and jam with yellow-jackets, who have a home on the bush by the road, twenty trees and one distant from the garden. Today I climbed upon the old rail fence close to their home, with a piece and a half of bread and jam — and the half piece for them, and the piece for myself. But they all wanted to be served at once, so it became necessary to turn over all bread and jam on hand. I broke it into little pieces, and they had a royal feast there on the old fence-rail. I wanted my bread and jam — but then yellowjackets are such interesting fairies, being among the world's first paper-makers; and baby yellowjackets are such chubby youngsters. Thinking of these things makes it a joy to share one's bread and jam with these wasp fairies.

When I was coming back from feeding them, I heard a loud noise. That Rob Ryder was out there by the chute, shouting at God in a very quick way. He was begging God to dam that chute right there in our back yard. Why, if God answered his prayer, we would be in an awful fix — the house we live in would be under water, if God dammed the chute! Now I think anger had Rob Ryder, or he would not pray kind God to be so unkind.

When I came again to the house we live in, the mamma was cutting out biscuits with the baking-powder can. She put the pan of biscuits on the wood-box, back of the stove. She put a most clean dish-towel over the biscuits. Then she went to gather in clothes. I got a thimble from the machine drawer. I cut little round biscuits from the big biscuits. The mamma found me. She put the thimble back in the machine drawer. She put me under the bed. Here under the bed, I now print.

By-and-by, after a long time, the mamma called me to come out from under the bed. She told me to put on my coat, and her big fascinator on my head. She fastened my coat with safety-pins. Then she gave me a lard-pail with its lid on tight. She told me to go straight to the grandpa's house for the milk, and to come straight home again.

I started to go straight for the milk. When I came near the hospital, I went over to it to get the pet mouse, Felix Mendelssohn. I thought that a walk in the fresh air would be good for his health. I took one of the safety-pins out of my coat. I pinned up a corner of the fascinator. That made a warm place next to my curls for Felix Mendelssohn to ride in. (I call this mouse Felix Mendelssohn because sometimes he makes very sweet music.)

Then I crossed to the cornfield. A cornfield is a very nice place, and some days we children make hair for our clothes-pin dolls from the silken tassels of the corn that grow in the grandpa's cornfield. Sometimes, which is quite often, we break the cornstalks in getting the silk tassels. That makes bumps on the grandpa's temper.

Tonight I walked zigzag across the field, to look for things. Into my apron pocket, I put bits of little rocks. By a fallen cornstalk, I met two of my mouse friends. I gave them nibbles of food from the other apron pocket. I went on, and saw a fat old toad by a clod. Mice and toads do have such beautiful eyes. I saw two caterpillars on an ear of corn, after I turned the tassels back. All along the way, I kept hearing voices. Little leaves were whispering, "*Come, petite Françoise*," over in the lane. I saw another mouse with beautiful eyes. Then I saw a man and woman coming across the field. The man was carrying a baby.

Soon I met them — it was Larry and Jean, and their little baby. They let me pat the baby's hand and smooth back its hair, for I do so love babies. When I grow up, I want twins and eight more children, and I want to write outdoor books for children everywhere.

Tonight after Larry and Jean started on, I turned again to wave good-bye. I remembered the first time I saw Larry and Jean, and the bit of poetry he said to her. They were standing by an old stump in the lane, where the leaves whispered. Jean was crying. He patted her on the shoulder, and said:

> "There, little girl, don't cry —
> I'll come back and marry you, by-and-by."

And he did. And the angels looking down from heaven saw their happiness and brought a baby real soon, when they had been married most five months — which was very nice, for a baby is such a comfort, and twins are a multiplication table of blessings. And Felix Mendelssohn is yet so little a person, and the baby of Larry and Jean is growed more big. On the day I did hear him say to her that poetry, it was then I did find Felix Mendelssohn there in the lane next to them. He was only a wee little mouse, then. And every week that he did grow a more week old, I just put one more gray stone in the row of his growing. And there was nineteen more gray stones in the row when the angels did bring the dear baby to Larry and Jean than there was stones in the row when they was married. And now there are a goodly number more stones in the row of Felix Mendelssohn's weeks of growing old.

I have feels that there will be friendship between the dear mouse Felix Mendelssohn and the dear baby of Larry and Jean. For by the stump where he did say that poetry to her was the abiding place of Felix Mendelssohn, when I did have finding of him. This eventime, he did snuggle more close by my curls. I have so much likes for him. I did tell him that this night-time, he is to have sleeps close by.

When we were gone a little way, I did turn again to wave good-bye to the baby of Larry and Jean. After I waved good-bye to the dear baby, I thought I'd go around by the lane where I first saw them and heard him say to her that poetry. It is such a lovely lane. I call it *our* lane. Of course, it doesn't belong to Brave Horatius and Lars Porsena of Clusium and Thomas Chatterton Jupiter Zeus and I and all the rest of us; it belongs to a big man that lives in a big house. But it is our lane more than it is *his* lane, because he doesn't know the grass and flowers that grow there, and the birds that nest there, and the lizards that run along the fence, and the cater-pillars and beetles that go walking along the roads made by the wagon wheels. And he doesn't stop to talk to the trees that grow all along the lane.

All those trees are my friends. I call them by names I have given to them. I call them Hugh Capet, and Saint Louis, and Good King Edward I — and the tallest one of all is Charlemagne, and the one around where the little flowers talk most is William Wordsworth; and there are Byron, and Keats, and Shelley. When I go straight for the milk, I do so like to come around this way by the lane, and talk to these tree friends. I stopped tonight to give to each a word of greeting. When I got to the end of the lane, I climbed the gate, and thought I had better hurry straight on to get the milk.

When I went by the barn, I saw a mouse run around the corner, and a graceful bat came near unto the barn door. I got the milk. It was near dark-time, so I came again home by the lane, and along the corduroy road. When I got most home, I happened to remember the mamma wanted the milk in a hurry, so I began to hurry.

I don't think I'll print more tonight. I printed this sitting on the wood-box, where the mamma put me after she spanked me, after I got home with the milk. Now I think I shall go out the bedroom window and talk to the stars. They always smile so friendly. This is a very wonderful world to live in.

# Four

# Peter Paul Rubens goes to School; Peter Paul Rubens goes Home

In the morning of today, when I was come part way to school, when I was come to the ending of the lane, I met a glad surprise. There was my dear pet pig, a-waiting for me! I gave him three joy pats on the nose, and I did call him by name ten times, I was so glad to see him. Being as I got a late start to school, I didn't have enough time to go around by the pig-pen, for our morning talk. And there he was, a-waiting for me at the ending of the lane! And his name, it is Peter Paul Rubens.

His name is that because the first day I saw him was on the twenty-ninth of June. He was little, then — a very plump young pig with a little red-ribbon squeal, and a wanting to go everywhere I did go. Sometimes he would squeal, and I wouldn't go to find out what he wanted. Then one day when his nose was sore, he did give such an odd pain squeal. Of course, I run a quick run to help him. After that, when he had a chance, he would come to the kitchen door and give that same squeal. That Peter Paul Rubens seemed to know that was the only one of all his squeals that would bring me at once to where he was.

And this morning when I did start on to school, he gave that same squeal, and came a-following after. When he was caught up with me, he gave a grunt, and then he gave his little red-ribbon squeal. A lump came up in my throat, and I couldn't tell him to turn around and go back to the pig-pen. So we just went along to school together.

When we got there, school was already took up. I went in first. The new teacher came back to tell me I was tardy again. She did look out the door. She saw my dear Peter Paul Rubens. She did ask me where that pig came from. I just started in to tell her all about him, from the day I first met him.

She did look long looks at me. She did look those looks for a long time. I made pleats in my apron with my fingers. I made nine on one side, and three on the other side. When I was through counting the pleats I did make in my apron, I did ask her what she was looking those long looks at me for. She said, "I'm screwtin-eyesing you." I never did hear that word before — it is a new word. It does have an interest sound. I think I will have uses for it. Now when I look long looks at a thing, I will print I did *screwtineyes* it.

After she did look more long looks at me, she went back to her desk by the blackboard. She did call the sixth grade fiziologie class. I went to my seat. I only sat halfway in it. I so did so I would have seeing of my dear Peter Paul Rubens.

He did wait at the steps; he looked long looks toward the door. It wasn't long until he walked right in. I felt such an amount of satisfaction, having him at school. Teacher felt not so.

Now I have wonders about things. I wonder why was it teacher didn't want Peter Paul Rubens coming to school. Why, he did make such a sweet picture as he did stand there in the doorway, looking looks about. And the grunts he gave, they were such nice ones. He stood there saying, *"I have come to your school — what class are you going to put me in?"* He said in plain grunts the very same words I did say the first day I came to school.

The children all turned around in their seats. I'm sure they were glad he was come to school, and him talking there in that dear way. But I guess our teacher doesn't have understanding of pig talk. She just came at him in such a hurry, with a stick of wood. And when I made interferes, she did send us both home, in a quick way.

We did have a most happy time coming home. We did go on an exploration trip. Before we were gone far, we did have hungry feels. I took the lid off the lard-bucket that my school lunch was in. I did make divides of all my bread and butter. Part I gave to Peter Paul Rubens, and he did have appreciations. He did grunt grunts for some more. Pretty soon, it was all gone. We did go on.

We went on to the woods. I did dig up little plants with leaves that do stay green all winter. We saw many beautiful things. Most everything we did see, I did explain about it to Peter Paul Rubens. I told him why — all about why I was digging up so many of the little plants. I did want him to have understanding that I was going to plant them again.

When I did have almost forty-five, and it was come near eventime, Brave Horatius and Lars Porsena of Clusium did come to meet us. When I did have forty-five plants, we all did go in the way that does lead to the cathedral, for this is the borning day of Girolamo Savonarola. And in the cathedral, I did plant little plants, as many years as he was old. Forty-five I did so plant. And we had prayers, and came home.

# Five

# Opal has a Hard Day at School; she finds Crayons in the Moss-Box, and visits the Mill by the Far Woods

Aphrodite has got a nice blue ribbon all her very own, to wear when we go walking down the lane, and to services in the cathedral. The man that wears gray neckties and is kind to mice did give to Sadie McKibben the money to buy it last time she went to the mill town. That was on the afternoon of the day before yesterday.

On yesterday, when I was coming my way home from school, I did meet with Sadie McKibben. It was nice to see her freckles, and the smiles in her eyes. She did have me to shut my eyes, and she did lay in my hand the new blue ribbon for Aphrodite that the man that wears gray neckties and is kind to mice did have her to get. I felt glad feels all over. I gave her all our thanks. I did have knowing all my animal friends would be glad for the remembers of the needs of Aphrodite for a blue ribbon.

I did have beginnings of hurry feels to go to the pig-pen. I have thinks Sadie McKibben saw the hurrys in my eyes. She said she would like to go hurrys to the pig-pen too, but she was on her way to the house of Mrs. Limberger. She did kiss me good-bye — two on the cheeks, and one on the nose.

I run a quick run to the pig-pen, to show it to Aphrodite. I gave her little pats on the nose, and long rubs on the ears, and I did tell her all about it. I did hold it close to her eyes, so she could have well seeing of its beautiful blues, like the blues of the sky. She did grunt thank grunts, and she had wants to go for a walk, right away.

I did make invest tag ashuns where there used to be a weak place in the pig-pen. It was not any more. I did look close looks at it. I made pulls, but nothing made little slips. Before, it was not like that. I have thinks that chore boy is giving too much at ten chuns to the fence of this pig-pen that Aphrodite has living in all of the time I am not taking her on walks.

I did feel some sad feels when I could not take her walking down the lane with her nice new blue ribbon on. While I did feel the sad feels so, I did carry bracken ferns to make her a nice bed. It brought her feels of where we were going for walks, where the bracken ferns grow.

When I did have her a nice bed of bracken fern, and some more all about her, I went goes to get the other folks. Back with me came Brave Horatius, and Lars Porsena of Clusium, and Thomas Chatterton Jupiter Zeus, and Lucian Horace Ovid Virgil, and Felix Mendelssohn, and Louis II, le Grand Condé. When we were all come, I did climb into the pig-pen and I did tie on Aphrodite's new ribbon, so they all might have seeing of its blues like the sky. I sang a little thank song, and we had prayers, and I gave Aphrodite little scratches on the back with a little stick, like she does so like to have me do. That was to make up for her not getting to go for a walk where the bracken ferns grow.

Now teacher is looking very straight looks at me. She says, "Opal, put that away." I so do.

Today it is I do sit here at my desk, while the children are out for play at recess-time. I sit here and I do print. I cannot have goings to talk with the trees that I do mostly have talks with at recess-time. I cannot have goings down to the rivière across the road, like I do so go sometimes at recess-time. I sit here in my seat. Teacher says I must stay in all this whole recess-time.

It was after some of our reading lessons this morning — it was then teacher did ask questions of all the school. First she asked Jimmy eight things at once. She did ask him what is a horse and a donkey and a squirrel and a engine and a road and a snake and a store and a rat. And he did tell her all. He did tell her in his way. Then she asked Big Jud some things, and he got up in a slow way and said, "I don't know," like he most always does, and he sat down. Then she asked Lola some things, and Lola did tell her, all in one breath. And teacher marked her a good mark in the book, and she gave Lola a smile. And Lola gave her nice red hair a smooth-back, and smiled a smile back at teacher.

Then it was teacher did call my name. I stood up real quick. I did have thinks it would be nice to get a smile from her, like the smile she did smile upon Lola. And teacher did ask me eight things at once. She did ask me what is a pig and a mouse and a baby deer and a duck and a turkey and a fish and a colt and a blackbird. And I did say in a real quick way, "A pig is a *cochon* and a mouse is a *mulot* and a baby deer is a *daine* and a duck is a *canard* and a turkey is a *dindon* and a fish is a *poisson* and a colt is a *poulain* and a blackbird is a *merle*." And after each one I did say, teacher did shake her head and say, "*It is not*," and I did say, "*It is*."

When I was all through, she did say, "You have them all wrong. You have not told what they are. They are not what you said they are." And when she said that, I did just say, "They are. They are. They are."

Teacher said, "Opal, you sit down." I so did. But when I sat down, I said, "A pig is a cochon, a mouse is a mulot, a baby deer is a daine, a duck is a canard, a turkey is a dindon, a fish is a poisson, a colt is a poulain, a blackbird is a merle." Teacher says, "Opal, for that you are going to stay in next recess, and both recess-times tomorrow, and the next day, and the next day." Then she did look a look at all the school, and she did say as how my not getting to go out for recess-times would be an egg sam pull for all the other children in our school.

They are out at play. It is a most long recess. But I do know a pig is a cochon, and a mouse is a mulot, and a baby deer is a daine, and a duck is a canard, and a turkey is a dindon, and a fish is a poisson, and a colt is a poulain, and a blackbird is a merle. So I do know, for Angel Father always did call them so. He knows. He knows what things are. But no one hereabouts does call things by the names Angel Father did. Sometimes I do have thinks this world is a different world to live in. I do have lonesome feels.

This is a most long recess. While here I do sit, I do hear the talkings of the more big girls, outside the window most near unto my desk. The children are playing Black Man, and the ones more little are playing tag. I have thinks as how nice it would be to be having talks with Good King Edward I, and lovely Queen Eleanor of Castile, and Peter Paul Rubens, and Brave Horatius, and Lars Porsena of Clusium, and Thomas Chatterton Jupiter Zeus, and Aphrodite. And I do think this is a most long recess.

I still do have hearings of the talkings of the girls outside the windows. The more old girls are talking what they want. Martha says she wants a bow. I don't have seeings why she wants *another* one. Both her braids were tied back this morningtime with a new bow, and its color was the color of the blossoms of *camarine*. Lola says she wants a white silk dress. She says her life will be complete when she does have on a white silk dress — a white silk dress with a little ruffle around the neck, and one around each sleeve. She says she will be a great lady, then. And she says all the children will gather around her and sing, when she has her white silk dress on. And while they sing, and while she does have her white silk dress on, she will stand up and stretch out her arms and bestow her blessing on all the people, like the deacon does in the church at the mill town.

Now teacher is come to the door. She does say, "Opal, you may eat your lunch — at your desk." I did have hungry feels, and all this is noontime, instead of short recess-time. It so *has* been a long recess-time. I did have thinks when came noontime of all the things I would do, down by the rivière.

Now I do gather seeds along the road, and in the field. I lay in rows side by side the seeds I gather. With them I do play *comparer* [comparison]. I look near looks at them. I do so to see how they look not like one another. Some are big, and some are not so. And some are more large than others are large. And some do have wrinkles on them, and some have little wings, and some do have silken sails.

Many so of all I did see on my way coming home from school on this eventime; and too I did see four gray squirrels, and two chipmunks. And when I was come near the meeting of the roads, I saw a tramper coming down the railroad track where the dinkey-engine comes with cars of lumbers from the upper camps. This tramper, he did have a big roll on his back, and he walked steps on the ties in a slow, tired way.

When I was come more near to the track, I did have thinks he might have hungry feels. Most trampers do. While I was having thinks about it, I took the lid off my dinner-pail. There was just a half a piece of bread and butter left. I was saving that. I was saving it to make divides between Peter Paul Rubens and Aphrodite and Felix Mendelssohn and Louis II, le Grand Condé, and the rest of us. I did look looks from that piece of bread and butter in the dinner-pail to the tramper going down the railroad track. I did have little feels of the big hungry feels he might be having.

I ran a quick run to catch up with him. He was glad for it. He ate it in two bites.

And I came a quick way to our lane. I went along it. I made a stop by a hazel bush. I did stop to watch a caterpillar making his cradle. He did not move about while he did make it — he did roll himself up in a leaf. That almost hid him. He did weave white silk about him. I think it must be an interesting life, to live a caterpillar life. Some days, I do think I would like to be a caterpiller, and by-and-by make a silk cradle. The silk a caterpillar makes its cradle from does come from its mouth. I have seen it so. But not so have I seen come the silk the spider does make its web of — this silk does come from the back part of the back of the spider.

When I was come to the house we live in, I did do the works the mamma did have for me to do. Then I made begins to fill the wood-box. When I did have ten sticks piled on its top, I looked to the door, where the mamma was talking with Elsie. I did have sorry feels for the mamma — I heard her say she lost ten minutes. I did have wants to help her find them. I looked looks under the cupboard, and they were not there. I looked looks in the cook-table drawers, and they were not there. I looked looks into every machine-that-sews drawer, and I didn't find them. I crawled under the bed, but I had no seeing of them. Then I did look looks in all the corners of the house that we do live in. I looked looks all about, but I didn't find them. I have wonders where those ten minutes the mamma lost are gone. While I did look more looks about for them, she did say for me to get out of her way. I so did.

I went to look for the fairies. I went to the near woods. I hid behind the trees, and made little runs to big logs. I walked along the logs, and I went among the ferns. I did tiptoe among the ferns; I looked looks about. I did touch fern-fronds, and I did have feels of their gentle movements. I came to a big root. I hid in it. I so did to wait waits for the fairies that come among the big trees.

While I did wait waits, I did have thinks about that letter I did write on the other day, for more color pencils that I do have needs of to print with. I thought I would go to the moss-box by the old log. I thought I would have goes there to see if the fairies yet did find my letter.

I went. The letter — it was gone. Then I did have joy feels all over — the color pencils, they were come! There was a blue one, and a green one, and a yellow one. And there was a purple one, and a brown one, and a red one. I did look looks at them a long time. It was so nice, the quick way the fairies did bring them.

While I was looking more looks at them, someone did come near the old root. It was my dear friend, Peter Paul Rubens. I gave him four pats, and I showed him all the color pencils. Then I did make a start to go to the mill by the far woods. Peter Paul Rubens went with me, and Brave Horatius came a-following after. All the way along, I did feel glad feels, and I had thinks how happy the man that wears gray neckties and is kind to mice would be when he did see how quick the fairies did answer my letter and bring the color pencils.

When we were come near the mill by the far woods, it was near graylight-time. The lumber men were on their home way. They did whistle as they did go. Two went side by side, and three came after. And one came after all. It was the man that wears gray neckties and is kind to mice. Brave Horatius made a quick run to meet him, and I did follow after.

I did have him guess what it was the fairies did bring this time. He guessed a sugar-lump for William Shakespeare every day next week. I told him it wasn't a right guess. He guessed some more. But he couldn't guess right, so I showed them all to him. He was so surprised. He said he was so surprised the fairies did bring them this soon. And he was so glad about it. He always is.

He and I, we do have knows the fairies walk often in these woods. And when I do have needs of more color pencils to make more prints with, I do write the fairies about it. I write to them a little letter on leaves of trees, and I do put it in the moss-box at the end of the old log. Then after they do come walking in the woods and find the letter in the moss-box, they do bring the color pencils, and they lay them in the moss-box. I find them there, and I am happy.

No one does have knowing of that moss-box but one.

He is the man that wears gray neckties and is kind to mice. He has knowing of the letters I do print on leaves and put there for the fairies. And after he does ask me, and after I do tell him I have wrote to them for color pencils that I have needs of, he does take a little fern plant and make a fern wish with it that the fairies will bring to me the color pencils I have needs of. Then we do plant the little fern by the old log. And the time is not long until I do find the color pencils in the moss-box by the old log. I am very happy.

# Six

# The Potato Field, a Washing, and Thomas Chatterton Jupiter Zeus

Today the grandpa dug potatoes in the field. Too, the chore boy did dig potatoes in the field. I followed along after. My work was to pick up the potatoes they got out of the ground. I picked them up, and piled them in piles. Some of them were very plump. Some of them were not big. All of them wore brown dresses.

When they were in piles, I did stop to take looks at them. I walked up close; I looked them all over. I walked off and took a long look at them. Potatoes are very interesting folks. I think they must see a lot of what is going on in the earth — they have so many eyes. And after I did look those looks as I did go along, I did count the eyes that every potato did have, and their numbers were in blessings.

To some piles, I did stop to give geology lectures. And some I did tell about the nursery, and the caterpillars in it — the caterpillars that are going to *hiver* [winter] sleep in silken cradles, and some in woolen so go. To more potatoes, I did tell about my hospital at Saint-

Germain-en-Laye in the near woods, and all about the folks that were in it, and that are in it, and how much prayers and songs and Mentholatum helps them to have well feels.

And to some other potatoes, I did talk about my friends — about the talks that William Shakespeare and I do have together; and about how Lars Porsena of Clusium does have a fondness for collecting things, and how he does hide them in the oak tree near unto the house we live in; and about Elizabeth Barrett Browning, and the poetry in her tracks. And one I did tell about the new ribbon Aphrodite has to wear, and how she does have a fondness for chocolate creams. To the potato most near unto it, I did tell of the little bell that Peter Paul Rubens does wear to cathedral service. To the one next to it, I did tell how Louis II, le Grand Condé, is a mouse of gentle ways, and how he does have likings to ride in my sleeve.

And all the times I was picking up potatoes, I did have conversations with them. Too, I did have thinks of all their growing days there in the ground, and all the things they did hear. Earth-voices are glad voices, and earth-songs come up from the ground through the plants; and in their flowering, and in the days before these days are come, they do tell the earth-songs to the wind. And the wind in her goings does whisper them to folks to print for other folks, so other folks do have knowing of earth's songs. When I grow up, I am going to write for children — and grownups that haven't grown up too much — all the earth-songs I now do hear.

I have thinks these potatoes growing here did have knowings of star-songs. I have kept watch in the field at night, and I have seen the stars look kindness down upon them. And I have walked between the rows of potatoes, and I have watched the star-gleams on their leaves. And I have heard the wind ask of them the star-songs the star-gleams did tell in shadows on their leaves. And as the wind did go walking in the field talking to the earth-voices there, I did follow her down the rows. I did have feels of her presence near. And her goings-by made ripples on my nightgown. Thomas Chatterton Jupiter Zeus did cuddle more close up in my arms. And Brave Horatius followed after.

Sometimes, when a time long it is I have been walking and listening to the voices of the night, then it is Brave Horatius does catch the corner of my nightgown in his mouth and he pulls — he pulls most hard, in the way that does go to the house we live in. After he does pull, he barks the barks he always does bark when he has thinks it is home-going time. I listen. Sometimes I go back. He goes with me. Sometimes I go on. He goes with me. And often it is, he is here come with me to this field where the potatoes grow. And he knows most all the poetry I have told them.

On the afternoon of today, when I did have a goodly number of potatoes in piles, I did have thinks as how this was the going-away day of Saint François of Assisi, and the borning day of Jean François Millet — so I did take as many potatoes as they years did dwell upon earth. Forty-four potatoes I so took for Saint François of Assisi, for his years were near unto forty-four. Sixty potatoes I so took for Jean François Millet, for his years were sixty years. All these potatoes I did lay in two rows — in one row was forty-four, and in the other row was sixty.

And as I had seeing of them all there, I did have thinks to have a choir. First I did sing, "*Sanctus, sanctus, sanctus, Dominus Deus.*" After I did sing it three times,

I did have thinks as how it would be nice to have more in the choir. And I did have remembers as how tomorrow is the going-away day of Philippe III, roi [king] de France; and so for the forty years that were his years, I did bring forty more potatoes in a row. That made more in the choir. Then I did sing three times over, "*Gloria Patri, et Filio, et Spiritu Sancto. Hosanna in excelsis.*"

Before I did get all through the last time with *Hosanna in excelsis*, I did have thinks as how the next day after that day would be the borning day of Louis Philippe, roi de France, and the going-away day of Alfred Tennyson. And I did bring more potatoes for the choir. Seventy-six I did so bring for the years that were the years of Louis Philippe, roi de France; eighty-three I so did bring for the years that were the years of Alfred Tennyson. And the choir, there was a goodly number of folks in it, all potato folks wearing brown robes. Then I did sing one "*Ave Maria.*"

I was going to sing one more, when I did have thinks as how the next day after the next day after the next day would be the going-away day of Sir Philip Sidney — so I did bring thirty-one more potatoes for the choir. It did take a more long time to bring them, because all the potatoes near about were already in the choir.

Brave Horatius did walk by my side, and he did have seeing as how I was bringing potatoes to the choir. And so *he* did bring some — one at a time, he did pick them up and bring them, just like he does pick up a stick of wood in his mouth when I am carrying in wood. He is a most helpful dog. Today I did have needs to keep watches — I did so have needs to see that he put not more potatoes in the other choir-rows. First time he did bring a potato, he did lay it down by the choir-row of

Alfred Tennyson. Next potato he did bring, he did lay it by the choir-row of Jean François Millet. Next time, I made a quick run when I did have seeing of him going to lay it down by the choir-row of Philippe III, roi de France. I did pat my foot, and tell him where to lay it for the choir-row of Sir Philip Sidney. He so did. We did go for more.

When there were thirty-one potatoes in the choir-row of Sir Philip Sidney, we did start service again. I did begin with "*Sanctus, sanctus, sanctus, Dominus Deus,*" and Brave Horatius did bark Amen. Then I did begin all over, and he did so again. After we had prayers, I did sing one more "*Ave Maria.*" Then I did begin to sing, "*Deo Gratias, Hosanna in excelsis,*" but I came not unto its ending — Brave Horatius did bark Amen before I was half done. I just went on. He walked in front of me and did bark Amen, three times.

I was just going to sing the all of it. I did not so. I so did not, because the chore boy did have steps behind me. He gave me three shoulder-shakes, and he did tell me to get a hurry on me and get those potatoes picked up. I so did — I so did in a most quick way. The time it did take to pick them up, it was not a long time.

And after that, there was more potatoes to pick up. Brave Horatius did follow after. He gave helps. He did lay the potatoes he did pick up on the piles I did pick up. He is a most good dog.

When near graylight-time was come, the chore boy went from the field. When most dark-time was come, Brave Horatius and I so went.

When we were come to the house we live in, the folks was gone to visit at the house of Elsie. I did take my bowl of bread and milk, and I did eat it on the back steps. Brave Horatius ate his supper near me. He did eat his all long before I did mine, so I did give him some of mine. Then we watched the stars come out.

I did not have goings to school today, for this is wash-day, and the mamma did have needs of me at home. There was baby clothes to wash. The mamma does say that is my work, and I do try to do it in the proper way she does say it ought to be done. It does take quite a long time. And all the time it is taking, I do have long-ings to go on exploration trips. And I do want to go talk with William Shakespeare, there where he is pulling logs in the near woods. And I do want to go talk with Elizabeth Barrett Browning in the pasture, and with Peter Paul Rubens and Aphrodite in the pig-pen. All the time it does take to wash the clothes of the baby — it is a long time. And I do stop at in-between times, to listen to the voices. They are always talking. And the brook that does go by our house is always bringing songs from the hills.

When the clothes of the baby were most white, I did bring them again to the wash-bench that does set on the porch that does go out from our back door. Then there was the chickens to feed, and the stockings were to rub. Stockings do have needs of many rubs — that makes them clean. While I did do the rubs, I did sing little songs to the grasses that grow about our door. After the stockings did have many rubs, the baby it was to tend. I did sing it songs of songs Angel Mother did sing to me, and sleeps came upon the baby. But she is a baby that does have wake-ups between times. Today she had a goodly number.

By-and-by, when the washing was part done, then the mamma went away to the grandma's house to get some soap. When she went away, she did say she wished she didn't have to bother with carrying water to scrub the floor. She doesn't. While she has been gone a good while, I have plenty of water on the floor, for her to mop it when she gets back. When she did go away, she said to me to wring the clothes out of the wash. There were a lot of clothes in the wash — skirts and aprons, and shirts and dresses, and clothes that you wear under dresses. Every bit of clothes I took out of the tubs, I carried into the kitchen and squeezed all the water out on the kitchen floor. That makes lots of water every-where — under the cook-table, and under the cupboard, and under the stove. Why, there is most enough water to mop the three floors, and then some water would be left over. I did feel glad feels, because it was so as the mamma did want it. While I did wait for her coming, I did make prints and mind the baby.

When the mamma was come, she did look not glad looks at the water on the floor. She did only look looks for the switches over the kitchen window. After I did have many sore feels, she put me out the door, to stay out. I did have sorry feels for her — I did so try hard to be helps.

When a little way I was gone from the door, I did look looks about. I saw brown leaves, and brown birds. Brown leaves were *érable* [maple] leaves and *chêne* [oak] leaves, and the brown birds were wrens. And all their ways were hurry ways.

I did turn about, and I did go in a hurry way to a root in the near woods. I so went to get my little candle. Then I did go to the Jardin [garden] des Tuileries. Often it is I do go there, near unto the near woods. Many days after I was here come, I did go ways to look for Jardin des Tuileries. I found it not. Sadie McKibben did say there is none such here. Then, being needs for it, and it being not, I did have it so. And in it I have put statues of *hiver* and all the others, and here I do plant plants and little trees. And every little tree that I did plant, it was for someone that was. And on their borning days, I do hold services by the trees I have so planted for them.

Today I did go in quick steps to the tree I have planted for Louis Philippe, roi de France; for this is the day of his borning, in 1773. I did have prayers; then I did light my little candle. Seventy-six big candles Angel Father did so light for him, but so I cannot do, for only one little candle I have. It did burn in a bright way. Then I did sing, *"Deo Gratias."* I so did sing for the borning day of Louis Philippe, roi de France. Then I did sing, *"Sanctus, sanctus, sanctus, Dominus Deus."*

Afterwards, I did have thinks about Thomas Chatterton Jupiter Zeus — about his nose, its feels. I so went in the way that does go to the hospital. That dear pet rat's nose is getting well. Some way, he got his nose too near that trap they set for rats in the barn. Of course when I found him that morning, I let him right out of the trap. He has a ward all to himself in the hospital. For breakfast, he has some of my oatmeal; for dinner, he has some of my dinner; and for supper, I carry to him corn in a jar lid. Sadie McKibben, who has on her face many freckles and a kind heart, gives me enough Mentholatum to put on his nose seven times a day. And he is growing better.

And today, when I was come to the hospital, I took him in my arms. He did cuddle up. Too, he gave his cheese squeak. That made me have lonesome feels. I can't carry cheese to him anymore, out of the house we live in. I can't because, when the mamma learned that I was carrying cheese to Thomas Chatterton Jupiter

Zeus, she said to me while she did apply a kindling to the back part of me, "Don't you dare carry any more cheese out to that rat!" And since then, I do not carry cheese out to Thomas Chatterton Jupiter Zeus. But I do carry *him* into the kitchen to the *cheese*. I let him sniff long sniffs at it. Then I push his nose back, and I cut from the big piece of cheese delicate slices for Thomas Chatterton Jupiter Zeus. This I do when the mamma isn't at home.

Today, she being come again to the house we live in, I could not have goings there for Thomas Chatterton Jupiter Zeus to the cheese. I did go the way that goes to the house of Sadie McKibben. I did go that way so she might have knowings of the nose-improvements of Thomas Chatterton Jupiter Zeus.

When I was most come here, he did squeak more of his cheese squeaks. It was most hard, having hearing of him and not having cheese for him. I could hardly keep from crying. He is a most lovely wood-rat, and all his ways are ways of gentleness. And he is just like the mamma's baby — when he squeaks, he does have expects to get what he squeaks for. I did cuddle him up more close in my arms, and he had not squeaks again for some little time.

It was when I was talking to Sadie McKibben about the château [castle] of Neuilly, that I do have most part done — it was then he did give his squeaks. He began, and went on, and did continue so. I just couldn't keep from crying. His cheese longings are like my longings for Angel Mother and Angel Father. He did just crawl up and put his nose against my curls. I did stand first on one foot, and then on the other. The things I was going to say did go in a swallow down my throat.

Sadie McKibben did wipe her hands on her blue

gingham apron with cross-stitches on it. She did have askings what was the matter with Thomas Chatterton Jupiter Zeus. And I just said, "O Sadie McKibben — it's his cheese squeak." And she said not a word, but she did go in a quick way to her kitchen. She brought back a piece of cheese. It wasn't a *little* piece; it was a great *big* piece. There's enough in it for four breakfasts and six dinners. When Sadie McKibben did give it to me for him, she did smooth back my curls and she did give me three kisses — one on each cheek, and one on the nose. She smiled her smile upon us, and we were most happy.

And we did go from her house to the cathedral. There I did have a thank service for the goodness of God and the goodness of Sadie McKibben, and the piece of cheese that did bring peace to the lovely Thomas Chatterton Jupiter Zeus.

# Seven

# The Tramper and
# the Ham, and
# How Trampers Differ

Today was a falltime-is-here day. I heard
the men say so that were talking at the meeting of the
roads. From the meeting of the roads, I did hurry on. I
so did in a quick way because, when I was come to the
meeting of the roads, I did have remembers as how the
mamma did say at morningtime there was much work
to be done before eventime.

When I was come to the house we live in, the
mamma and the little girl and the baby, they were all
gone to the house of Elsie. I made a start at the works.
I did feed the chickens, and there was much wood to
bring in, and baby clothes to wash, and ashes to empty
from the stove. These four things I did. I looked looks
about, to see what other works did have needs to be
done.

I had remembers that when the papa went away to
work this morning, he said he did not have time to cut
the ham before he went. I have knows if he is too busy
in the morning to get a thing done, it mostly don't get
done when he comes home from work at night — it so

does not because he has so tired feels. Today I had thinks the time was come when I better help about that ham.

I went out to the wood-shed. I went not out to get wood; I went out to the wood-shed to tend to that ham. I had thinks I better make an early start, or that ham wouldn't be cut up by evening.

I piled wood high enough so I could stand on tiptoes and reach to the flour-sack the ham was tied in. But I could not get that sack down. I pulled and pulled, but it wouldn't come down. I didn't have knows what I was going to do.

Pretty soon, by having concentration of my thinks, I thought of a way. I got the scissors, and cut the bottom out of that sack. That ham came down right quick. It landed on its back on the woodpile. My foot slipped, and I landed on top of it. I got up, and dragged it up on the chopping-block. Then I got the butcher-knife from its place in the cook-table drawer. I went to work.

That knife didn't seem to make moves like the moves it does make when it is in the hands of the papa. I tried to make it go down in a quick way. It went not so. I looked close looks at it. Its appears did have looks like it did have needs of a sharp pennying. I have seen the papa sharp pen it on the grindstone by the singing brook.

So did I. I poured a goodly amount of water on that stone wheel. Most of the water splashed off. The rest did trickle away. Then I did hold that knife to the stone wheel, and I did make tries to turn it in a quick way, like I have seen the papa do. But I could not make that wheel go in quick turns. It would not so go. I made big tries, for a long time.

When I had thinks the knife did look some better, I did go again to my work. I walked three times around that ham there on the chopping-block. I so did to take looks at it, to see where I better make begins. I did have thinks in under its outside where it is most big would be the proper place.

I made begins. I did make the knife to go a little way. Then I made a stop to rest. Then I made the knife go some more. I made another stop to rest. I went on.

Pretty soon, a slice of ham landed. It fell off the chopping-block onto a stick of wood. I picked it up. I held it up to take a look at it. My, I did feel such proud feels, from my toes to my curls! I had it cut in such a nice way. It had frills around it, and holes in-between, just like Elsie's crochet doily that she keeps on her best stand-table. I have knows the papa never did cut a slice of ham that way. The slices of ham *he* cuts — they never do have frilly looks, with holes in-between.

After I did hang that slice of ham on a nail by the door, I did cut another slice. It was not so wide, but it had more longness, and some strings on it like the little short strings on the nightcap of Jenny Strong. I had not decides yet where to hang it. It was when I was having thinks about it — it was then I did hear a heavy step.

I turned me all about, and there was a tramper by the wood-shed door. He had not gentle looks, like some trampers have. His beard did grow in the hobo way, and his appears did look like he knew not knowings of neatness. He stood there, looking looks at that ham. He kept his looks on it, and he did walk right into the wood-shed.

He had asking if the mamma was at home. I said, "No, she is not — she is at the house of Elsie." Then he says, "I guess I'll take this *ham* along with me."

I almost lost my breathings, because I did have re-members of all the days the papa has plans to have that ham for breakfast and dinner and supper. So I just sat down on the chopping-block — I sat on the ham, and I spread my blue calico apron out over it. I put my hand on its handle that it hangs in the wood-shed by. Me and my apron covered that ham, so he couldn't have seeing of it. And while I sat on the ham, I did pray God to keep it safe for the breakfasts and dinners and suppers of the papa and the mamma.

The tramper looked queer looks at me. He came a little more near. I did pray on. And God in his goodness sent answers to my prayer, in a quick way. Brave Horatius came on a run from somewhere. He made a stop at the wood-shed door; he looked a look in; he gave a growl. Then he went at that tramper. He did grab him by his ragged pants. I have thinks maybe his teeth did touch the ankle of the tramper, because he gave a little pain squeal, and shook his leg. Then he did go in a hurry, away. Brave Horatius followed after.

I was just going to start work again on that ham, when the mamma was come home from her visit. She did soon give me a whipping, and put me here under the bed. Now I have wonders what that whipping was for. I did feed the chickens, and carry in the wood, and do the baby's washing, and empty the ashes. And more I did, besides — I cut two slices of ham, with frills on them.

Now I have thinks about trampers — how they do differ. Many of them follow the railroad track. They make goes to the upper camps, beyond the rivière. They do carry a roll on their backs. They so carry their blankets. They go that way, and some of them come down the track very soon again. Some stay nowhere long.

Some of the trampers that go the way that goes to the upper camps do have stops when they go by here. They stop to get a bite to eat. And some come to the front door, and some do come to the back door. They knock on the door. Some rap their knuckles hard, and some tap in a gentle way.

There was one who so did, one week ago. Sleeps was just come upon the baby, after I did sing it le chanson de Saint Firmin [the song of Saint Firmin]. And I did go to the door, to see who it was. The man that it was, he said he was on his way to get work at the upper camps. He was a man with a clean, sad face, and a kind look in his eyes. And the roll upon his back was a heavy roll. I straightway did go and get my bowl of bread and milk, that I was going to have for dinner. I gave it to him. He ate it in a hungry way, like Brave Horatius does eat his supper when we are come back from a long explore trip. Then when the man did eat all the bread and milk, he did split some wood, out in the woodshed. He did pile it up in a nice way. Then he went — he went on to the upper camps. When he did go, he said, "The Lord's blessing be with you, child." I said, "It is." And I did tell him, "We have a cathedral in the woods, and this eventime when we have prayers there, we will pray that you may get work at the upper camps."

And at coming of eventime, we did. And Peter Paul Rubens did grunt Amen at in-between times. Now every day, we do pray for the man that was hungry, and had a kind look in his eyes.

Some days are long. Some days are short. The days that I have to stay in the house are the most long days of all.

In the morningtime of now, I had thinks to go on explores. I was going to Saint Firmin, and adown the Nonette. I was going to listen to its singings. And Peter Paul Rubens and Brave Horatius and Lars Porsena of

Clusium and Thomas Chatterton Jupiter Zeus, we were all going together. When I did have the wood in the wood-box, the mamma hollered at me. She said when she got back from Elsie's, she was going to make me stay in the house all the rest of the day.

While she was gone to the house of Elsie, I did make prepares. I took all the safety-pins out of the machine drawer. I took all the patch-pieces out of the mamma's work-basket. I made patches all over my underskirt, except where I do sit down. I put Louis II, le Grand Condé, in one of the pockets I did so make. I put Lucian Horace Ovid Virgil in another one. In one more pocket, I put Felix Mendelssohn. He peeked out. Then he settled down. He so does like to take naps in the pockets I pin on my underskirts. I put Nannerl Mozart in another pocket. Then when the mamma was come, I did walk into the house in a quiet way.

Before she did go, she told me do's to do while she was gone. She told me to keep the fire going, and to tend the baby — to fix its bottle for it, and to mind it all the time. Then she shut the door and locked it, and went in the way that does go to the house of the grandma, by the meeting of the roads. I did watch her out the window. Then I did put some more wood in the fire. After that, I did look looks about.

There are no rows and rows and rows of books in this house, like Angel Mother and Angel Father had. There is only three books here. One is a cook-book, and one is a doctor-book, and one is a almanac. They all are on top of the cupboard, most against the top of the house. They have not interest names on their backs.

The alarm-clock does set on the shelf, where it always sets all day long. At night-time, it sets on a chair by the bed that the mamma and the papa sleep in — it sets on the chair all night, with its alarm set. It is so the papa will be made awake early in the morning. That clock has interest looks. Someday when there is not a fire in the stove, I have thinks I will take that clock apart, to see what its looks are inside. On a day when there is no fire in the stove, I will climb upon it. I can reach that shelf when I stand on tiptoe on top of the stove.

After I did look looks at the clock, I did look looks out the front window. There are calf-tracks by our front door. These tracks are there because when I went walking with Elizabeth Barrett Browning on yesterday, I had her wait at the front step while I did go into the kitchen to get her some sugar-lumps. She has a fondness for sweet things. I think she will grow up to be a lovely cow. Her mooings now are very musical, and there is poetry in her tracks. She does make such dainty ones. When they dry up in the lane, I dig up her tracks and I save them. There is much poetry in them. And when I take her track out that I keep in the back part of the cook-table drawer, I look at it and think: *This way passed Elizabeth Barrett Browning.*

After I did look looks out the front window, I did look looks out the back window. William Shakespeare and the others, they were pulling in logs. That Rob Ryder was trying to make them go more fast. All the horses do have to pull so hard when they pull logs in. Sometimes they look tired looks. And when they are come in from work, I go to the barn; I rub their heads. For when the mamma is tired, she does like rubs on her head.

While I did watch the horses, the baby had wake-ups. I went to sing her to sleep. I sang her about William Wordsworth.

When sleeps was come upon the baby, I had remembers when she went away, the mamma wished she did have some varnish to shine up the furniture with. So while she is gone, I have given the furniture a shine-up with Vaseline. Vaseline gives just as bright a shine as varnish does. I have aunt tis a pay shuns the mamma will be pleased when her arrives come home.

When the furniture was all fixed proper, I looked a look out the window. Raindrops were beginning to come down from the sky. Their coming was in a gentle way. I had longs to be out with them. I so do like to feel the raindrops patter on my head, and I like to run runs and hold out my hands to meet them. There was more rain, and there was sunshine. There came across the sky the *arc-en-ciel* [rainbow]. Then was its going, and grayness after. I watched the raindrops in the brook, going on and on. When I grow up, I am going to write a book about a raindrop's journey.

While I did watch the raindrops, I had longs to go to the forêt [forest] de Chantilly, and adown by Nonette. I did have thinks more about it. I took some of the wood out of the wood-box. I stood it up for trees. I called them all forêt de Chantilly. We went a walk between them, Lucian Horace Ovid Virgil and I did. Then I took the dipper full of water, and I let it pour in little pours a rivière on the kitchen floor. That was for Nonette. Then all of us went a walk by Nonette. We went in little steps, to make the time go longer. Felix Mendelssohn perched on my shoulder. Louis II, le Grand Condé, did ride in my hands, and Nannerl Mozart in my apron pocket. I took some more water and the dipper, and I made it go a little rivière to join Nonette. Then we went a walk by Lounette. And more I did pour in little pours, to join Nonette. That was for Aunette.

After we did have walks all in-between the forêt de Chantilly, I took more sticks from the wood-box back of the stove, and I made another forêt. Then we went walking in the forêt d'Ermenonville.

When we were come back from that walk, I made some lions out of cheese. Two I made. I made them to put in forêt de Chantilly, at the begins of route du Connétable. Then we went a walk again in forêt de Chantilly. I had to have carefuls not to go a step too big, because I did stand the sticks of wood near unto one another, and if I took a big step, they might have falls over.

While I was standing up more sticks of wood for more trees in forêt de Chantilly, the baby did have wake-ups. I went to sing it to sleep. I sang it about Good King Edward I.

When I went again into the kitchen, there was Louis II, le Grand Condé, and Felix Mendelssohn, and Nannerl Mozart, all in the forêt de Chantilly. They were at the begins of the route du Connétable — they were nibbling nibbles at the two lions there of cheese. Already they did have ragged noses, where all of the three mouses did nibble nibbles. I have thinks I will have to make lions of *stone* for the begins of route du Connétable.

The baby had wakes-up again. I did sing it to sleep with *"Chant d'Automne"* ["Song of Autumn"].

Now I sit here and I print. The baby sleeps on. The wind comes creeping in under the door. It calls, *"Come, come, petite Françoise, come."* It calls to me to come go exploring. It sings of the things that are to be found under leaves. It whispers the dreams of the tall fir trees. It does pipe the gentle song the forest sings on gray days. I hear all the voices calling me. I listen. But I cannot go.

# Eight

## Opal listens to What The Brown Leaves Say, and dances with the Wind; she explains Shadows to The Girl Who Has No Seeing

Now are come the days of brown leaves. They fall from the trees; they flutter on the ground. When the brown leaves flutter, they are saying little things. They talk with the wind. I hear them tell of their borning days, when they did come into the world as leaves. And they whisper of the hoods they wore then. I saw them — I used to count them, on the way to school. Today they were talking of the time before their borning days of this springtime. They talked on and on, and I did listen on to what they were telling the wind and the earth in their whisperings. They told how they were a part of earth and air, before their tree-borning days. And now they are going back. In gray days of winter, they go back to the earth again. But they do not die.

And in the morning of today it was that I did listen to these talkings of the brown leaves. Then I faced about. I turned my face and all of me to the way that leads to the house we live in, for there was much works to be done.

When I was come to the house, I went around and I did walk in the back doorway. The mamma wasn't in. I took long looks about, to see what works I best do first. There was washed-up dishes in a bake-pan, so I did dish-towel them all and put them away. There was needs to climb upon a chair and upon a box, to put those dishes where they ought to be put. While I was up there, I took looks about, to see what there was. I saw a cake of Bon Ami. Bon Ami is to give things a shine-up. And this morning I gave the knives a shine-up, and the forks, too. Then I tried Bon Ami on the black kettles and the bake-pans. It did not give unto them such nice appears, so I gave them a shine-up with Vaseline.

After that, I did take the broom from its place, and I gave the floor a good brooming. I broomed the boards up and down and crossways. There was not a speck of dirt on them left. What I did sweep off with the broom, I did place into a shoe-box lid, and dust it in the stove. Then the floor did look clean, like the mamma does say it ought to look all the time. I put the broom back in its place, where the mamma does say it ought to be.

Then I did look looks from the floor to the window. I thought I better clean the window, too, while I was fixing things. Just when I started to put Bon Ami on the window, I did look out to see what I could see. I saw Agamemnon Menelaus Dindon going in a slow walk by. He was giving his neck a stretch-out. He gave it another one, and when he made a swallow, his throat did look appears of croup. And croup does always have needs of being fixed up. So I laid down the Bon Ami, and I went and I did pour a whole lot of coal-oil down the throat of Agamemnon Menelaus Dindon. That was to make his croup go away. Now he will be feeling well feels, real soon. He didn't want to take the coal-oil

— I had to hold him tight. Some turkey gobblers can kick most hard.

When I did have him fixed, I thought I better take looks about, to see if any more folks did have croup appears. I yet did have some coal-oil left in the bottle. Few folks were about, and none did have croup looks; so I did go again to the cleaning of the window. When that was done in the proper way the mamma says it ought to be done, I did stop to eat some bread and milk, for it was after dinner-time, and it was a long time before supper-time.

After that, I went out in the wood-shed, where the papa keeps his tools. He keeps them in a big box. Some days he forgets to lock the box. Those days, I have very interesting times in the wood-shed. There are all kinds of queer-looking things in that tool-box.

Just when I did have the lid open, the mamma did call. She was come again home. And she sent me back to Elsie's, to get the tidy she was crocheting that she did forget and leave there. So I did go the way that does lead to the house of Elsie. It is not far from the house we live in. And Elsie has not been married long; she only has one baby. She has much liking for it. Elsie is a very young girl — a very young girl to be married, the mamma says.

Today when I came to the house of Elsie, she was trotting on her knee that dear baby boy the angels brought her when she did live at the other camp where we did live, too. To him she was singing a song. It was:

> "Gallop-a-trot,
> Gallop-a-trot,
> This is the way the gentlemen ride,
> Gallop-a-trot."

She tossed her head as she did sing, and the joy-light danced in her eyes.

I have thinks it must be wonderful happiness to be married. I have seen the same joy-light in the eyes of her tall young husband. It is there much when he is come home at eventide from work in the woods. Then she does have many kind words and kisses for him. He has adoors for her. And too he has a pumpadoor that he smooths back with Vaseline. Why, today I did see he had used most all of the Vaseline out of that jar that sets on their kitchen shelf. That Vaseline jar has an interest look. I have been watching it. And every day when I do stand on tiptoe and take peeks at it, there is not so much Vaseline in it as there was in it the day before. I have thinks it does take a goodly amount to keep his pumpadoor smooth.

While I was bringing home the tidy the mamma did leave at the house of Elsie, I met a *chapine** [hooded (?)] baby. He did sail away. *Érable* leaves did go in little hops, and so went I. Soon I saw a gray board. I did turn it over. Under that old gray board were five little silk bags. They were white, and they did feel lumps. I know baby spiders will come out of them when comes spring days, because last year I found bags like these, and this year in the spring, baby spiders walked out. They were very fidgety youngsters.

Just when I did most have decides to take them to the nursery, I heard the mamma calling. I put the board back again, in the way it was before I came that way; then I did run a quick run to the house. And the mamma did send me in a hurry to the wood-shed — it was for two loads of wood she wanted.

* Probably an Opal-invented word.

I did bring in the first load in a hurry. The second load, I brought not so. I did pick up all the sticks my arms could hold. While I was picking them up, I looked long looks at them. I went not to the kitchen with them in a quick way. I was meditating. I did have thinks about the tree they all were, before they got chopped up. I did wonder how *I* would feel, if I was a very little piece of wood that got chopped out of a very big tree. I did think that it would have hurt my feelings. I felt of the feelings of the wood. They did have a very sad feel.

Just when I was getting that topmost stick a bit wet with sympathy tears, then the mamma did come up behind me with a switch. She said while she did switch, "Stop your meditations!" And while she did switch, I did drop the wood. I felt the feels the sticks of wood felt when they hit the floor. Then I did pick them up with care, and I put them all in the wood-box, back of the cook-stove. I put them there because the mamma said I must put them there. But all the time I was churning, I did hum a little song — it was a good-bye song to the sticks in the wood-box, back of the kitchen stove.

When the churning was done and the butter was come, the mamma did lift all the little lumps of butter out of the churn. Then she did pat them together in a big lump, and this she put away in the butter-box in the wood-shed. When she went to lay herself down to rest on the bed, she did call me to rub her head. I like to rub the mamma's head, for it does help the worry lines to go away. Often I rub her head, for it is often she does have longings to have it so; and I do think it is very nice to help people have what they do have longings for.

By-and-by, when the mamma did have sleeps, and

after I did print, I did go to listen to the voices. The wind was calling. His calling was to little wood-folk and me. He did call more again: *"Come, petite Françoise, come go explores!"* He was in a rush. I raced. Brave Horatius ran. We played tag with the wind. The wind does have many things to tell. He does toss back one's curls, so he can whisper things in one's ears. Today he did twice push back my curls three times, that I might better hear what he did have to say. He whispered little whispers about the cradles of moths-to-be, that hang a-swinging on the bushes in the woods.

I went around to see about it. I looked looks on many bushes. Some brown leaves were swinging from some bushes. No cradles I found.

By-and-by, I came to a log. It was a nice little log. It was as long as three pigs as long as Peter Paul Rubens. I climbed upon it. I so did to look more looks about. The wind did blow in a real quick way — he made music all around. I danced on the log. It is so much a big amount of joy to dance on a log when the wind does play the harps in the forest. Then do I dance on tiptoe. I wave greetings to the plant-bush folks that do dance all about. Today a grand pine tree did wave its arms to me, and the bush branches patted my cheek in a friendly way. The wind again did blow back my curls — they clasped the fingers of the bush-people most near. I did turn around to untangle them. It is most difficult to dance on tiptoe on a log when one's curls are in a tangle with the branches of a friendly bush that grows near unto the log, and does make bows to one while the wind doth blow.

When I did turn to untangle my curls, I saw a silken cradle in a hazel branch. I have thinks that the wind did just tangle my curls so I would have seeing of that cradle. It was cream, with a hazel leaf halfway round it. I put it to my ear, and I did listen. It had a little voice. It was not a tone voice; it was a heart voice. While I did listen, I did feel its feels. It had lovely ones.

And I did hurry away in the way that does lead to the house of the girl that has no seeing. I went that way so she too might know its feels, and hear its heart voice. She does so like to feel things — she has *seeing* by feels. Often I do carry things to her when I find them. And she knows some of my friends. Peter Paul Rubens has gone with me to visit her. So has gone Felix Mendelssohn and Nannerl Mozart, the two mices with voices that squeak mouse-songs in the night. And Plato and Pliny, the two bats, and others go, too. And their goings, and what she has thinks about them, I have printed here in my prints. And it is often I go the way that does lead to her house, for the girl who has no seeing, she and I, we are friends.

One day, I told her about the trees talking. Then she did want to know about the voices. And now I do help her to hear them. And too, I tell her about *comparer*, that Angel Father did teach me to play, and I show her the way. She cannot *look* long looks at things, to see how they look not looks alike, because she has no seeing. So she is learning to play *comparer* by feels.

Today, after she did feel the feels of the cream cradle and we did play *comparer*, then she asked me what the trees were saying. And I led her out across her yard and away to the woods, and Brave Horatius did follow after. I led her in the way that does lead to that grand fir tree Good King Louis VI. And when we were come unto him, I did touch his finger-tips to her cheeks. She liked that. Then we did stand near unto him, and I told her of the trees in the night — of the things they tell to the shadows that wander through the woods. She said she didn't think she would like to be a shadow.

And just then, she stubbed her toe. She did ask me what that was there, near unto her foot. I told her it was a *ville* [town] I did build there — the ville of St. Denis. She wanted to know why I builded it there. I told her there was needs of it being near unto Good King Louis VI, for he so loved it; so I builded it there, where his branches shelter it and his kindness looks kind looks upon it. And I did tell her about his being on his way to St. Denis when he died. While I builded up again the corner of the abbey, I did give explanations about how lovely it is to be a gray shadow, walking along and touching the faces of people. Shadows do have such velvety fingers.

After that, we did go on. We went on to where dwell Alan of Bretagne, and Étienne of Blois, and Godefroi of Bouillon, and Raymond of Toulouse. To each I led the girl who has no seeing, and she was glad to know them all. They are grand trees.

As we went our way, we did listen unto the voices. And I took all the hairpins that was in her hair out of it. I so did so the wind could blow it back and whisper things into her ears. The wind does have so much to tell of far lands, and of little folks that dwell near unto us in the fields and in the woods.

Today near eventime, I did lead the girl who has no seeing a little way away into the forest, where it was darkness, and shadows were. I led her toward a shadow that was coming our way. It did touch her cheeks with its velvety fingers. And now she too does have likings for shadows, and her fear that was is gone.

And after that, we turned about to the way that does lead out of the forest. And so we went, and I led her again home. We did hurry a bit. We so did because it was most time for her folks to be there. Often she does say I mustn't be thereabout when her folks are thereabout. I don't be.

At the steps of the door that does go into her house, she did tell me good-bye. When she so did, she kissed me on each cheek, like she always does. Then I did turn my face to the way that leads to the house we live in. Cloud-ships were sailing over the hills. They were in a hurry. The wind was in a hurry. Brown leaves, little ones and big ones, were hurrying along. I thought *I* had better get a hurry on me. I did.

When I was come near unto the barn, I did go in to get Plato and Pliny. I put them in my apron pockets. The barn was rather dark. There were friendly shadows in its corners.

When I came out, I thought of Peter Paul Rubens — I did have thinks cathedral service would be good for his soul. I went again into the barn, to get his little bell that he does always wear around his neck to service. And I did put it on.

There was a time when there was no little bell for Peter Paul Rubens to wear to service. That was in the days before one day when I did say to the man that wears gray neckties and is kind to mice, "I do have needs of a little bell for Peter Paul Rubens to wear to church." I got it. And Peter Paul Rubens always knows he is going to the cathedral when I put that little bell around his neck. It does make lovely silver tinkles as he goes walking down the aisle to the altar.

Tonight so we did go, and too with us was Elizabeth Barrett Browning. When we were come near unto the hospital, I went aside for Thomas Chatterton Jupiter Zeus. In the cathedral, the wind and the trees sang a vesper song. And I prayed for quite a time long, little prayers and long prayers for the goodness of us all. Peter Paul Rubens did grunt Amen at in-between times.

Now I hear the mamma say, "I wonder where Opal is." She has forgets. I'm still under the bed where she did put me, quite a time ago. And all this nice long time, light is come to here from the lamp on the kitchen table — light enough so I can print prints. I am happy. I think I better crawl out now, and go into the bed for sleeps.

# Nine

## Opal goes Walking with Brave Horatius and Peter Paul Rubens, and gives Comfort to Elizabeth Barrett Browning

Near eventime today, I did go out the house when the works were done. I went out the front door and a little way down the path. I made a stop to watch the clouds. They first did come over the hills in a slow way; then they did sail on and on. They were like ships. I did have wonders what thoughts they were carrying from the hills to somewhere. While I did watch, Brave Horatius did come and stand by my side. He looked up at me. In his eyes were askings. I made explainings. I told him, "Le ciel est plein de nuages, qui ont l'air de navires." ["The sky is filled with clouds, which look like ships."]

While I did talk with him, the mamma did call. I went in. Brave Horatius followed after. She made him go out the other door. I went, too — I went to get the potatoes the mamma wanted for supper. I got them out of a sack in the wood-shed.

When she did make prepares to peel the potatoes, the mamma reached away back in the cook-table drawer for the paring-knife. When she did reach so far back, she did feel the track of Elizabeth Barrett Browning. Then she pulled it out, real quick. She threw it out the window. When I went to pick it up, it was broken into eleven pieces. I did gather up all the pieces. They got a little bit wet, from tears that trickled down my nose. When I did get the pieces together, I did put them in the back part of the machine drawer.

While I so did, I heard a grunt by the bedroom window. I climbed out. There was Peter Paul Rubens, and near unto him was Brave Horatius. To each, I gave four pats on the nose. They have likes for pats on the nose. Then I went adown the path. They walked beside me. I saw the cloud-ships sailing on. I made a stop to tell Peter Paul Rubens what I did tell Brave Horatius. I didn't get it all told. When I did say, "Le ciel est plein de nuages," Peter Paul Rubens did grunt a grunt to go on. That was his own dear way of telling me that he already did have knowings those clouds looked like ships. I gave him a pat, and one to Brave Horatius, too.

I went on. They walked beside me. I went on a little way; then I did go aside from the path. I so went to the altar of Saint Louis. Three logs and four stumps and three trees it is distant from the path. And I took there with me all the little plants with green leaves, the ones I did dig up yesterday. I brought them to plant them in a crown there on his altar, for this day is the day of his crowning, in 1226. While I did plant them, the wind did sing a memory song. And the trees were talking — I have thinks they were saying of the goodness of Saint Louis. Peter Paul Rubens, he did have understanding of what they were saying. He did grunt Amen at in-between times.

.    .    .

Today in the morning, when the mamma was in the other room, I did take down from its hook the papa's big coat. I did put it onto me, and it did trail away out behind. I like to wear the papa's big coat. Jenny Strong, who comes to visit us, says the reason I like to wear the papa's big coat is because it makes me more grown-up. She's wrong. The reason I like to wear the papa's big coat is because it has pockets in it — *big* ones — nice ones to put toads and mice and caterpillars and beetles in. *That's* why I like to wear the papa's coat. Why, when I go walking in the papa's big coat, nearly the whole nursery can go along!

This morning, just as I was making a start out the door to the nursery, the mamma came into the kitchen. She did hurry to the door, and I did hurry out — but she caught me by the end of the coat. She did get that coat off of me in a quick way. She hung it back on its nail. When it was hung on its nail in the proper way, she gave to me a shoulder-shake. And I did go to feed the chickens.

After I did feed the chickens all and have some conversations with them, I went in to get the lard-pail that does have my school lunch in it. While I was putting my jacket on, the mamma did tie a new piece of asfiditee around my neck, to keep me from having disease. It was a big piece of asfiditee. It didn't stay a big piece very long. I divided it with my animal friends. Now each one of us has a bit of asfiditee tied around our necks, so we will not catch sickness. I do so like to share things. I could not find Brave Horatius, to give him his share — I did have it already to tie around his dear neck, but he did not answer when I did call. I called in the woods, and I called in the field. When he did not come, I went a little way back in the woods to a root. I hid his piece of asfiditee there. Tomorrow morning, I will tie it around his neck.

Near the root was a little wren. I made a stop to watch him. He was in a hurry — I thought he would tip over. I went in a hurry to help him. Before I was come to the root, he was gone. And I saw his short tail no more.

When I got to school, teacher was standing there in the door. She was looking far-off looks, in the way that does lead to the river. I thought maybe she was having dream-thoughts. I was just going to walk past her, when she turned me about for inspection. She felt the outside of my left apron pocket. But I didn't bring my pet toad again to school this morning. I am not going to risk his life again. Next time, I am going to bring him to school in a pocket in my underskirt.

Most all day in school today, I did study from the books Angel Mother and Angel Father did make for me. I did screwtineyes the spell of words.

When school was let out, I went in the way that does lead to a grove where many *chêne* trees do dwell. I so went to get brown leaves. After I did have a goodly number of leaves, I did face about in the way that does lead to the willow creek.

When I was come to the log that goes across the creek, I went halfway across. I went not all way across because this is the going-away day of Henry I in 1135, and I did pause to scatter leaves upon the waters. I let them fall, one by one. And they were sixty-seven, for his years were sixty-seven.

Then I went to bugle in the canyon. I did go by the pig-pen. I went that way to get Peter Paul Rubens. He does so like to go for walks in that canyon of the far woods when I go to bugle there, and I do so like to have him go. I have thinks the trees and the ferns and the singing brook all have gladness when Peter Paul Rubens comes a while to walk in the woods. He does carry so much joy with him, everywhere he goes.

Today near eventime, we did walk our way back unto near the cathedral. We made a stop there, for a short prayer service. First I said "Our Father," and then I said two short prayers — one was a thank prayer and one was a glad prayer. As always, Peter Paul Rubens did grunt Amen at in-between times. Then he did go his way to the pig-pen to get his supper, and I went aside to see if there was any sheeps on the hillside. I saw not one. And so I come again to the field.

Elizabeth Barrett Browning was at the pasture-bars. There was lonesome feels in her mooings. I went and put my arm around her neck. It is such a comfort to have a friend near, when lonesome feels do come.

## Ten

## Brave Horatius is Lost and Found; Peter Paul Rubens is Lost Forever

I have wonders — where is Brave Horatius? He comes not at my calling. Two days he is now gone. For him I go on searches. I go the three roads that go the three ways from where they have meeting, in front of the ranch house. On and on, I go. To the Orne and Rille, I go — I go adown their ways; I call and call. Into the woods beyond the rivière, into the forêt de Saint-Germain-en-Laye, I go. I listen. The sounds that were in time of summer are not now. Brave Horatius is not there. I call and call. Then I come back again. I go to the house of the girl who has no seeing. I go on. I go across the fields of Auvergne and Picardie. But I have no seeing of my Brave Horatius. I come back again.

The man that wears gray neckties and is kind to mice, he does keep watch by the mill. But these two days, he has had no seeing of Brave Horatius. I have wonders — where can he be? Every time I see the chore boy, he does sing, "There was a little dog, and his name was Rover; and when he died, he died all over.

*And when — he died — he died — all o——ver."* The
last part he does wail in a most long way. I have not
listenings to what that chore boy says. I go on; I pray
on; I look and I look for Brave Horatius.

I go four straight ways, and I come back four
different ways. When I am alone, I go back and forth
by Jardin des Tuileries, and across Pont Royal, and
adown the singing creek where the willows grow. Lonesome feels are everywhere. I call and I do call. And I
do go on and on, to where Rhone flows around
Camargue.

I turn about, and I go in the way that does go to the
forêt de Montmorency. I go to the forêt de Montmorency. No tree here is a *châtaignier* [chestnut], but
anyway, I do call it forêt de Montmorency; and often
it is I come here — here I come with Brave Horatius.
I went in through, and out through, but no answerings
did come when I did call. I wonder where he is.

In the morning of today when I did go that way, I did
meet with the father of Lola, and I did ask if he had
seen my Brave Horatius. He did have no seeing of him.
And he did ask where all I was going on searches. I did
tell him to Orne and Yonne and Rille, and to Camargue
and Picardie and Auvergne, and to the forêt de Montmorency. And when I did so tell him, he did laugh.
Most all the folks do laugh at the names I do call places
hereabout — they most all do laugh, 'cepting Sadie
McKibben. She smiles and smooths out my curls and
says, "Name 'em what ye are a mind to, dearie." Sadie
McKibben has an understanding soul. She keeps watch
out of her window for seeings of Brave Horatius, and
she has promised me she will ask everybody that she
does see go by her house if they have had seeings of
Brave Horatius.

All my friends do feel lonesome feels for Brave
Horatius. Lars Porsena of Clusium hardly has knowing
what to do. And Peter Paul Rubens did have goings
with me three times on searches; and when I did have
stops to pray, he did grunt Amen. And he would like
to have goings with me on the afternoon of today. But
the pig-pen fence, it was fixed most tight, and I couldn't
unfix it with the hammer so he might have goings with
me. I did start on. He did grunt grunts to go. I did
feel more sad feels — I do so like to have him go with
me on explores and searches. Today I did go on, and
then I did come back to give him more good-bye pats
on the nose, until I was come again. So I did, four
times. I did tell him when Brave Horatius was found,
we would soon come to his pen. Then I went on.

On I went not far, for the mamma did call me to
come tend the baby. And I came again to the house we
live in. When sleeps was upon the baby, I lay me down
to sleep, for tired feels was upon me. Now I feel not so.
I have been making prints. The mamma is gone with
the baby to the house of Elsie. I go now again to seek
for my Brave Horatius.

A little way I went. A long way I went. When I was
come part way back again, I climbed upon the old gray
fence made of rails. I walked adown it to the gate-post,
and there I sat. I sat there until I saw the shepherd
bringing down the sheep from the blue hills. When he
was come in sight, I went up the road to meet him and
all the sheeps. And when I was come near unto them,
I did have seeing — there by the shepherd's side did
abide my Brave Horatius! I was happy. I was full of
glad feels. Brave Horatius showed his glad feels in his
tail, and he did look fond looks at the flock of sheep. I
so did, too.

And in the flock, there was Bede of Jarrow, and Alfric of Canterbury, and Albéric de Briançon, and Felix of Croyland. And there was Cynewulf, and Alcuin, and Orderic, and Gwian, and Elidor. And in the midst of the flock, there was Guy de Cavaillon, and Raoul de Houdenc, and Edwin of Diera, and Adamnan of Iona. I did give to each and every one a word of greeting, as I did walk among the flock. And there were others that I had not yet given names to. And last of them all, last of all the flock, was Dallan Forgaill.

And when we were come a little way, the shepherd did ask me again what were the names I did call his sheep. And I told him all over again, and he did say them after me. But the ways *he* did say them were not just the ways *I* say them, some of them. And he did ask me where I did have gettings of those names. And I did tell him I did have gettings of those names from my two books that Angel Mother and Angel Father did write in.

We went on. Pretty soon, I did tell him as how it was while he was gone away to the blue hills, I did choose for him another name. I told him how sometimes I did call him by that other name. He did have wantings to know what the other name was. I did tell him this new name I have for him is Aidan of Iona come from Lindisfarne. He liked it. I told him I did, too.

We went on. We did have talks. When we were come near unto the lane, I did say, "Good-bye, Aidan of Iona come from Lindisfarne. I am glad you and the flock are come." He gave my curls a smooth-back, and he said, "Good-bye, little one."

Then Brave Horatius and I went in a hurry, in the way that does go to the pig-pen. When we were gone part ways, I looked a look back, and in the road there

I saw Aidan of Iona come from Lindisfarne, still watching us. Then we went on.

And we were full of gladness when we did reach the pig-pen, for Brave Horatius and Peter Paul Rubens and I, we are friends. I did say a long thank prayer, for that we were together again. And Peter Paul Rubens did grunt Amen.

I am feeling all queer inside. Yesterday was butchering day. Among the hogs they butchered was Peter Paul Rubens.

The mamma let me go off to the woods all day, after my morning's work was done. Brave Horatius and Lars Porsena of Clusium went with me. A part of the time he perched on my shoulder, and then he would ride on the back of Brave Horatius. Felix Mendelssohn rode in my apron pocket, and Elizabeth Barrett Browning followed after.

We had not gone far, when we heard an awful squeal — so different from the way pigs squeal when they want their supper. I felt cold all over. Then I did have knowings why the mamma had let me start away to the woods without scolding. And I ran a quick run to save my dear Peter Paul Rubens — but already he was dying. And he died with his head in my lap. I sat there feeling dead, too, until my knees were all wet with blood from the throat of my dear Peter Paul Rubens.

After I changed my clothes and put the bloody ones in the rain-barrel, I did go to the woods to look for the soul of Peter Paul Rubens. I didn't find it. But I think when comes the spring, I will find it among the flowers — probably in the blossom of a *faon* [fawn] lily, or in the top of a fir tree. Today when Brave Horatius and I went through the woods, we did feel its presence near.

When I was come back from the woods, they made me grind sausage. And every time I did turn the handle, I could hear that little pain squeal Peter Paul Rubens always gave when he did want me to come where he was at once.

# Eleven

## Opal thinks of a way to remove the Miller's Brand from the Flour-Sack; she sings a New Song to the Baby, and visits William Shakespeare, who has Likings for Poems

This day when I was come home from school, I did have much wood to carry in, for cold days are come. I did make goes to the wood-shed, to get the wood. Going to the wood-shed, I passed that new flour-sack hanging on the clothes-line. It was flapping in the wind. By-and-by, that flour-sack is going to evolute into an underskirt for me to wear under my dress when I go to school. I got my arms full of wood, as much as they could hold. Then I came into the house, to put the wood into the box behind the stove.

The mamma was standing by the window. She looked worry looks at that new flour-sack hanging on the clothes-line, there. She said she wished she knew a quicker way to get that miller's brand out of the flour-sack. She put on her fascinator and went a-visiting. She told me to watch the baby, that was sleeping on the bed. While I was carrying in more sticks of wood, I tried to think of a quicker way to get that miller's brand out of that flour-sack a-flapping there in the window.

When enough wood was in and two more loads besides, I did sit on the wood-box. After I did sit still a most long time, thinks did come of a way. I got the scissors out — I got them out of the mamma's work-basket.

The time it did take to cut the miller's brand out of the flour-sack, it was only a little time. And when it was fixed, I did fold it in nice folds, with the nice crooks sticking out. The scissors did make those crooks in a nice way. Scissors are useful — I do find much use for them. But the mamma likes not the uses I find for the scissors. She does say I am a new sance. I guess a new sance is something some grown-up people don't like to have around at all.

I have wonders about things. I have sore feels in my heart, and sore feels on the back part of me. I so want to be helps to the mamma. But it's very hard. Why, today when I did run to meet her, I did say, "It's out! It's out! I've got it out!" And she looked no glad looks. She did only look looks about for a hazel bush. First one she saw, she did take two limbs of it. All the way to the door, she made tingles on me with them. I do not think she does have knowing how they feel — such queer, sore feels. I feel she would not like their feels.

When we were come to the door, she did tell me to stay outside. She said I couldn't come into her house. But I did have knowing where I could go. I went to talk with Good King Edward I and lovely Eleanor of Castile. I did climb onto the lane fence, and into the arms of lovely Queen Eleanor. I do so like to be in her arms when things do trouble me. She has understandings.

From her arms, I did go to hunt for the soul of Peter Paul Rubens. Lucian Horace Ovid Virgil rode in my left apron pocket, and Nannerl Mozart rode in my right apron pocket. She is a most shy mouse, and does keep her nose hid. As we did go along, I did gather gray leaves — forty-two gray leaves I did so gather. Then we went on.

We went on to the near woods. I had not findings today for the soul of my dear Peter Paul Rubens. But I did tell the wind that was walking in the woods to tell Peter Paul Rubens I was come a-seeking for his soul. Then I did turn my face to the way that does lead to the cathedral. On the way, I met with Elizabeth Barrett Browning and Brave Horatius and Isaiah. Together we did go to the cathedral.

We went unto the little tree that I have planted there for rememberings of good John Milton, for this day is the day of his borning, in 1608. We did have prayers. It was so lonesome, Peter Paul Rubens not being there to grunt Amen at in-between times. Brave Horatius came near unto me when prayers were most done. He did put his nose against my hand for a pat. I gave him two. One was for him, and one was for Peter Paul Rubens that was.

Then we all did go in the way that does lead to the singing creek where the willows grow. When we were come, all that were with me did stand very close by. They so did stand while I did drop the gray leaves upon the water. All the forty-two leaves I did gather, I did drop upon the water — for this is the day of the going-away of Antoine Van Dyck, in 1641; and his years, they were forty-two. When the leaves were all upon the water, I did say a little prayer.

And we came home. It was most dark-time, and the

lamp on the kitchen table did shine its light out the window. And it came down the path to meet us.

There were pictures on the window-panes when I woke up this morning. By-and-by, the fire in the stove made the room warm, and the pictures on the window-panes went away. I was sorry when they went away. I so did like to look looks at them.

When I did have my breakfast, the mamma did send me to take a bucket of something with eggs on top it to the ranch house. The outdoors did have coldness. It did make my fingers to have queer feels, and my nose felt like I didn't have any. Brave Horatius followed after me as I did go along. As I did go along, I did see ice on the mud-puddles. Every now and then, I did stop to break the ice on the mud-puddles. I broke the ice to see what was in the water. Under the ice that was over the cow-tracks, there was no water — only dirt, cold and stiff, with little crystals on it.

When I was come to the ranch house, the grandma did come to the door, and she took the bucket of something with eggs on top it that the mamma did send to her. I started on to school. I did go as far as the pump. I made a stop there. I was going to give its handle some lift-ups and some pull-downs, so water would come out. I have likes to see water come out of that pump. But today, water won't come out of the pump. The pump-handle won't go up and down. The grandpa said it froze in the night. I think it has got the croup. I expect it needs some coal-oil. I have thinks I must tend to that pump tonight.

All day here at school, I now do study. For little bits of times, I do study my school-book. But most of the time, I do study the books Angel Father and Angel Mother did write in. I do study these most every day at school. I do study the spell of the words. And after times and before times, I do sing the spelling of the words to the gentle Jersey cow, while I do ride her to pasture. And I sit in the manger at evening-time and sing the spellings of these words to William Shakespeare, when he is come home from work in the woods. I have thinks most of my animal friends do have knowings of the spelling of these words — it so often is I do sing the spellings of these words to them.

When I did come home from school tonight, I did make a stop at that pump, to see how much coal-oil it did need for its croup. But it had no needs to be tended — the croup that it did have on this morning was all gone. When I did give its handle some lift-ups and some push-downs, water did come out. I watched it. It stopped coming out when I did stop giving it lift-ups and push-downs.

I went on. I saw the black cat, by the barn. On cold nights, I have given that cat long rubs on its back, and sparks have come. I did have thinks about sparky things as I did come on home. Now I have knowings of these: Cats are sparky — black ones, on a cold night. Stoves are sparky, on cold days. Rocks are sparky — flint ones, when you give them a thump. The chore boy says some *people* are sparky. He doesn't know what he is talking about.

When I was come into the house we live in, I gave the baby a gentle thump. It squawked, but there were no sparks. Then the mamma came in the back door. She had not knows why it squawked, but she did tell me to mind it. I so did. The mamma went out again, to the house of Elsie.

When she was gone, I did sing to the baby a new song I did make up today. Most every day, I do make up a song. I sing them not when the mamma is in the house, for she does give me most hard spankings when I do start to sing them. Today I did teeter the baby on the bed, as she said. And more I did — I did sing to her the new song. I did sing to her:

> "Maintenant est hiver —
> Le ciel est gris,
> Le champ est tranquil,
> Les fleurs dorment —
> Maintenant est hiver."

> ["Now it is winter —
> The sky is gray,
> The field is quiet,
> The flowers sleeping —
> Now it is winter."]

Then she did kick many kicks in the air. I did tickle her toes. She likes to have her toes tickled; she has likes for it. This baby has likes for many things. She has likes to sit up on the bed. The mamma has me to prop it up, so it won't fall over. And this baby, it has likes to make bubbles with its mouth, and to stick its foot in its mouth. It does like to rattle all the rattles the grandma and Jenny Strong and Elsie bring to it. It does have such likes to be rocked. And most of the times when it is awake, it does want to be singed to, and carried about. It is a baby what has satisfaction looks on its face for a little time, when it gets what it wants. It only has those satisfaction looks a little time. Soon it does have some more wants, and it wants to *have* what it wants. The mamma does have me to rock it and rock it, and teeter it on the bed, and walk the floor with it. Sometimes it does get most heavy. Then I do let my knees bend under, and I do sit on the floor and rock it back and forth. The mamma, she does have much likes for it to have what it wants.

I am joy all over. I have found in the near woods a plant that has berries like the berries *symphorine* has. And its leaves are like the leaves symphorine has. I have had seeings of it before. And every time I do meet with this new old plant, I do say, "I have happy feels to see you, Symphorine!" And when the wind comes walking in the near woods, the little leaves of symphorine do whisper little whispers. I have thinks they are telling me they were come here before *I* was come here. I make a stop to have more listens. They do whisper, "*See, petite Françoise, we were a long time come.*" I can see they were, too, because their toes have grown quite a ways down in the ground.

Today as I did walk a walk to where they grow, I did tell them about the day that it is. I told them all about this being the borning day of Jeanne d'Albret, mère de Henri IV, in 1528. I told the year-numbers on my fingers. I had thinks they might have remembers better if I so told them on my fingers. (*I* do have remembers of numbers better when I do tell them on my fingers.) Brave Horatius did stand by and listen while I so told them. We went on.

I tied bits of bread on the tips of the branches of the trees. Too, I tied on popcorn kernels. They looked like snow-flowers blooming there on fir trees. I looked looks at them. I have knows the birds will be glad for them. Often I do bring them here for them. When I have hungry feels, I feel the hungry feels the birds must be having. So I have comes to tie things on the trees for them. Some have likes for different things — little gray one of the black cap has likes for suet, and other folks has likes for other things.

There is a little box in the woods that I do keep things for the pheasants and grouses and squirrels, and more little birds, and wood-mouses and wood-rats. In falltime days, Peter Paul Rubens did come here with me when I did bring seeds and nuts to this box for days of *hiver*. When we were come to the box, I did have more thinks of him. I think the soul of Peter Paul Rubens is not afar. I think it is in the forest. I go looking for it. I climb up in the trees. I call and call. And then when I find it not, I do print a message on a leaf, and I tie it onto the highest limb I can reach. And I leave it there with a little prayer for Peter Paul Rubens. I do miss him so.

Today after I so did leave a message on a leaf away up in a tree for him, I did have going in along the lane, and out across the field, and down the road beyond the meeting of the roads. There was grayness everywhere — gray clouds in the sky, and gray shadows above and in the canyon. And all the voices that did speak, they were gray tones: *"Petite Françoise, c'est jour gris."* And all the little lichens I did see along the way did seem a very part of all the grayness. And Felix Mendelssohn in my apron pocket, he was a part of the grayness, too. And as I did go adown the road, I did meet with a gray horse, and his grayness was like the grayness of William Shakespeare. Then I did turn about. I did turn my face to the near woods, where is William Shakespeare.

When Rob Ryder isn't looking, I give to William Shakespeare pieces of apple, and I pull grass for him. He so likes a nice bit to eat after he does pull a long pull on the logs. And while I do feed him bits of apple and bits of grass, I do tell him poems. William Shakespeare has likes for poems. And sometimes I do walk along by him when he is pulling in logs, and I do tell

156

the poems to him while he pulls. And I give his head rubs when he is tired, and his back, too. And on some Sundays when he is in the pasture, I go there to talk with him. He comes to meet me. William Shakespeare and I, we are friends. His soul is very beautiful. The man that wears gray neckties and is kind to mice says he is a dear old horse.

# Twelve

# Elsie's Brand-New Baby, and the New Young Folks who live by the Mill

Elsie has a brand-new baby, and all the things that go with it. There's a pink fleur on its baby brush, and a pink bow on its cradle-quilt. The angels brought the baby just last night, in the night. I have been to see it a goodly number of times. Most everything I did start to do, I went aside before I did get through doing it, to take peeps at the darling baby. I so did when I was sent to feed the chickens, and when I went to carry in the wood, and when I went to visit Aphrodite, and when I went to take eggs to the folks that live yonder, and when I went to get some soap at the ranch house, and when I went to take a sugar-lump to William Shakespeare, and when I went to take food to the folks in the hospital, and when I went to the ranch house to get the milk. And in the between-times, I did go in the way that does lead to the house of Elsie.

The baby, it is a beautiful baby, though it does have much redness of face from coming such a long way in the cold last night. Maybe it was the coldness of the night that did cause the angels to make the mistake. They stopped at the wrong house. I'm quite sure this is the very baby I have been praying for the angels to bring to the new young folks that do live by the mill by the far woods. Dear Love, her young husband does call her. And they are so happy. But they have been married seven whole months, and haven't got a baby yet. Twice every day for a long time, I have been praying prayers for the angels to bring them one real soon. And most all day today, I did feel I better tell Elsie as how this baby isn't her baby, before she does get too fond of it. She so likes to cuddle it, now. Both morning and afternoon, I did put off going to tell her about it. I did wait most until eventime. Then I couldn't keep still any longer — I felt I would just have to speak to her about it, at once.

I did have knowings that Mrs. Limberger, that was staying with Elsie until the other woman was come back, wouldn't let me come in the door to see the baby again, because she has opinions that nineteen times is fully enough to be a-coming to see a baby on the first day of its life on earth. So I went and got a wood box off the back porch, and I did go around to the bedroom window. I did get on top the wood box, and I made tappings on the window-pane. Elsie did have hearings. She did turn her head on the pillow. And she gave nods for me to come in. I pushed the window a push enough so I could squeeze in. Then I sidled over to the bed.

Elsie did look so happy with the baby. I did swallow a lump in my throat. She looked kind smiles at me. I did not like to bring disturbs to her calm. I just stood there, making pleats in my blue calico apron. I did have thinks of Dear Love and the house without a baby, by the mill by the far woods. Then I felt I couldn't wait any longer. I just said, "I know you are going to have a disappoint, Elsie, but I have got to tell you — this baby isn't yours. It's a mistake. It really belongs to Dear Love, in that most new, most little house by the mill by the far woods. It's the one I've been praying the angels to bring to her."

Just when I was all out of breath from telling her, there did come the heavy step of Mrs. Limberger's approaches. Elsie did say in a gentle way, "Come to me early in the morning, and we will talk the matter over." Then I went out the window.

From the house of Elsie, I did go to talk with Michael Angelo Sanzio Raphael. He does so understand. All troubles that do trouble me, I do talk them over with him.

While I was telling him all about how the angels did make a mistake and did bring Dear Love's baby to the house of Elsie, I did hear a little voice. It was a baby voice. It did come from the barn. I went in to see. It wasn't in the haystack. It seemed to come from away below. I slid down to the manger of the gentle Jersey cow. I thought she was in the pasture, but there she was in the barn — and with her was a dear new baby calf!

When I did ask the ranch folks when it was brought, they did say it was brought in the night, last night. I have thinks the same angel that did bring the new baby to the house of Elsie did bring also in her other arm that baby calf to the gentle Jersey cow. Tonight I will pick it out a name from the books Angel Mother and Angel Father did write in. Early in the morning, I will go again to the house of Elsie.

Early on the morning of today, I did go in the way that does lead to the house of Elsie. I did rap gentle raps on the door, and the young husband of Elsie did come to raise the latch. When the door did come open, I did have seeing that his black pumpadoor did seem to shine more than most times, and all the Vaseline was gone from the jar that sets on the kitchen shelf. I did tell him how Elsie did say for me to come early in this morning. And before he did have time for answers, Elsie did have hearing in the other room. She did call — she did call me to come in.

In I went. The baby, it was beside her. It was all wrapped in a blanket, so it couldn't even have seeings out the window how the raindrops was coming down so fast. The young husband of Elsie did look fond looks at that blanket. I did begin to have fears he did have thinks it was his baby.

Elsie did unwrap the blanket from its red face. It's just as red as it was yesterday, though the rain coming makes the weather more warm. Elsie did say, "See its long hair." And I did have seeing. It wasn't long, though — not more than an inch. It was most black. And its eyes, they were dark. It did have prefers to keep them shut. When I did see them, Elsie did say, "Now about what we were talking about yesterday — next time you go to the house of Dear Love, have seeing of the color of her eyes and hair, and also of her husband's. I hardly think this baby's hair and eyes are like theirs. And maybe it is where it does belong." "I feel sure about that," said her young husband. But I had not feels so.

Just then, the mamma did holler for me to come home, to bring wood in. I so come. Now she does have me mind the baby. I do print.

When sleeps was come upon the mamma's baby, I straightway did go in a hurry to the house of Dear Love, by the mill by the far woods. All the way along, the raindrops were coming in a hurry down. Many of them did say, *"Petite Françoise — too I wonder, I wonder."*

When I was come to the house of Dear Love, she was there and he was there. Her eyes were light blue, and her hair, it was very light. Most cream hair, she has got. And her husband that does call her Dear Love — his eyes they are blue, and he has red hair. I saw. And I was going right back, because I did feel sad feels.

Dear Love, she did lead me back into her house, and did have me to sit on a chair. I sat on its corner, and I felt lumps come up in my throat. She did take off my fascinator, and she did take off my shoes, so my feet would get dry. Then she did take me on her lap, and she did ask me what was the matter. And I just did tell her all about it — all about how I had been praying for the angels to bring a baby real soon to them, and how sad feels I did feel because they didn't have a baby yet. Her husband did smile a quiet smile at her, and roses did come on her cheeks. And I did have thinks that they did have thinks that this baby the angels did bring to the house of Elsie was their baby.

Then I did give them careful explanations as how I too did have thinks it was their baby the angels did bring to the house of Elsie, that I did pray for them to have real soon; and as how I did have thinks so yesterday, and last night, and right up until now — when I did come to their house and have seeings of their blue eyes, and his having red hair. I did tell them as how this baby couldn't be theirs, because it has most dark hair and dark eyes, like the eyes and the hair of the young husband of Elsie's:

"Angels do have a big amount of goodly wisdom. They do bring to folks babies that are like them. To mother sheeps, they do bring lambs. To mother horse, they do bring a *poulain*. To mother bats, they bring twin bats. To a mother mouse, they do bring a baby *mulot* and some more like it, all at the same time. To *mère daine*, they do bring a baby *faon*. To the gentle Jersey cow, they did bring a baby calf with creamness and brownness upon it, like the creamness and brownness that is upon the gentle Jersey cow. Angels do have a goodly amount of wisdom — they do bring to folks babies that do match them."

And after I did tell them that, I did have telling them as how, being as this baby didn't have eyes and hair to match theirs, it couldn't be their baby. But I did tell them not to have disappoints too bad, because I am going to pray on, and maybe she will get a baby next week.

When I did say that, her young husband did walk over to the window and look long looks out. I have thinks he was having wonders if two or three angels would be coming with the angel that will be bringing their baby, and if the cradle-quilt they bring with it will have a blue bow or a pink bow on it, and if its baby brush will have blue fleurs or pink fleurs on it. I have wonders. I think blue fleurs on its baby brush and a blue bow on its cradle-quilt will look nicer with red hair than pink fleurs and a pink bow. I have thinks I better put that in my prayers.

By-and-by, when my feets were dry, they did put my shoes on, and they laced them up. They didn't miss a string-hole like I do sometimes, when I am in a hurry to get them tied up. Then, when they did have them tied up, they did want me to stay to dinner. But I did have feels I must hurry back to the house of Elsie, and tell her that the baby was hers. She might be having anxious feels about it.

When I did say good-bye, they did give me two

163

apples — one for William Shakespeare and one for Elizabeth Barrett Browning. And they did give me some cheese for Thomas Chatterton Jupiter Zeus, and corn for Lars Porsena of Clusium. And they came a long way with me.

Then I did go in hurry steps to the house of Elsie. As quick as her young husband did open the door, I did walk right in, for I did have thinks maybe she did have some very anxious feels while I was gone. She smiled glad smiles when I told her it was hers. It must have been an immense amount of relief, her now knowing it really was her own baby. And when I did turn around to tell her young husband it was theirs, her young husband, he just said, "I knew it was mine." And he looked more fond looks at the blanket it was wrapped in. I have feels now it is nice for them to have it, and it is good that they will not have needs to give it up, being as it matches them. Angels do have a goodly amount of wisdom. This is a wonderful world to live in.

When I did say good-bye to Elsie and the *charmante* [charming] baby, I did go to the barn, where is the gentle Jersey cow and the baby calf that does match her. That baby calf I have named Mathilde Planta-genet. I have named her so for Mathilde that was daughter of Roi Henri I, and Mathilde that was daughter of Sainte Marguerite, that was reine d'Écosse [queen of Scotland]. Mathilde Plantagenet is her name, because the name of the man Mathilde did marry, it was Geoffroi Plantagenet. And too, in days of summer, the *gênet fleur* [broom] grows near unto here. I have had seeings of them by waters that flow by the mill town. And when their bloom time is come, I will make for Mathilde Plantagenet a guirlande of *les fleurs de gênet*. And we will go walking down the lane.

# Thirteen

## Opal carries her Friends home from School, and meets Sadie McKibben; Opal and Rob Ryder disagree

On the way home from school tonight, I did meet with Sadie McKibben, and it was very nice to see her freckles. And she wore her blue gingham apron with cross-stitches on it. First when we were met, she did kiss me on each cheek. Then she was going to shake hands with me. But I could not shake hands with her with my right hand, because Louis II, le Grande Condé, was asleep in my sleeve. I had fears shaking hands with my right hand would disturb his calm. So I gave explanations, and Sadie McKibben did have understanding. She gave me a kiss on my nose and smoothed back my curls, and shook hands with my left hand.

When she so did, Felix Mendelssohn did poke his nose out the cuff. He made a quick run up my arm, and settled down on my shoulder. He is a very quick-moving mouse. Sadie McKibben did see the movement his moving did make on my sleeve. She asked me if that was all my friends I did take to school today. Then I lifted up my apron, and I did show her Lucian Horace Ovid Virgil — he was riding in a pocket in my under-skirt. She did have wantings to know why it was that I was not carrying him in my apron pocket, as I used to do. I told her I did not so now for teacher does feel of my apron pockets when I do come into school in the morning. So I carry my friends in my sleeves, and in pockets in my underskirt.

Sadie McKibben did have understanding. And she did say she thought she would have to be getting me a little basket to carry them in. She said she was going to speak to the man that wears gray neckties and is kind to mice about the matter. I have thinks to be carried in a warm basket will please the souls of Louis II, le Grand Condé, and Felix Mendelssohn, and Lucian Horace Ovid Virgil, and all the little folk that do go walking with me. It will be almost as nice as to ride in the pockets of the papa's big coat. I have thinks I will have needs to put pockets in that basket, and divides, so there in it will be little rooms — little rooms for all the folks of the nursery. I will let them have their turns riding to school in the basket. And there is enough room in my seat so that basket can set right beside me. I can hardly wait waits until I do have that basket.

When Sadie McKibben did kiss me good-bye, she gave me a sugar-lump for William Shakespeare, and a piece of cheese for Thomas Chatterton Jupiter Zeus, and a bone for Brave Horatius, and ten corn-seeds for Lars Porsena of Clusium. She does have knowings of the likings of my friends. Then she went her way, and I did come my way home to the house we live in.

When I was come, first I did feed the chickens, and then I did go to carry in the wood. It was while I was carrying in wood that Rob Ryder came to borrow a hammer. I haven't been near unto where he has been since I did bite his hand the other day. And today the mamma tried to make me say to that Rob Ryder how sorry I was because I bit him on the hand. But I wasn't a bit sorry, and I wouldn't say I was sorry — and if I got a chance I'd bite him again, for his laying that big whip to the back of William Shakespeare when he doesn't pull logs fast enough. I know my William Shakespeare, and I know how hard he pulls to pull those logs. To pull those logs, he does his very best.

And when he was gone away, the mamma did spank me most hard with the hair-brush. Then she put me out the door. And I did go from the house we do live in to where do dwell King Edward III and Queen Philippa of Hainault. They are grand trees. We are friends. Often it is I go to where they dwell when the mamma does put me out of the house. Today I did stay long with them, and I did talk long with them. Mostly it was about the lovely England when they were there, we did have talks about today. And the wind was talking, too. I think the wind does have knowing of this being their wedding day, in 1328. As he did come near unto where they dwell, he did walk among the willows by the singing creek. And I did climb down from the arms of Queen Philippa of Hainault and go to gather watercress for the mamma — she does have such a fondness for it.

Then I did say good-bye, and I did say good-bye to all those twelve trees growing near unto them. And all those twelve trees that do grow near unto King Edward III and Queen Philippa of Hainault, those twelve trees are their twelve children. The tree most near unto Edward III, that is Edward, Prince of Wales; and the one next unto him is Lionel, Duke of Clarence; and the one most near unto him, that is John of Gaunt, Duke of Lancaster. The time was when there were only ten trees growing there, and I did have needs to plant two more. Two little ones I did plant. And one is for baby Blanche, and one is for baby William, the other one.

# Fourteen

## The Window Lesson, and the Long Ride on William Shakespeare

After I did dish-towel all the dishes that we did use in the breakfast meal, the mamma did send me to get barks for the warming stove. While I was getting barks, I did stop to screwtineyes the plump wiggles that were in and under all the barks. Those plump wiggles will grow and change — they will grow and change into beetles. I have seen them do so. I have taken them from the bark, and they did so grow into beetles, after some long time. In the nursery I kept them, while they did so change.

After the barks was in, I did go my way to school. I went aside to Saint Firmin, by Nonette. I made a stop where the willows grow. I love to touch fingers with the willows — then I do feel the feels the willows feel. I did tell them all and every one about this being the going-away day of Charlemagne in 814, and the borning day of Henry VII, in 1457. Each pussy-willow baby did wear a gray silk *tricot* [sweater]. He did look warm. He smiled, *"Bonjour, petite Françoise!"* in a friendly way. I think he does remember the days in summer when I did drink in inspirations, dabbling my toes by his toes, there in the singing brook.

When I did have talks with them for a little time, I did go on. And all along, I stopped very often on the way, to talk to the other pussy-willows.

I was quite late to school. Teacher made me stand in the corner, to get my lesson with my face to the wall. I didn't mind that at all. There was a window in that part of the wall. It was near the corner. I looked looks at my book, sometimes. Most of the times, I looked looks out the window. I had seeing of little plant folks just peeping out of the earth to see what they could see. I did have thinks it would be nice to be one of them, and then grow up and have a flower, and bees a-coming, and seed-children at falltime. I have thinks this is a very interest world to live in. There is so much to see out the window when teacher does have one to stand in the corner to study one's lesson.

When teacher did send me to my seat to get my slate for arithmetic, I did put Lucian Horace Ovid Virgil in my desk by my *Cyr's Reader*. I keep my books in one little corner of my desk, and that does leave a lot of room for my animal friends. There was room enough for Lucian Horace Ovid Virgil to take nice little hops. But while I was having recites with arithmetic, he hopped a little hop too far, and he fell out of my desk. I had quivers, and it was hard to pay attentions to arithmetic.

When our lessons were done, I made a quick go to my seat. I looked a look-under for him. He was not there. I looked more looks about. He was rows away, over by the seat-row where Lola has her sitting. I did almost sit sideways in my seat, I had such anxious feels about him.

Lola had seeing. She made a reach-over. She picked him up in a gentle way; she put him in her apron pocket. She made a begin to study her geography. She asked teacher if she might get a drink from the dipper in the wrap-room. She went. She made a come-back from the wrap-room down our row, going to her geography class. When she went by my desk, she put her hand in my pocket. She went on to the recite bench. Lucian Horace Ovid Virgil was back again in my apron pocket. I felt an immense amount of satisfaction feels.

Some days there is cream to be shaked into butter. The mamma does have me to make a handle go up and down a lot of times in the churn. This makes the butter come. When there is only a little cream to be shaked into butter, then the mamma has me to shake it to and fro in a glass jar. Sometimes it gets awfully heavy, and my arms do get ache feels up and down. There are most ache feels when the butter is a long time in coming. It so was today. I gave it many shakes, and I was having hopes it soon would be come. After some long time, when it was most come, the lid came off and it all shaked out. Then the mamma did have cross feels, and the spanks she gave made me to have sore feels, on the back part of me. I was making tries to be helps to her. That butter was almost come.

After I did give the floor washes and mops-up where the splashes of buttermilk did jump, then the mamma put me out the door, and told me to get out and stay out of her way. I so did. I went out across the field, and in along the lane. Lars Porsena of Clusium had going with me. I looked looks away, to the meeting of the roads. There was a horse come near unto it. A man was riding on this horse. I like to ride upon a horse. I like to stand up when I ride upon a horse — it is so much joy. I feel the feels the horse does feel when he puts each foot to the ground.

When I did see that horse go on and on, then I did have feels it would be nice to go a long way on explores. I did have thinks William Shakespeare had wants to go. He was in the lane. I gave him pats on the nose, and I talked with him about it. We did start on.

When we were come to the end of the lane, there was the gate. It did take some long time to get it open. The plug did stick so tight, and more yet. I did pull, and I made more pulls. It came out — it did come out in a quick way. I did have a quick set-down. I got up in a slow way. I did show William Shakespeare the way to go out the gate. He went. I went.

We went adown the road. A little way we went, and we were come to a stump. I made a climb-up on it. From the stump, I did climb upon the back of William Shakespeare. We went on.

When we were come to the meeting of the roads, we went the way of the road that goes to the upper camps. We made no stops until we were come to where a long time ago the road had a longing to go across the rivière, and some men that had understanding made it a bridge to go across on. When we were come to the bridge, we made a stop, and I did sing to the rivière a song. I sang it *le chant de Seine, de Havre et Essonne et Nonette et Roullon et Iton et Darnetal et Ourcq et Rille et Loing et Eure et Audelle et Nonette et Sarc.* I sang it as Angel Father did teach me to, and as he has wrote it in the book. And after I did sing it all, we did watch the water splash itself against the legs of the bridge. The water goes not now slow, as it did in summer days.

We went on. And the boards of the bridge did make

squeaks as we went across; and they said in their squeaks, "*Petite Françoise, we have been waiting a long time for you to go across the rivière.*" And I did have William Shakespeare to make a little stop, so I could tell the boards, "I have been waiting waits a long time to go across." While I so was doing, they did not squeak. When we made a start to go on, they did squeak.

After we were across the rivière, we went in a more slow way. There was so many things to see. Trees and trees were all along the way. There were more ranch houses. I did have seeing of them set always back from the road, and smoke did come in curls from out their chimneys. At a bend in the road, there was a big chêne tree — it was a very big one. On its arms there was bunches of mistletoe. I made a stop to have looks at them. I had thinks I might reach up to them. I stood on tiptoe on the back of William Shakespeare. I could reach a reach to one limb. I put my arms around it, and had a swing. It was very nice to swing — *one*, forward and *two*, back again.

But when I was ready to stand on William Shakespeare again, he was not there. I looked a look down and about. He was gone on a little way. I had wonders what to do. There was most too many rocks to drop down on. Lars Porsena came and perched on the limb above. I did call William Shakespeare four times, and in between, I called him by the bird-call that does mean I have needs of him. He did come, and he made a stop under the limb. I was most glad. My arms did have a queer feel, from hanging there. I was real glad just to sit quiet on the back of William Shakespeare while he did walk on. And Lars Porsena of Clusium did sit behind me.

We went on. We had seeing of the section men

working on the railroad track where the dinkey-engine goes with the cars of lumbers to the mill town. They were making stoop-overs. I had seeing they did screw-tineyes the rails, and the ties they stay upon. The men did wave their hands to us, and I did wave back. And on the fence, there was a bird with a yellow chest and a little black moon across his front. His back, it was like the grasses of the field grown old. And his song is the song of all the voices of the field. We have seeing of him and his brothers all days of the year.

After we had going past the next turn in the road, I did look a look back. A little bush with some tallness was yet a-nodding. It was asking a question. I gave William Shakespeare two pats on the shoulder. That means *"Turn about."* He did. When we were come to the bush a-nodding, I leaned over to the tallness of it. I put my ear close, so I could have hearing. It had wants to know what day this was. I did tell it this day was the going-away day of John of Gaunt, and the borning day of Felix Mendelssohn, in 1809. It had hearings, but it did not stop nodding. But it was asking no questions — it was nodding nods of the day this is. I felt the satis-faction feels it did feel when it did know the answer to its question. I do too have likes to ask questions about things, so to have knows.

We went on in a slow way. I did look looks about, and there were birds — robins, and two bluebirds, and more larks of the meadow, and other crows like unto Lars Porsena of Clusium.

When we was come to another bend in the road, William Shakespeare made a stop. I made a slide-off. I went to pick him some grass. A wagon went by. Two horses were in front of it, and on its high seat was a man with his hat on sideways and a woman with a big fascinator most hiding her face. There was seven children in the wagon — two with sleeps upon them, and a little girl with a tam-o'-shanter and a frown and a cape on her. I have thinks from the looks on their faces they all did have wants to get soon to where they were going to. I brought the grass back to the road to William Shakespeare. I smiled a smile, and waved to the last little girl of all on the wagon. She smiled and waved her hand. Then three more of them waved. I waved some more. The wagon had its going on. And William Shakespeare had begins to nibble at the grass I was holding in my fingers. While he did nibble nibbles, I did tell him poems. William Shakespeare does have such a fondness for poetry, and nibbles of grass, and apples, and sugar-lumps.

While we did have waiting at the bend of the road, I saw a maple tree with begins of buds upon it. I did walk up to the tree. I put my ear to it, to have listens to the sap going up. It is a sound I like to hear — there is so much of springtime in it.

While I did listen, in the other ear that was not to the maple tree I did have hearings of the talkings of the wind, and petite plants just having begins to grow out of the earth. The wind did say, *"Je viens, je viens."* ["I come, I come."] The plants did answer make: *"Nous entendons, nous entendons."* ["We hear, we hear."] So they did speak. Then the wind did say, *"Le printemps viendra bientôt."* ["The spring will come soon."] And the plants did answer make: *"Nous fleurirons bientôt."* ["We will soon blossom."] I did have glad feels. William Shakespeare moved a little move. I had some doubts if he did hear all plainly they did say, so I went up to his nose and said it all over to him. He had understanding.

We went on. When we were come again to a stump, I did climb again upon his back.

We went by a big mill with piles of lumber to its near side, and a long, wide roof it had. There was a row of lumber-shanties, and some more. There was children about, and dogs. They did smile and wave, and I did, too.

We went on. More fir trees of great tallness was on either side the road — they did stretch out their great arms to welcome to us. I so do love trees. I have thinks I was once a tree, growing in the forest. Now all trees are my brothers.

When we were gone a little way on from the very tall trees, in the sky, the light of day was going from blue to silver. And thoughts had coming down the road to meet us. They were thoughts from out the mountains where are the mines. They were thoughts from the canyons that come down to meet the road by the rivière. I did feel their coming close about us — very near they were, and all about. We went on a little way, only. We went very slow. We had listens to the thoughts. They were thoughts of blooming-time and coming-time — they were the soul-thoughts of little things that soon will have their borning-time.

When we did go on, we did hear little sounds coming from a long way down the road. They were like the shoe on the foot of a horse making touches on the road in a hurry way. The sound, it came more near. We made a stop to have a listen. It was coming more near graylight-time, and we could not have plain sees until the horse was come more near a way down the road. Then we had sees a man was riding on the horse. They came on in the quick way that made the little fast patter sounds on the ground.

When he was most come to where we were, the man did have the horse to go in a more slow way. When he was come to where we were, he did have the horse to stop. The man upon the horse was the man that wears gray neckties and is kind to mice. He did seem most glad that we were on the road he was on. He did breathe some satisfaction breathes, just like Sadie McKibben does when she finds I haven't broken my bones when I fall out of a tree. Then he made begins. He said, "The fairies —" And I said, "What?" He said, "The fairies have left a note on a leaf in the moss-box by the old log. It was a note for me to go until I find you and William Shakespeare, to bring you home again before starlight-time." There was a little fern-plant with the note on the leaf. He gave them to me. And we came our way home.

Now I have thinks it was God in his goodness did send the fairies to leave that fern-note on the leaf. And William Shakespeare and I were glad he was come to meet us, for the stars were not and dark was, before we were come home. But the man that wears gray neckties and is kind to mice, he did have knows of the way of the road by night.

# Fifteen

## Jenny Strong comes to Visit, with Ruffles and a Pink Rosebud

Jenny Strong is come to visit us. She came in the morning of today. She came on the logging train. She brought her bags with her. The mamma did send me to meet her, at the meeting of the roads. The bags, they were heavy to carry, and my arms got some tired.

As we did go along, in-between times I did look looks at Jenny Strong. There is so much of interest about her. The gray curls about her face did have the proper look she wants them to have. To get that proper look, she does them up on curl-papers. I have seen her so do, when she was come to visit us before. And this morning her plump cheeks were roses, and all her plumpness did most fill the gray dresses she was wearing. Jenny Strong has little ruffles around the neck of that dress, like the little ruffles that was around the neck of the man with the glove, when Titian made his picture. Those ruffles on the neck of the gray dress of Jenny Strong did look like it was their joy to cuddle up against the back of her black bonnet. That black bonnet has a pink rosebud on it. And every time that Jenny Strong does give her head a nod, that pink rosebud does give itself a nod. It must be interest to be a pink rosebud on a black bonnet that Jenny Strong wears.

When we were come to the gate, Jenny Strong did hold her cape and her gray dress up in a careful way. She had blue stockings on, and they was fastened up with pink ribbons. She went on while I did shut the gate. I did come after. I could not come after in a quick way, because the bags was heavy. Pretty soon, Jenny Strong did have seeing I was not there beside her; and she did wait waits for me a little while, and I did come to where she was.

We went on. The way was dampness near the singing creek, and Jenny Strong did take dainty steps as we did go along. Lars Porsena of Clusium did come to meet us, and so came Brave Horatius; and Lars Porsena of Clusium did perch upon his back. We went on. The pink rosebud on the black bonnet of Jenny Strong did nod itself twelve times as we did go along.

When we were come near unto the house, there was a rooster by our front door — he was strutting along. He was that same rooster that I tied a slice of bacon around his neck this morning, because he had queer actions in the throat. When Jenny Strong saw him strutting along with the bacon wrapped around his throat, she did turn her head to the side, with a delicate cough.

After Jenny Strong took off her cape and her black bonnet with the pink rosebud on it, I did pull the best rocking-chair out in the middle of the room for her. She sat down in it and she did start to have talks with the mamma. I did go to teeter the baby on the bed, as the mamma did say for me to do. Jenny Strong did rock big rocks in that rocking-chair while she did talk. One time, she did almost rock over. She breathed a big breath. Then, that she might not rock over again, I did put a stick of wood under the rocker. That helped some. But too, it did keep her from rocking. She went on talking. I went back to the bed, to teeter the baby.

While I did teeter the baby, I did look looks out the window. In a bush that I do tie pieces of suet to, there was a little gray bird with a black cap, and his throat it was black. He was a fluffy ball. And he almost did turn himself upside-down on that branch. Then he went a go-away. Only a little way he went — then he was with more like himself. They went on together.

By-and-by, the mamma's baby did go to sleep, and I climbed off the bed and made a start to go to the nursery. Jenny Strong did ask me where I was going. I did tell her. She said she thought she would like to go with me. We did go out the door. Then I ran a quick run back, to get her black bonnet with the pink rosebud on it. I brought it to her. She said being as I did bring it to her, she would wear it, but she had not in tent chuns to when we started. She had forgot it. But *I* didn't have forgets — I do so like to see that pink rosebud nod itself.

We went on. We went a little way down the path; then I did go aside. Jenny Strong did follow after me. She came over the little logs in a slow way. I did make stops to help her. The pink rosebud on the black bonnet did nod itself fifteen times on the way — I did count its times.

When we were come to the nursery, first I did show her the many baby seeds I did gather by the wayside in the falltime. I did tell her how I was going to plant them, when comes springtime. She did nod her head.

Every time she so did, the pink rosebud on the black bonnet did nod itself.

After I told her most all about the seeds, I did show her the silk bags with spider eggs in them. Then I did show her all the cradles the velvety caterpillars did make at falltime. I did give her explainings how butterflies and moths would be a-coming out of the cradles when springtime was come. She looked concentration looks at them. She gave her head some more nods. And the pink rosebud on the black bonnet gave itself some more nods.

I moved on to where the wood-mouse folks are. I was just going to show her what a nice nose and little hands Nannerl Mozart has, and what a velvety mouse Felix Mendelssohn is. When I did turn about to so do, there was Jenny Strong going in funny little hops over the logs. She was going in a hurry way to the house.

I did have a wonder — why was it she so went? I gave Felix Mendelssohn more pats, and I put him in my apron pocket. And Nannerl Mozart did curl up in the bed I have fixed for her in the nursery. Then I did sing a lullaby song to all the wood-mice in the nursery. And they are a goodly number. I did sing to them the song La Nonette sings as it goes on its way to Oise.

Then I did go through the near woods, to the mill by the far woods. I so did go to see the man that wears gray neckties and is kind to mice.

When he had seeing that I was come by the big tree, he did say in his gentle way, "What is it, little one? Is Thomas Chatterton Jupiter Zeus not well?" "Oh, yes," I said, "he is most well, and he did have likes for that piece of cheese you did give to him on yesterday. He is a most lovely wood-rat — and what I have come to tell you about is, we got company. She has a fondness for pinkness. Her name is Jenny Strong, and she has a pink rosebud on her black bonnet, and ties her blue stockings up with pink ribbons."

And then I did ask him if he did not have thinks a pink ribbon would be nice for Thomas Chatterton Jupiter Zeus to wear on some days — on days when he goes to cathedral service with me. And too, I did tell him how I did have thinks a pink ribbon would be nice for William Shakespeare, and Felix Mendelssohn, and Lars Porsena of Clusium, and Brave Horatius.

The man that wears gray neckties and is kind to mice did have thinks like my thinks. He did say for me to go write the fairies about it. And I did.

I did write it on a gray leaf. I put the gray leaf in a moss-box at the end of an old log, near unto the altar of Saint Louis. The man that wears gray neckties and is kind to mice knows about that moss-box where I do put letters for the fairies. He believes in fairies, too. And we talk about them. He does ask me what I write to them about, and what things I have needs for them to bring. I do tell him. And when the fairies do leave the things at the end of the old log, I do take and show them to the man that wears gray neckties and is kind to mice. He is so glad. He does believe in fairies, too.

As I did come back through the near woods, I did stop by some grand fir trees to pray. When one does look looks up at the grand trees growing up almost to the sky, one does always have longings to pray.

When I did come on, I did hear the mamma calling. When I was come to the door, she made me go stand in the corner of the wood-shed. Soon she came out. She did shut the door tight behind her. Then she did ask me what for was it I gave Jenny Strong such a scare. And she did spank me, most hard. Now I have sore feels, and I have thinks it would be nice to have a cushion to sit on. And I do have wonders what it was Jenny Strong got scares about. I think grownups are queer, sometimes.

When I did go into the house, all the scares was gone off Jenny Strong. The mamma soon did make me to go under the bed. Here I print. Jenny Strong sits by the fire. She does sit in a rocking-chair, with her feet propped up on a soap-box. She hums as she sits; she crochets as she hums. She does make lace in a quick way.

Now Jenny Strong and the mamma is gone to the house of Elsie, to see the new baby. When she did go, the mamma did tell me to put the baby to sleep. I so did — I did sing it to sleep in the rocking-chair. I did sing it the *rivière* and *fleuve* [river that falls into the sea] song: "A is for *Adour, Avre, Ain, Aube, Arroux,* and *Allier.*" When I did get to "D is for *Douze,* and *Dordogne,* and *Durance,*" the baby did move its arm. When I did get to "G is for *Garonne,* and *Gers,* and *Gard,*" the baby did open its eyes. When I did get to "I is for *Indre,* and *Isère,* and *Iraouaddy,*" it did *close* its eyes. I did sing on, and sleeps did come upon the baby.

We had lots on the table to eat tonight, because Jenny Strong is come. And most everything I did get to eat, I did make divides of it for my animal friends. They will all have a good share. And they will be glad. There is enough for all to have a good amount to eat, which often isn't. I did feel a goodly amount of satisfaction, sitting there at the supper-table tonight for a little time. I was thinking how glad the mice will be for the corn I have saved for them. And too, Brave Horatius will have good feels in his mouth when he sees that big bone. And the birds will like all the scraps that are on the plate of Jenny Strong, if I can get them before the mamma gives them to that big gray cat.

I have seeings that the folks, they are almost through eating. I now am not at the table — I was only there for a very little while. I now am under the bed. The mamma did send me away from the table. It seems a long time ago. She did send me away from the table because, when Jenny Strong asked me if I liked her dress, I said, "Yes — and the ruffles around your neck are like the ruffles around the neck of the man with the glove, when Titian made his picture." Jenny Strong looked a queer look, and she said to the mamma, "What a naughty child!" The mamma did straightway tell me to crawl under the bed, and to stay there. I so am. I have feels Jenny Strong has not had seeing of the picture of the man with the glove, that Titian did make. I thought it was nice to tell her her ruffles were like his. They did look so nice.

I have wonders about folks. They are hard to understand. I think I will just say a little prayer.

My, I do have such hungry feels, now. They at the table are not through yet. I make swallows down my throat. It is most hard not to eat what I have saved for my animal friends. But they will like it. So I can wait waits until breakfast-time. I can. In-between times, I will have thinks and prayers.

# Sixteen

# The Talk of the Lichens on a Lonely Day

This day — it was a lonely day. I did have longings all its hours, for Angel Mother and Angel Father. In-between times all day at school, I did print messages for them on gray leaves I did gather on the way to school. I did tell on the leaves the longings I was having.

Too on the leaves, I did tell of William Shakespeare and our talks as we do go walking down the lane, and the poetry I do tell him in the manger. And I did print on more leaves how I do read out of the books they did make — how I do sit in the manger and read what is in them, and he does have understandings. And on other leaves, I did tell them as how the nose of Thomas Chatterton Jupiter Zeus that was soreness has now well feels, with prayers and Mentholatum that Sadie McKibben did give; and as how the headache of the most big rooster has now well feels, with camphoratum and vaselineatum; and as how the stomachache of Aphrodite did get well feels, with castor oilatum that Sadie McKibben did give.

And after, I did tell of how on many days in gray-light-time, I have had going on searches for the kisses of Angel Father — what he did tell me to keep watches for in the fleurs, while he was away, gone to the far lands. And on more leaves, I did tell them as how Peter Paul Rubens that was is not now, and how I do carry about with me the little bell he always did wear in the cathedral.

And when these leaves were so done, I did not go on for a time little. For a little time, I did have thinks. And the thinks I did have, they were about the glad song. The glad song in my heart sings not bright today. It is lonesome feels I have. But I do try to have thinks as how I can bring happiness to folks about. That is such a help when lonesome feels do come. Angel Mother did say, "Make earth glad, little one! That is the way to keep the fire-tongue of the glad song ever in your heart. It must not go out!" I so do try to keep it there. I so do try, for it is helps on cold days, and old days. And I did have remembers as how it was Angel Mother did say, "When one keeps the glad song singing in one's heart, then do the hearts of others sing."

So I did make hard swallows, to swallow all the lonesome feels. And I did have thinks as how I would stop to get watercress for the mamma on the way home from school. She does have such a fondness for it. And too, she does have longings for singing lessons. I am saving my pennies to buy her one. All the pennies that the man that wears gray neckties and is kind to mice does give to me, I save. I put them in the corner of the wood-shed where Brave Horatius sleeps at night. I think I have most enough pennies to buy her a singing lesson, now. I have nineteen pennies. And when I grow up, I am going to buy her a whole rain-barrel full of singing lessons.

And then I did have thinks as how tomorrow I will
be taking Elizabeth Barrett Browning to visit the girl
who has no seeing. They do both have likings for one
another. The girl who has no seeing has an understanding soul. All my friends do have appreciations of the
pats she does give to them, and the words she does say.
And sometimes a goodly number of them do have
goings to her house with me — that is, when her folks
are not at home. Then does Elizabeth Barrett Browning
walk right by my side, up to the door. And Thomas
Chatterton Jupiter Zeus cuddles up in my arms, and
in my pockets do ride other folks. And Brave Horatius
follows after.

When we are come, she does smooth back my curls
and give me a kiss. She says when we are come, "Here
is come the kingdom of heaven!" (I have feels she has
mistakes about that, because the kingdom of heaven,
being up in the sky, is there beyond the stars.) And
when we are come, she does have asking about the
voices, and I do help her to get understandings of the
thoughts growing with the fleurs and the trees and the
leaves. And I do tell her as how those are God's
thoughts, growing right up out of the earth. And she
wants to know more — always she does ask for more.
Tomorrow we will go, Elizabeth Barrett Browning and
me; we will go the way that does lead to the house of
the girl that has no seeing.

Today, after I did have thinks about it in school, I
did print more messages on leaves for Angel Father
and Angel Mother. I did tell them about the girl who
has no seeing. And on more leaves, I did print all about
the cathedral, and how the presence of Saint Louis is
always near unto it. And then it was come time for
school to let out.

I went adown the road. I went the way by the field,

where Aidan of Iona come from Lindisfarne was on yesterday. I climbed the fence; I looked looks about. He was not there today. But there were Bede of Jarrow and Felix of Croyland. I did have talks with them. I went on.

I went on to the singing creek where the willows grow. I gathered watercress for the mamma. Then I did go my way to the house we live in. No one was there. I put the watercress for the mamma on the cook-table. Then I did bring much wood in, and put it in the wood-box back of the kitchen stove.

After the chickens did have their supper feed, I did go into the near woods. I so went to tie the messages I did print on gray leaves to the trees. And I tied one on one tree, and one on another. I tied them there that they may go in thoughts to Angel Mother and Angel Father, up in heaven, there. And I did have thinks when the angels come to walk in the near woods, they would see and carry them on. And I did say a little prayer every time I did tie on a leaf-message.

I did look looks about. This woods is gray in winter, when come cold days. And gray shadows walk among the trees. They touch one's face with velvet fingers, when one goes walking there in the woods. In the winter, old gray leaves grow to look like lace. They are very beautiful.

As I did go along, I saw many gray rocks. Some gray rocks had gray and green patches on them. Some of these patches had ruffles all around their edges. The gray patches on gray rocks are lichens. My Angel Father said so.

Lichen folks talk in gray tones. I think they do talk more when come winter days — I hear their voices more in December than I do hear their voices in July and June-time. Angel Father did show me the way to listen to lichen voices. Most grownups don't hear them at all. I see them walk right by in a hurry, sometimes. And all the time, the lichen folks are saying things; and the things they say are their thoughts about the gladness of a winter day. I put my ear close to the rocks, and I listen. That is how I do hear what they are saying. Then I do take a reed for a flute. I climb on a stump — on the most high stump that is near. I pipe on the flute to the wind what the lichens are saying. I am piper for the lichens that dwell on the gray rocks, and the lichens that cling to the trees grown old.

## Seventeen

## Opal finds the Pink Ribbons the Fairies brought, and sees The Man Of The Long Step Who Whistles Most All Of The Time

Morning works is done, and some more already, too. There is enough barks in for today and tomorrow, and many kindlings are now in on the floor by the big wood-box.

I have had my dinner at the noontime, and I went into the barn. There were little sad sounds in the stall — it was the moos of Mathilde Plantagenet. Now I have thinks her moos were moos for some dinner at noontime. She has breakfast at morningtime, and supper she has at graylight-time. But when noontime is come, Mathilde Plantagenet is here in the barn and her mother, the most gentle Jersey cow, is away out in the pasture. I have thinks there is needs for me to take Mathilde Plantagenet from the barn to the pasture at noontimes, so she may have her dinner. I go now to so do.

I did give the latch of the barn door a slip-back. Then I led Mathilde Plantagenet out by the little rope I did

use to use to lead Elizabeth Barrett Browning out by
when she was a little calf.

We went our way to the pasture-bars. I did give to
one a push, and it made a drop-down. Then I gave two
more pushes, and they went drop-downs. We went on
through in-between. It took a more long time to fix *up*
the pasture-bars — they have so heavy feels when I go
to put them back again. When I did have them so put,
we made a go-on.

We went a little way on. We did not have goes far,
for the gentle Jersey cow had sees of our coming, and
she came to meet us. We was glad to have it so. I have
thinks Mathilde Plantagenet did have most joy feels
about it — she did start to get her dinner from her
mother in a quick way. I watched her suck, and suck
some more. Seeing her have her dinner from her mother
a long time before suppertime did make me to have such
a big amount of satisfaction feels.

The grandpa felt not so. There was disturbs on his
temper. He was at our house when I was come home
from leading Mathilde Plantagenet back to the barn,
after she had sucked her mother a long time. The
mamma did spank me some, and some more. Now I have
wonders: Why was it the grandpa felt not satisfaction
feels at Mathilde Plantagenet having her dinner near
noontime, just like most all other children?

After the mamma did spank me, she told me more
works to do. And she went with her father to the ranch
house, to see her mother that was newly come back from
the mill town, where she did go early on this morning.

When the more works was done, I went in a quick,
soft way to the woods. I made little hops over the bushes
— the *little* bushes — as I did go along. I went along
the path until I came near unto the way that does lead

to the big old log where is the moss-box. I hid behind a tree when I was almost come there. I so did to wait a wait to see if the fairies were near about. I had not seeing of one about the moss-box. I looked looks about.

I looked looks about the old root by the log. I turned a big piece of bark over. Under it was something between two layers of moss, tied up with a pink ribbon. I felt glad feels. When I did untie the pink ribbon around the moss, there was lots more of pink ribbons. They did have little cards. And the little card on a nice long piece of pink ribbon said, "For Thomas Chatterton Jupiter Zeus." Another card on a more long piece did say, "For William Shakespeare." Another card on a more short piece did say, "For Lars Porsena of Clusium." And there was a ribbon for Brave Horatius, and Isaiah, and Elizabeth Barrett Browning, and for Mathilde Plantagenet — and there was more.

I did take them all in my arms, and I did go to the mill in the far woods. I so went to show all those pretty pink ribbons to the man that wears gray neckties and is kind to mice. I did show him all the cards that was on them. He was glad — I had seeing of the glad light in his eyes. He and I, we do believe in fairies.

Near him today was working the man of the long step that whistles most all of the time. He is a man with an understanding soul. When Brave Horatius did get his leg hurt the other day, this man did wash it and Mentholatum it, and he wrapped his handkerchief in rounds around it. Brave Horatius has likes for him, too.

Today when I did show to the man that wears gray neckties and is kind to mice all the pink ribbons the fairies did bring, he did say he thought the other man would like to see Brave Horatius's new pink ribbon that he was going to wear to cathedral service come a-Sunday.

And he did have likes to see it. When I told him how it was brought by the fairies to the moss-box by the old log, he said, "By jolly — that's fine!" And the man that wears gray neckties and is kind to mice gave me pats on the head, and I brought the ribbons back to a box where I do keep things in the woods.

I went on. When I was come to the house we live in, I had sees the mamma was come back. When I was come into the house, I had sees with her the mamma brought back a little bottle. It is called *"China-Mending Glue — Guaranteed to Stick."* That sounds great. I believe that bottle is quite a blessing. It has an interest look. It will be of much use, in many ways. I'm glad the mamma set it on the lamp-shelf, because I can climb on the stove and reach up to the shelf.

Now I go to talk with the willows where Nonette flows. I am going to tell them about this being the borning day of Queen Elizabeth of York, in 1465. Then I am going goes to tell William Shakespeare and Lars Porsena of Clusium about it.

# Eighteen

# Opal learns How To Mend Things Quickly

The nipple on Elsie's baby's milk-bottle has not stay-ons. It has had come-offs a lot of times today. The last time it did come off, Elsie did say, "I wish it would stick tight this time." I was standing by with the bacon she was sending back that she did borrow from the mamma, when I did hear her express her wish. I did tell her I had knows of a way to make that nipple stick tight on the baby's milk-bottle. She said, "That's nice — *I* don't know of a way." Inside me, I had feels she *ought* to have knows of a way, now that her babies are two. But I had sees how it was she had not knows of a way: On her lamp-shelf back of the stove, there is no bottle of china-mending glue, guaranteed to stick. I looked looks up to the shelf, and there was not any.

She had asks for me to show her the way. I told her it was as I would have to go first to the house we live in.

I so went in a quick way. The mamma was not in. I put the bacon on the cook-table. Then I made a climb-up on the stove, to get the bottle of china-mending glue. I most fell off the stove, but I didn't. If I did, I might have broke the bottle of china-mending glue guaranteed to stick. That would have been a cal lamb of tea.

When I was come to the house of Elsie, she had askings what was she to do. I told her to go in the bedroom and shut her eyes, while her wish came true. She filled the baby's bottle that used to be a brandy bottle with warm milk. She gave it and the nipple to me, and she went into the bedroom to wait waits for her wish to come true.

A little time it took. I had to have carefuls, so there wouldn't be glue in top of the bottle, too. I made it in a nice ring around the top. Then I put some more china-mending glue guaranteed to stick in a ring around the edge of the nipple. That fixed it. When I put it on, I had knows it would stick.

I put the china-mending glue in my pocket, and when I did say, "It is fixed!" Elsie did come. I felt a big amount of satisfaction. It is nice to help people to have what they wish for. It was as Elsie did have wishes for it to be. When I did hand it to her, she did have askings how was she going to have it stick on on other days, when I was not there to make it so do. She did have asks how did I do it. I told her it wasn't me, it was the china-mending glue guaranteed to stick — *that* was what did it.

She had a spell of cough. It came in a sudden way upon her, while I was telling her what it was that made the nipple stick like she had wishes for it to. I had not knows in the morning of this day she had a cold. Whenever she does have a cold, or feels of a one coming, she does send in a quick way for her mother. And her mother does come — she comes down the road that goes up to the mines. She has not come yet. And it's an awful cough Elsie did have then, and tears in her eyes.

When she did get better of the cough, I did give

more explains how she could always make the nipple stick on tight on the baby's bottle by keeping there on her lamp-shelf a bottle of mending glue guaranteed to stick. She started to have coughs again, and I gave her some pats on the back, like I have seen a man by the mill by the far woods pat his brother on the back. The pats on the back did help her some.

When she had coughs no more, I went out the door. She stepped out on her back steps. She gave my curls a smooth-back, and told me thanks for making her wish come true. And she told me more thanks for the in form ashun about how to make the nipple stick on the baby's bottle other times.

When I was come into the house we live in, I had thinks to go to visit Dear Love. When I did give my dress a smooth-out, I did have feels of that tear I got in it yesterday on top the barn door, when I did go to talk with Michael Angelo Sanzio Raphael. That was not a little tear — it was quite a big one. I had thinks it might get some *more* tear, if I did not mend it.

I got a patch. It was almost like the dress. It was a piece of a piece that was left when the mamma did make for her baby a jacket of light blue outing flannel. The patch of light blue looked nice on my dark blue calico dress, and the patch did have a soft feel. I mended it onto my dress with china-mending glue guaranteed to stick. Mending it that way saves so much time. It is quicker than mending it with a needle and thread, in the regular way.

Then I went to get the cap of the husband of Dear Love. The husband of Dear Love has given me one of his old caps, to carry some of my pets in. Sometimes caterpillars do ride in it — black and brown ones that do roll up in a ball and sleep the all of the time that I have them out for a walk. And sometimes Felix Men-

delssohn and Nannerl Mozart and Louis II, le Grand
Condé, do all ride in it. It is a nice warm place for them
to ride when we do go on winter walks. But mostly
Louis II, le Grande Condé, has prefers to ride in the
sleeves of my warm red dress.

Sometimes Brave Horatius does wear this cap that
was the cap of the husband of Dear Love. It so was today — when Brave Horatius and I did go to visit Dear
Love, Brave Horatius did wear the cap of her husband.
I put little pink-ribbon strings on it, and I did tie them
under his chin in a nice way. He was very quiet while
I did so do, and his being quiet did help me to get them
tied in a nice way. He is such a lovely dog. And he does
have appreciations for all the things I do for him. When
I did have that cap tied on in a nice way, he did bark a
joy bark, and he gave his tail three wags. And we did
start to go to the house of Dear Love.

As we did go along, I did make stops to look for cones,
and to get a piece of long moss. I put them in my pocket.
I put them there for the girl who has no seeing. She has
likes for the things I bring her to feel. She says she has
likes to have them near her, in the house she does live
in. So most every day I do find something for her, so
she can have joy with its feels. She so does like pine-
needles. I did gather for her my little basket full of
pine-needles, under the most tall pine tree of all.

We went on. Little blue fleurs are early blooming
now, before the oak and maple trees have yet their
leaves. I do so like blue — it is glad everywhere. When
I grow up, I am going to write a book about the glads of
blue, and about the *dauphinelle* and *lin* and *cornette*
and *nigelle* and *herbe-de-la-trinité*.

We made more stops, to tell the willows by Nonette
about this day being the borning day of Galileo in 1564,
and the going-away day of Michael Angelo in 1564.

And I did say another little thank prayer to God for their borning. This morning, we did have prayers of thanks in the cathedral for the works they did on earth. And Elizabeth Barrett Browning was there, and Brave Horatius, and most of the rest of us except Louis II, le Grand Condé.

When we were come to the house of Dear Love, the husband of Dear Love was making for her a chair. He was putting much work on all the little pieces. He did make all little rough places to have much smoothness. He so did with tools out of a tool-box he does keep in the kitchen of their little house. When he is not having uses of the tools in the tool-box, then the tool-box has its lid down, and it is a seat to sit on. Sometimes on rainy days when I do take Thomas Chatterton Jupiter Zeus to visit Dear Love, we all do sit on the tool-box, and Thomas Chatterton Jupiter Zeus does allow Dear Love to give him gentle pats on his nice white paws. He does have such beautiful ones. Today he did have allows for her to pat his paws while we did sit on a little bench.

Dear Love had thinks the appears of the cap of her husband on the head of Brave Horatius was very nice. And the husband of Dear Love did say the pink ribbons now on his cap made it a better-looking cap. I had thinks so, too.

Before I did have comes back to the house we live in, Dear Love did get out a piece of calico, just like my dress. Then she cut out the light blue patch that I did mend on with china-mending glue guaranteed to stick. She did sew on the blue calico patch in a nice way. She so did because she thought the light blue patch of outing flannel would be nice for a crib-robe for Felix Mendelssohn.

While Dear Love was sewing that blue calico patch

on my blue calico dress with little stitches, her husband did smile and look at her, and he did say, *"Another reason."* Now I have thinks the other reason was that he had fears if I longer wore that light blue patch of outing flannel on my dress, some of its soft feels would get wored off, and wouldn't be there for the joys of Felix Mendelssohn. He is a mouse that has likes for soft feels to go to sleep in.

# Nineteen

# The Ways of Lumber-Camp Folk, the End of the China-Mending Glue, and the Long Sleep of William Shakespeare

The papa is again come home from one of the upper camps — one of those by the rivière. I had seeing of him when I went to look for Lucian Horace Ovid Virgil, under the front step. He said he was going to make early garden. He said he thought he would set some onions out, and plant some radishes and some seeds that will grow into lettuce. I did make a stop to help him. He said for me to carry off the rocks where he did make spade-ups. I did — I picked up the rocks in a quick way. I carried them a little way away, by the brook. When summertime is come, I have thinks I will put them in the brook with some more, to make the brook have more wideness. And the man of the long step that whistles most all of the time has made me a water-wheel to go rounds in the brook when summertime is come.

The time it took to pick up those rocks, it was a time long. I did like to do it — I had thinks it would be of helps to the papa. After they was all picked up and carried over by the brook, I did go to the papa to see what more helps I could be. He was talking with the husband of Elsie. When I did ask him what helps I could be, he told me to run away from there — he wanted to talk.

I so did. I got Thomas Chatterton Jupiter Zeus, and we went to the woods. Brave Horatius did come a-following after, and Louis II, le Grand Condé, did ride in the sleeve of my warm red dress.

As we did go along, the leaves of salal did make little rustles. They were little askings. They had wants to know what day this was. I made stops along the way to tell them it was the going-away day of Gentile Bellini in 1507, and Sir Joshua Reynolds in 1792, and John Keats in 1821; and the borning day of George Frederick Handel, in 1685. I have thinks they and the tall fir trees were glad to know.

Brave Horatius barked a bark, and we went on. He looked a look back, to see if we was coming. Thomas Chatterton Jupiter Zeus did cuddle up more close in my arms. We saw six birds, and I did sing to Brave Horatius the bird song of grandpère, of *roitelet* and *ortolan* and *bruant* and *étourneau* and *rossignol* and *tourterelle* and *durbec* and *orfraie* and *roussette* and *loriot* and *nonnette* and *sarcelle* and *draine* and *épeiche* and *cygne* and *hirondelle* and *aigle* and *ramier* and *tarin* and *rousserolle* and *émerillon* and *sittelle*. Brave Horatius and William Shakespeare do have likes for that song. Sometimes I do sing it to them four times a day.

We all did go on, until we were come near to where were two men of the mill by the far woods. They were making divides of a very large log. They were making it to be many *short* logs. There was a big saw going moves between — one man did push it, and one man did pull it. I went on. I did look a look back. I had sees there was a tall fern growing by the foot of one man, and he did have his new overalls cut off where they do meet the boots.

I wonder why it is the lumber-camp folk do cut off their overalls where they do meet the boots. When they so cut them, they get fringy, and such fringes are more long than other fringes. I wonder why it is they so cut them. It maybe is because they so want fringes about the edge of the legs of their overalls. I would have prefers for ruffles.

We did go on. We went a little way on, and we had sees of more folks of the camp by the mill by the far woods. I did make a climb-up on an old tree-root, to have sees of them at work. Brave Horatius made a jump-up, and he came in a walk-over to where me and Thomas Chatterton Jupiter Zeus were sitting. We had seeing of them all working.

I have thinks the folks that live in the lumber camps, they are kindly folk. When they come home from work at eventime, I do so like to sit on a stump and watch them go by. They come in twos and threes. They do carry their dinner-pails in their hands. And some do whistle as they come, and some do talk. And some that do see me sitting on the stump do come aside and give to me the scraps in their dinner-pails. Some have knowing of the needs I do have for scraps in the nursery and the hospital. And too, when they come home from work in the far woods, the men do bring bits of moss, and nice velvet caterpillars, and little rocks. Some do. And these they give to me, for my nature collections. And I feel joy feels all over. Brave Horatius does bark joy barks. He does know, and I do know, the folks that live in the lumber camps — they are kindly folks.

.    .    .

Morning is glad on the hills. I hear a song like unto the song of the *verdier* [greenfinch]. The sky sings in blue tones; the earth sings in green. I am so happy.

The mamma is gone for a visit away. Before her going, she did set me to mind the baby. I do so. Inbetween times, I print, and I do spell over and over the words in my two books Angel Father and Angel Mother did make. I sing-song the letters of the words when I go adown the road. So I do when I am in the house, when the mamma isn't at home. I do not so when she is at home, because she won't let me.

Now Elizabeth Barrett Browning is calling me, out in the pasture. I expect she wants an apple or a sugar-lump. But I cannot have goes out there to the pasture, because the mamma did say for me to mind the baby, and mind the house. I sing to the baby words out of the two books, and the song about Iraouaddy, and the bird-song of grandpère.

And I have minded the house, as the mamma did say for me to do. First I swept the floors in a careful way. The broom made bobby moves. That broom in my hands makes not moves like the moves it does make in the hands of the mamma. It has so much of tallness — I look looks up its handle. And afterwards, I did the windows a wash-up-and-down with a cloth that did have Bon Ami on it. When the windows do get dirt on them, it is quite a worry on the mamma's mind — she so likes to have all things clean. I have thinks maybe she will have some glad feels way down in her heart where one cannot see them, when she is come home and has seeing of the windows made clean.

And more helps I have done. Most every week, there is patches to fix on clothes that have needs of them. Patching is quite a worry on the mamma's mind. It will be so no more. I have found a better way. While she was gone away today, I did get all the week's patching done. First I began on the papa's undershirt. It needed a big patch on the elbow. The mamma had cut out the patch and pinned it there on the sleeve, near unto the hole. I patched it on with china-mending glue guaranteed to stick.

Then I did do all the other patching that was in the basket. It did take most all the china-mending glue. When I did see it was most all gone, I did have remembers of that kettle that I have heard the mamma say she has wishes its lid would stick on tight. It is always a-coming off. I did fix that lid on that kettle so it will stay as tight as the mamma has wishes for it to. And then I did put the bottle that used to be full of china-mending glue back in its place on the lamp-shelf.

The baby had wake-ups, and I did sing it to sleep. When sleeps was come upon the baby, the mamma did come in the door. First she went to look upon her dear baby, sleeping there on the bed. She said now she was going to mend those two mush-dishes. And she got the pieces of them from the cupboard. She put them on the cook-table. And then the mamma went to get the china-mending glue guaranteed to stick. There was none in the bottle. I knew where it was gone. The mamma knew, too.

After she did spank for some long time, she did ask me what I did with all that glue. It took quite some time to tell her about Elsie's baby's bottle that she had wishes for the nipple to stick on tight, and about all the patches the china-mending glue did fix, and all the other things that it did fix.

When I got to the end, she did spank me again. She said that was to be good on. Now I do think it was real kind of her to tell me what that last spanking was for. Most times, I don't know what I get spanked for. And I do like to know, because if I did have knows what I was spanked for, I'd be real careful about doing what it was again — if it was not helping folks of the fields and woods. I have to do *that*, no matter how many spanks I do get for it. But there is so much joy in the woods, and it does help spank feels to hurt not so much. Now I think I will go feed the folks in the nursery, and then I will go to have vesper service in the cathedral.

Most all this afternoon-time, I have been out in the field — the one that is nearest unto the woods. I have been having talks with William Shakespeare. Today he is not working in the woods with the other horses. He is having a rest-day.

He was laying down near unto one of the altars I have builded for Saint Louis. He did lay there all the afternoon. Tiredness was upon him. I gave his nose rubs, and his neck and ears, too. And I did tell him poems, and sing him songs. He has likes for me to so do. After I did sing him more, sleeps did come upon him. The breaths he did breathe while he was going to sleep, they were such long breaths. And I gave unto him more pats on the nose, and pats on the neck. We are chums, William Shakespeare and me. This evening, I will come again to wake him. I'll come just before suppertime, so he may go in with the other horses to eat his supper in the barn.

I did. Sleeps was yet upon him. He looked so tired, laying there. I went up to pet his front leg, but it was stiff. I petted him on the nose — and his nose, it was so cold. I called him, but he did not answer. I said again, "William Shakespeare, don't you hear me calling?" But he did not answer. I have thinks he is having a long rest, so he will have ready feels to pull the heavy poles on tomorrow.

I now go goes to tell the man that wears gray neckties and is kind to mice about William Shakespeare having all this rest-day, and how he has sleeps in the field with the pink ribbon around his neck that the fairies did bring. Thomas Chatterton Jupiter Zeus is going goes with me. We will wait on the stump by that path he does follow when he comes home from work at eventime.

We are come back. The man that wears gray neckties and is kind to mice did go with us to see William Shakespeare having his long sleep there in the field by the altar of Saint Louis. Now I do have understanding. My dear William Shakespeare will no more have wake-ups again. Rob Ryder cannot give him whippings no more. He has gone to a long sleep — a very long sleep. He just had goes because tired feels was upon him. I have so lonesome feels for him. But I am glad that Rob Ryder cannot whip him now no more.

I have covered him over with leaves. To find enough, I went to the far end of the near woods. I gathered them into my apron. Sometimes I could hardly see my way, because I just could not keep from crying. I have such lonesome feels. William Shakespeare did have an understanding soul. And I have knows his soul will not have forgets of the willows by the singing creek. Often I will leave a message there on a leaf for him. I have thinks his soul is not far gone away. There are little blue fleurs a-blooming, where he did lay him down to sleep.

# Twenty

## Opal watches Elsie's Baby, christens Solomon Grundy, and visits Dear Love

Today was wash-day come again. After I did do my parts of the washing, I did go to feed the folks in the nursery. When I was come back again, I did start to make things out of clay. I was making vases out of clay when the mamma called me to come empty the wash-water. There were two tubs full of water. That's an awful lot of water to empty. But I carry it out in the wash-pan. And wash-pans full of water are not so much water at a time, but they soon empty the tub.

Then the mamma did have me to weed onions. There were an awful lot of weeds trying to grow up around those onions. It took a very long time to pull all the weeds, and my back did get some tired feels; but I did get those weeds pulled out. I have thinks the onions were saying when the wind did rustle them, *"We thank you for the more room we now have got to grow in."* Folks growing in a garden do say interest things.

From the onion garden, I did go to the Jardin des Tuileries. I so did go to have a little service there, for this is the borning day of Charles de Valois in 1270, and the going-away day of Saint Grégoire I, in 604. Felix Mendelssohn did ride in my pocket to service. He did sleep most of the time, though. I did begin to sing by the two little trees I have planted for Saint Grégoire and Charles de Valois. I first did sing, "*Sanctus, sanctus, sanctus, Dominus Deus, Hosanna in excelsis.*" While I was singing, Brave Horatius and Lars Porsena of Clusium came. They did wait while I did sing two more songs. Then I said a long prayer, and a little prayer.

Afterwards, we did start to go along the path. We went a little way; then I did go aside. I went aside to the house of Elsie, to see the new baby.

It was sleeping in its cradle that the husband of Elsie made out of a box. He put rockers on the box, and Elsie put soft feels in it. After the box did have rockers on it and soft feels in it, they did take the baby girl from the bed and lay her in the cradle. And now everyday, except the day she does go with her mother Elsie to visit her grandma, the baby does lay in the cradle. And Elsie does rock the cradle with her foot while she sews. She sings and sings. She sings, "Rock-a-by baby, in the tree-top; when the wind blows, the cradle will rock." And while she does sing, I have knowings that the little song-notes do dance about the cradle of the baby.

Today I did stay quite a time long to look upon the face of the baby. I so do love babies. Every night, I pray for the twins I want when I grow up. Some nights, I pray that they may have blue eyes and golden hair. Other nights, I pray for them to have brown eyes and brown hair. Sadie McKibben tells me I better stop changing my prayers about so much, or the angels may bring to me when I grow up twins with streaked hair and variegated eyes.

After I did look upon the little baby at the house of

Elsie, I did have thinks to go to the house of Sadie McKibben. I so did go. As I did go along, I did have wonders if mothers can see the little song-notes that dance about their babies's cradles when they sing lullaby songs to them.

I went on across the field. When I was come to a stump by the fence corner, I stopped. I heard a *criard* [squealing] noise. It came from near the stump. I think it was a mulot. I looked looks about. I had not seeing of it. I went on. I saw a blue jay nearby the old log where I did hide nineteen acorn children on a gray day in September. He was looking looks about. I watched him make a flyaway with one of my acorns. I did count what was left. There was only a few. I went on.

When I was come to the house of Sadie McKibben, she was washing clothes. On washing days, Sadie Mc-Kibben does look a bit different from her appears on other days. On wash-days along in the afternoon, her hair does hang in strings about her face, her dress does have crinkles all adown it, and her nice blue gingham apron with cross-stitches on it does have rumples and soapy smells. I do know so, for I do smell those soapy smells when I cuddle close to her apron on wash-days.

Today I did stay by the side of Sadie McKibben for a little time. Then I did go to weed her onions for her. They did have looks like they did have needs for more room to grow in. And while I did weed her onions, I did see many beautiful things about. There is so much to see near about, and a little way off, and there is so much to hear. And most all the time I am seeing, I am hearing, and I do have such glad feels.

Today we did christen Solomon Grundy. He was borned a week ago yesterday, on Monday. That's why we did name him Solomon Grundy. And this being

Tuesday we did christen him, for in the rhyme, the grandpa does sing to the children about Solomon Grundy being christened on Tuesday.

Yesterday I made him a christening robe out of a new dish-towel that was flapping in the wind. But the aunt had no appreciation of the great need of a christening robe for Solomon Grundy. And my ears were slapped until I thought my head would pop open, but it didn't. It just ached. Last night when I went to bed, I prayed for the ache to go away. This morning when I woke up, it had gone out the window. I did feel good feels, from my nightcap to my toes. I thought about the christening. And early on this morning, before I yet did eat my breakfast, I went out the window that the ache went out in the night. I went from the window to the pig-pen.

I climbed into the pig-pen. I crawled on my hands and knees back under the shed, where he and his sisters five and his little brother were all having breakfast from their mother. I gently did pull away by his hind-legs, from among all those dear baby pigs, he who had the most curl in his tail. I took him to the pump and pumped water on him, to get every speck of dirt off. He squealed, because the water was cold. So I took some of the warm water the mamma was going to wash the milk-pans in, and I did give him a warm bath in the wash-pan. Then he was the pinkiest white pig you ever saw. I took the baby's talcum-powder can, and I shook it lots of times all over him. When the powder sprinkled in his eyes, he did object with a regular baby-pig squeal. And I climbed right out the bedroom window with him, because the mamma heard his squeal, and she was coming fast. I did go to the barn in a hurry, for in the barn yesterday I did hide the christening robe. When I reached the top of the hay, I stopped to put it on Solomon Grundy. Then we proceeded to the cathedral.

A little ways we did go, and I remembered how on the borning day of him, I did ask that grand fir tree, Good King Edward I, to be his godfather. And that smaller fir tree growing by his side, the lovely Queen Eleanor of Castile, I did ask to be his godmother. We went aside from the path that leads unto the cathedral. We went another way. We went adown the lane to where dwell Good King Edward I and the lovely Queen Eleanor. And there beside them, Solomon Grundy was christened. They who were present at the christening were these: Saint Louis, and Charlemagne, and Hugh Capet, and King Alfred, and Theodore Roosevelt, and William Wordsworth, and Homer, and Cicero, and Brave Horatius, and Isaiah. These last two did arrive in a hurry, in the midst of the service. Being dogs with understanding souls, they did realize the sacredness of the occasion, and they stood silent near Charlemagne.

When we got most to the end of the service, just at that very solemn moment while I was waiting for Good King Edward I and his lovely Queen Eleanor of Castile to bestow their blessing upon the white head of the babe, he gave a squeal — just the kind of squeal all baby pigs give when they are wanting their dinner.

After the naming of him, I placed around his neck a little wreath that I made in the evening yesterday for him. Then I did sing softly a hymn to the morning, and came again home to the pig-pen with Solomon Grundy.

When I got to the corner of the barn, I pulled off his christening robe. I did hide it again in the hay. Then I climbed into the pig-pen. I did say the Lord's Prayer softly over the head of Solomon Grundy. After I said Amen, I did poke him in among all his sisters, and near unto his mother. Aphrodite gave a grunt of satisfaction. Also did Solomon Grundy.

I went to the house. I climbed in the window again. I took off my nightcap and my nightgown. I did get dressed in a quick way. The little girl was romping in the bed. I helped her to get her clothes on. Then we went to the kitchen for our breakfast. The mamma was in the cellar. She did hear me come into the kitchen. She came in. With her came a kindling and a hazel switch.

After she did spank me, she told me to get the mush for the little girl's breakfast. It was in a kettle. I spooned it out into a blue dish that came as premium in the box of mush, when they brought it new from the mill town. After we did eat our mush and drink our milk, the mamma told me to clear the table and go tend chickens.

I carried feed to them. I scattered it in shakes. The chickens came in a quick way. Fifteen of those chickens I did give names to, but it's hard to tell some of them apart — most of them have about the same number of speckles on them. I counted all the chickens that were there. There weren't as many there as ought to be there. Some came not. These were the hens setting in the chicken-house. I went in; I lifted them off. They were fidgety and fluffy and clucky. I did carry them out to the feed.

While they were eating breakfast, I counted their eggs. I made a discovery: Minerva hadn't as many eggs as the others. That meant she wouldn't have as many children as the others would have. I did begin to feel sorry about that, because already I had picked out names for her fifteen children, and there in her nest there were only twelve eggs. I didn't know what to do. And then I had a think what to do. I did it. I took an egg from each nest of the three other setting hens. That fixed things.

Then I thought I would go on an exploration trip and to the nursery, and there I would give the folks a talk on geology. But then the mamma called me, to scour the pots and pans. That is something I do not like to do at all. So all the time I'm scouring them, I keep saying lovely verses. That helps so much, and by-and-by, the pots and pans are all clean.

After that, all day the mamma did have more works for me to do. There was more wood to bring in. There was steps to scrub. There was cream to be shaked into butter. There was raking to do in the yard. There was carpet-strings to sew together. In-between times, there was the baby to tend. And all the time, all day long, I did have longings to go on exploration trips. The fields were calling. The woods were calling. I heard the wind — he was making music in the forest. It was soft music; it was low. It was an echo of the songs the flowers were singing. Even if there was much works to do, hearing the voices helped me to get the works done in the way they ought to be done.

The most hurry time of all was the time near even-time, for there was going to be company to eat at the table. The mamma was in a hurry to get supper, so I helped her. She only had time to give one shake of salt to the potatoes, so I gave them three more. She did not have time to put sauce on the peas, so I flavored them with lemon extract, for the mamma is so fond of lemon flavoring in lemon pies. When she made the biscuits, she was in such a hurry she forgot to set them on a box back of the stove for an airing, as usual, before putting them in the oven. Being as she forgot to do it, while she was in the cellar to get the butter, I did take the pan of biscuits out of the oven and put them under the stove, so they would not miss their usual airing. Then I did go to the wood-shed for more wood.

When I did put it in the wood-box, the mamma reached over for me. She jerked me. She spanked me with her hand, and the hair-brush, and the pancake-turner. Then she shoved me out the door. She said for me to get out, and stay out of her way.

I came here to the barn. I sit here printing. In-between times, I stretch out on the hay. I feel tired and sore all over. I wonder for what it was the mamma gave me that spanking. I have tried so hard to help her today.

Solomon Grundy is grunting here beside me. I went by and got him, as I came along. Here on the hay, I showed to him the writings in the two books my Angel Father and Angel Mother made for me. These books are such a comfort; and when I have them right along with me, Angel Father and Angel Mother do seem nearer.

I did bow my head and ask my guardian angel to tell them there in heaven about Solomon Grundy being christened today. Then I drew him up closer to my gingham apron, and I patted him often. And some of the pats I gave to him were for the lovely Peter Paul Rubens that used to be. And the more pats I gave Solomon Grundy, the closer he snuggled up beside me. Tonight I shall sing to him a lullaby song, as I cuddle him up all snowy white in his christening robe, before I take him out to his mother Aphrodite in the pig-pen.

I now have a bottle with a nipple on it for Solomon Grundy. But he won't pay much attention to it. He has prefers to get his dinner from his mother Aphrodite, out in the pig-pen.

After he so did have his dinner today, and after my morning works were done and I did have that hen started on a set — that hen had wants to set so much; I did have an awful time getting her off the nest at feeding-time. I had thinks I would set her myself, being as the mamma doesn't want to bother about it. I had thinks I would put three eggs under her today, and three more when comes tomorrow, and three on the next day, and three on the next. That will give her a good setting of eggs to start on.

Today, after I so did have her started on a set with three eggs, then I went to visit Dear Love. I did cuddle up Solomon Grundy in one arm, and Thomas Chatterton Jupiter Zeus in the other arm. And so we went to visit Dear Love. Solomon Grundy wore his christening robe, and he looked very sweet in it. I gave him a nice warm bath before we did start, so as to get all the pig-pen smells off. Sometimes smells do get in that pig-pen, though I do give it brush-outs every day, and I do carry old leaves and bracken ferns and straws in for beds for Aphrodite. After I did give Solomon Grundy his bath, I did dust talcumatum powder over him. I was real careful not to get any in his eyes.

As we did go along, I did sing to them a lullaby about Nonette and Saint Firmin, and more I did sing about Iraouaddy. We went on. Then I did tell them about the beautiful love the man of the long step that whistles most all of the time does have for the *pensée* [pensive] girl with the far-away look in her eyes. But he is afraid to tell her about it — Sadie McKibben says he is. Sadie McKibben says he is a very shy man. Thomas Chatterton Jupiter Zeus did go to sleeps while I was telling them about it, and Solomon Grundy did grunt a little grunt. It was a grunt for more sings. So I did sing to him:

> "Did he smile his work to see?
> Did he who made the Lamb make thee?"

He had likes for that song, and he grunted a grunt with a question in it. So I did sing him some more: "Indeed he did, Solomon Grundy, indeed he did. And the hairs of thy baby head, they are numbered." Soon I shall be counting them, to see how many they are.

We went on to the house of Dear Love. When we were come to there, the husband of Dear Love was digging in the ground, under the front window of their little house. As he did dig, he did pick up the little rocks that were under the window, and he did lay them aside. I did have asks what for was he digging up the ground under their window, and he did give explanations. He is making a flower-bed, and when it is made, Dear Love is going to plant morning-glory seeds in it. And then morning-glory vines will grow up around the window. I think that will be so nice.

I did ask him how far up they would grow. And he reached up his hand to where they have thinks the morning-glory vines will grow to. I looked up — it was high up. It was lots more up than I have growed to. Now I think it would be nice to be a morning-glory vine, and grow up and up. In the fields, I have had seeing that the little white ones there do grow out and out.

I did ask them how many leaves does the morning-glory have that is going to grow up by their window. They both did say they were sorry, but they did not know. Then I did tell them that they did not need to have cry feels about it, because when it is growing up, we can learn together how many leaves it has. And he did stop digging digs, to take Solomon Grundy in his arms; and Thomas Chatterton Jupiter Zeus had allows for Dear Love to pet his paws.

# Twenty-one

# Cathedral Service in the Barn; a Lamb for Opal, and a Lily for Peter Paul Rubens

Today was a very stormy day — more rainy than other stormy days. So we had cathedral service on the hay, in the barn.

Mathilde Plantagenet was below us in her stall, and she did moo moos while I did sing the choir-service. Plato and Pliny, the two bats, hung on the rafters in a dark corner. Lars Porsena of Clusium perched on the back of Brave Horatius. Thomas Chatterton Jupiter Zeus sat at my feet and munched leaves while I said prayers. Lucian Horace Ovid Virgil was on my right shoulder, and Louis II, le Grand Condé, was on my left shoulder, part of the time; then he did crawl in my sleeve, to have a sleep. Solomon Grundy was asleep by my side in his christening robe, and a sweet picture he was in it. On my other side was his little sister, Anthonya Mundy, who has not got as much curl in her tail as has Solomon Grundy.

Clementine, the Plymouth Rock hen, was late come to service. She came up from the stall of the gentle

Jersey cow, just when I was through singing *"Hosanna in excelsis."* She came and perched on the back of Brave Horatius, back of Lars Porsena of Clusium. Then I said more prayers, and Brave Horatius did bark Amen. When he so did, Clementine tumbled off his back. She came over by me. I had thinks it would be nice if her pretty gray feathers were blue. I gave her a gentle pat, and then I did begin the talk service. I did use for my text, *"Blessed be the pure in heart, for they shall see God."*

And all of the time, the raindrops did make little joy patters on the roof. They were coming down from the sky in a quick way.

Now is the begins of the borning-time of the year. I did hurry home from school in a quick way, in the afternoon of this day. Aidan of Iona come from Lindisfarne has said I may name the little lambs that now are coming. All day, I did have thinks about what names to call them by. There are some names I do so like to sing the spell of. Some names I do sing over and over again when I do go on explores. I could hardly wait waits until school-getting-out-time. I had remembers how Sadie McKibben says no child should grow a day old without having a name. Now some of those dear baby lambs are two and three days old, since their borning-time.

When I was come to where was Aidan of Iona come from Lindisfarne, I did tell him, "Now I have come to name all your lambs!" He did have one little lamb in his arms. He did tell me as how it was it didn't belong to anyone, and it was lonesome without a mother. He said he had thinks he would give it to *me* to mother. I was so happy. It was very white, and very soft, and its legs was slim. And it had wants for a mother. It had likes for me to put my arms around it. I did name it first of

218

all — I called it Menander Euripides Theocritus Thucydides. It had likes for the taste of my fingers when I did dip them into the pan of milk on the rock and then put them in its mouth. Its woolly tail did wiggle joy wiggles, and I did dance on my toes. I felt such a big amount of satisfaction feels, having a lamb to mother. I am getting quite a big family, now.

After I did dip my fingers in the milk for Menander Euripides Theocritus Thucydides, I was going goes to see about getting a brandy bottle somewhere and a nipple, so this baby lamb could have a bottle to nurse, like other babies hereabouts. When I did make a start to go, Aidan of Iona come from Lindisfarne did say, "You are not going away before you name the others, are you?" Of course I was not. And he said Menander Euripides Theocritus Thucydides was full up of milk for today, and I could bring his bottle on the morrow.

Then I did make begins to name the other lambs. They were dear, and so *dear*. First one I did come to, I did name Plutarch Demosthenes. The next one I did name Marcus Aurelius. And one came close by Aidan of Iona come from Lindisfarne, and I called it Epicurus Pythagorus. One did look a little more little than the others. I called him Anacreon Herodotus. One was more big than all the others. I named him Homer Archimedes Chilon. He gave his tail a wiggle, and came close to his mother. One had a more short tail, and a question-look in his eyes. I called him Sophocles Diogenes. And one more, I called Periander Pindar; and one was Solon Thales; and the last one of all that had not yet a name, I did call him Tibullus Theognis. He was a very fuzzy lamb, and he had very long legs.

The shepherd did have likes for the names I did give to his little lambs, and the names I did give to his sheep, a long time ago. And today, when he did tell me how he did have likes for their names, I did tell him how I have likes for them too, and how I have thinks to learn more about them, when I do grow up more tall. I told him how I did sing the spell of the words to the fishes that live in the singing creek where the willows grow.

After I said good-bye to all the other lambs, I did kiss Menander Euripides Theocritus Thucydides on the nose. I have thinks every eventime I will kiss him good-night, because maybe he does have lonesome feels too, and maybe he does have longs for kisses, like the longs I do have for them every night-time.

Before I was come to the house we do live in, I did make a stop by the singing creek where the willows grow. I did print a message on a leaf. It was for the soul of William Shakespeare. I tied it on a willow branch.

Then I did go by the cathedral, to say thank prayers for Menander Euripides Theocritus Thucydides. And I did have remembers that this was the going-away day of Reine Marie Amélie in 1866, and Queen Elizabeth, in 1603. And I did say a thank prayer for the goodness of them. It was near dark-time. There were little whispers in the woods, and shadows with velvet fingers. I did sing, "*Sanctus, sanctus, sanctus, Dominus Deus.*"

Before I did come on to the house we live in, I did go aside to have sees of a cream lily that has its growing near unto the cathedral. I have watched the leafing of that lily, and I have watched its budding. A long time, I have had thinks about it. Today its blooming-time was come. There it was.

I went close unto it. My soul was full of thank feels. Ever since the day when Peter Paul Rubens did go away, I have looked for his soul in tree-tops, and all about. Now I have knows his soul does love to linger by this lily. I did kneel by it, and say a thank prayer for the blooming of this fleur Peter Paul Rubens's soul does love to linger near. If ever I go from here, I will take with me this lily plant. I did have feels that my dear Peter Paul Rubens was very near this eventime.

Today is more rain come again. I like rain. I like the music patters it does make. I like to have feels of it on my head. When it rains, I like to go barefooted. I like to feel the clean mud by the lane ooze up between my toes.

When I did see the rain coming down in so fast a way, I did go to the barn; and after I did have them off, I did put my shoes and stockings in the hay. I went out to talk with Michael Angelo Sanzio Raphael about this day being the borning day of Sanzio Raphael, in 1483. Then I came down by the lane. I was so glad to have my shoes and stockings off — the feel was so good. Having my shoes and stockings off made my heels feel like they were getting wings. I went up and down the lane. Brave Horatius came a-following after.

I had thinks to go see how was Minerva in the henhouse. I saw her feathers were more fluffy, and there was some more heads than hers in her nest — there was the heads of the little chickens I did pick out names for, before they was yet hatched. And now I cannot tell them apart.

Minerva had one baby chicken to hatch four days ago, and one baby chicken three days ago, and one more baby chicken two days ago. I heard the grandpa say it was a puzzle what was making that hen to have her chickens begin hatching so soon, and then no more to hatch until today. Too, I have thinks it is a puzzle. But anyway, she is going to have fifteen chickens, because that day a little time ago, I took one egg each from those hens that was set before she was, so Minerva would have the fifteen children I had already picked out names for.

I did tell Minerva again the names I did pick out for all her children, before they was yet hatched. I told her Edmund Spenser, and John Fletcher, and Francis Beaumont, and Jean Racine, and Sir Walter Raleigh, and Jean Molière, and Sir Francis Bacon, and Nicolas Boileau, and Sir Philip Sidney, and Jean de la Fontaine, and Ben Jonson, and Oliver Goldsmith, and Cardinal Richelieu, and Samuel Taylor Coleridge, and Pius VII. And Minerva had joy feels when I did tell her. And she ate all the grain in my hand while I was telling her.

Minerva is a very nice hen, and it is so nice she has so many children at once. I so do like to pick out names for children. Now I have thinks there is needs for me to hurry to get those christening robes done for her children, being as they are hatching now. On the day of their christening, I will carry them in a little basket to the cathedral. There is needs to carry little chickens in a basket, for they are delicate. Today I did show Minerva the little cap with ruffles on it that I have just made for her to wear to the cathedral at their christening. I made it like Jenny Strong's morning-cap with ruffles on it.

After I did talk some more with Minerva and she did chuckle some more chuckles, I did make a start to go to the cathedral, to have a thank service for the borning of Sanzio Raphael, in 1483. As I did go, I went aside to the pig-pen. Every time my way goes near to the way that goes to the pig-pen, I do go that way. I so go to take a peep at Aphrodite. She does have such a motherly look, with those dear baby pigs about her. How nice it must be to be a mother pig. It must be a big amount of satisfaction, having so many babies at one time.

# Twenty-two

## Opal carries Solomon Grundy to The Man Who Wears Gray Neckties, takes the Baby Chickens to the Cathedral, and brings Flowers to The Girl With The Far-Away Look In Her Eyes

Today I went not to school. For a long time after breakfast, the mamma did have me to cut potatoes into pieces. Tonight and tomorrow night, the grownups will plant the pieces of potatoes I cut today. Then by-and-by, after some long time, the pieces of potato with eyes on them will have baby potatoes under the ground. Up above the ground, they will be growing leaves and flowers. One must leave an eye on every piece of potato one plants in the ground to grow — it won't grow if you don't. It can't see how to grow, without its eye.

All day today, I did be careful to leave an eye on every piece. And I did have meditations about what things the eyes of potatoes do see there in the ground. I have thinks they do have seeing of black velvet moles, and large earthworms that do get short in a quick way. And potato flowers above the ground do see the doings of the field, and maybe they do look away and see the willows that grow by the singing creek. I do wonder if potato plants do have longings to dabble their toes. I have supposes they do, just like I do. Being a potato must be interest, specially the having so many eyes. I have longings for more eyes — there is much to see in this world all about. Every day, I do see beautiful things, everywhere I do go.

Today it was near eventime, the time I did have all those potatoes ready for plants. Then I did go to see Solomon Grundy in the pig-pen. I did take a sugar-lump in my apron pocket for his dear mother, Aphrodite. She had appreciations and well looks. But the looks of Solomon Grundy — they were *not* well looks. He did lay so still, in a quiet way. I gave to him three looks. I felt a lump come in my throat. His looks, they were so different.

I made a run for the wood box — the wood box I did bring before for the getting in of Brave Horatius to service in the pig-pen. I did step on it in getting Solomon Grundy out of the pig-pen. I did have fears if I did it in jumps, as I always do, the jumps might bother the feelings of Solomon Grundy. So I did have needs for that box — it is such a help. Every time I do get a place fixed in the pig-pen so some of the pigs can get out to go to walks and to go to the cathedral service, the grownups at the ranch house do always fix the boards back again. So a box is helps to get the little pigs that aren't too big over the top.

When I did have Solomon Grundy over the top, I did cuddle him up in my gray calico apron. I have thinks he does like the blue one best. But today he had not seeings it wasn't the blue one I had on. He did not give his baby squeaks. He was only stillness. I did have fears that sickness was upon him. He has lost that piece of asfiditee I did tie around his neck the other day. That was the last piece I did have. It was the little piece that was left of the big piece that the mamma did tie around my neck, and I did make divides with my friends. But Solomon Grundy, he has lost his share both times. He does lose it in a quick way. And I did have no Castoria to give him, because the mamma has gone and put away the baby's bottle of Castoria where I cannot find it.

I did not have knowings what to do for him. But I did have thinks the man that wears gray neckties and is kind to mice would have knowings what to do for the sickness of Solomon Grundy. I made starts to the mill by the far woods.

Brave Horatius was waiting at the barn — he gave his tail two wags, and followed after. We went by Michael Angelo Sanzio Raphael. I did tell him the baby in my arms was sick. I said a little prayer over his head. We went along the lane. When we were come to Good King Edward I and lovely Queen Eleanor, we made stops. I did tell them of the sickness of the baby. I said a little prayer for his getting well, and I did hold him up for their blessing. Then we went on, and Brave Horatius came a-following after. When we were come to the ending of the lane, I said another little prayer. Then we went on. When we were come near unto the altar of Good King Edward I, I said another little prayer. Then we went on. Elizabeth Barrett Browning was in the woods, and she went with us. She mostly does so. And we went on.

By-and-by, my arms was getting tired. Solomon Grundy, now that he is older grown, does get a little heavy when I carry him quite a long ways.

When I was come to the far end of the near woods, I

met the man that wears gray neckties and is kind to mice. He smiled the gentle smile he always does smile, and he took Solomon Grundy into his arms. I have thinks he did see the tiredness that was in my arms. When he sat down on a log with the dear pig, I said I had fears Solomon Grundy was sick. He said he did, too. But he smoothed my curls back and he said, "Don't you worry — he will get well." Hearing him say that made me have better feels.

Men are such a comfort — men that wear gray neckties and are kind to mice. One I know. He looks kind looks upon the forest, and he does love the grand fir trees that do grow there. I have seen him stretch out his arms to them, just like I do do in the cathedral. He does have kindness for the little folks that do live about the grand trees. His ways are ways of gentleness. All my friends have likes for him. And so had Solomon Grundy.

Today he said he would take Solomon Grundy back to camp by the mill, to his bunk-house. A warming he did need, so he said, and he said he would wrap him in his blanket and take care of him until morningtime was come. Then he did go the way that goes to the far woods, and I did go the way that does go to the cathedral. I so went to have a little thank service for the getting well of Solomon Grundy. I do have knowings he will be well when morningtime is come. With me to the cathedral did go Elizabeth Barrett Browning and Brave Horatius.

This morning before breakfast, I did go to the cathedral to say thanks for the goodness of one William Wordsworth; for this is the day of his borning, in 1770. With me did go Thomas Chatterton Jupiter Zeus, and Brave Horatius came a-following after.

After the morning's work was done, I took my little

basket most full of christening robes to the pen-place near the hen-house, where is Minerva and her fourteen baby chickens. (One baby chicken didn't hatch.) I had most enough christening robes ready on yesterday afternoon but one. When I did go to sing her baby to sleeps, Elsie did help me to fix that one, while I did carry in some wood for her. She put a little ruffle of lace on it, and a little blue bow of ribbon. It looked very nice. I did have thinks how nice they would look if *all* of the christening robes for the baby chickens of Minerva did have little bows of ribbon on them.

Elsie had asks what was my thoughts about, and I did tell her. And she did say she had thinks that way, too. And she did make a go to her work-basket that was under the shelf where does set the bottle of Vaseline that her young husband does smooth back his pumpadoor with. That Vaseline jar is most empty again. When Elsie did find some little ribbons in her work-basket, she did go and raise up the trunk-lid, and she did find some more little ribbons in the tray of the trunk. She tied them all into little bows. And some were pink, and some were *lavande* [lavender], and some were blue, and some were rose. There was enough for every baby chicken to have one on his christening robe. And I did sew them all on at night-time on yesterday, when the mamma did put me under the bed. Light enough came from the lamp on the kitchen table, so I could have sees to sew them all on.

When we was come near unto the cathedral, I made a stop to put on their christening robes. Nicolas Boileau and Jean Molière did have lavande ribbon bows on theirs. They waited waits in a corner of the basket while I did put on the others. Sir Walter Raleigh had a little pink bow on his. He would not keep still while I was getting him into his robes. He peeped three times. But

Sir Francis Bacon was more fidgety than *he* was — it took quite a time to get *his* christening robe on. Ben Jonson did wear the christening robe with the ruffle of lace around it, and before I did get him put back in the basket there, he did catch his toe in that ruffle of lace. Then he peeped. I took his toe out of the ruffle, and put a christening robe with a rose ribbon bow on it on Francis Beaumont, and one like it on John Fletcher, because their names was together in the book Angel Mother did write in.

After I did get little brown Oliver Goldsmith and all the rest of the children of Minerva into their christening robes, then I did take out of my pocket her little white cap with the ruffles on it like the ruffles on the morning-cap of Jenny Strong. I tied it under Minerva's bill. She was a sweet picture in it, coming down the cathedral aisle by my side. Minerva is a plump hen of gentle ways. It is not often she does talk, but she did chuckle all of the time while her baby chickens was getting christened.

Brave Horatius stood by the altar, and Lars Porsena of Clusium did perch upon his back. Lucian Horace Ovid Virgil did sit on a log close by. And Mathilde Plantagenet watched from the pasture-bars. Menander Euripides Theocritus Thucydides did walk by my side when we went goes to have asks for the blessing of Saint Louis on all Minerva's baby chickens, after they were christened. Then I did sing *"Hosanna in excelsis."* And Ben Jonson peeped, and so did Francis Beaumont and Pius VII. He was wiggling so that his christening robe was most off him. I put it on again. Then I did stop to straighten up Minerva's cap with the ruffles on it. It had had a slip-back. Then we had more prayers.

Afterward, we all did have goes back to the chicken-yard pen. I took off Minerva's cap, so it would be clean for cathedral service on Sundays. Then I put her and all her children back in their pen, after they did have their christening robes off.

After I did give Minerva some good-bye pats and advices about bringing up her children, then I did go goes to the house of Sadie McKibben. Menander Euripides Theocritus Thucydides did walk by my side, and Brave Horatius came a-following after.

When I was come to the house of Sadie McKibben, there was Dear Love. They was glad we was come, and they had likes for Minerva's little cap with the ruffles around it, like the morning-cap of Jenny Strong. Dear Love did give Thomas Chatterton Jupiter Zeus some pats on his nice white paws.

And they did talk on. I did have hears of them saying of the *pensée* girl with the far-away look in her eyes, that is come again to visit her aunt of the gray calico dress with the black bow at its neck. I was glad she is come again. I whispered to Thomas Chatterton Jupiter Zeus about my glad feels in his left ear. He cuddled up more close. We listened more listens.

Dear Love too did say to Sadie McKibben as how it is the man of the long step that whistles most all of the time has great love for the *pensée* girl with the far-away look in her eyes, and how it is he is afraid to speak to her about this great love he has for her. And more Dear Love did say, of how it is he does pick bunches of flowers in the woods for her, and then he does lay them by an old log, because he has too shy feels to take them on to her.

Thomas Chatterton Jupiter Zeus did stick out his right front foot. I gave it a pat, and I did give him some throat rubs that he had likes for. And all of the time, I was having thinks.

I looked looks out the side window of the house of Sadie McKibben. A white cloud was sailing in the sky. A little wind was in the woods. It was calling, "*Petite Françoise — come, petite Françoise.*"

I did tell Dear Love and Sadie McKibben there was needs for me to hurry away. They did have understanding. And Sadie McKibben did say it was not long I was staying today, and she would wait waits for my return, coming on the morrow. Dear Love did tell me of the pieces she did find in the top of her trunk, that were waiting waits to be made into christening robes for little folks that now do have their borning-time. I was glad, for there is needs of more.

After I did say good-bye, I went goes on to the woods. I did not follow the trail that does go to the moss-box where I do leave letters on leaves for the fairies. The wind was calling. I followed after it. It was not adown the path that does lead to the nursery. It was calling over logs, in the way that does lead to where is that old log with the bunches of flowers by it, and under its edges. They was the flowers that the man of the long step that whistles most all of the time did gather for the *pensée* girl with the far-away look in her eyes.

Some of the bunches of flowers was all faded. It is days, a long time, since he did put them there; and it is only a little time since he did put the last ones there.

I set down on the moss my basket that I did carry Minerva's baby chickens to christening in. Then I made begins. First I put some moss in the basket. Then I did put in some of the bunches of flowers. I put in the most faded ones, because they had been waiting waits the longest. Then we all did go in a hurry to the house of her aunt of the gray calico dress with the black bow at its neck.

The aunt was not there, and we were glad — but the *pensée* girl with the far-away look in her eyes was there. She came to the door when we did tap upon its handle. I did tell her all in one breath that we was making begins to bring the flowers that the man of the long step that whistles most all of the time did gather for her on many days. We gave her explanations how it was too shy feels he had to bring them to her himself, so he did lay them by the old log. I told her as how it was we did bring the most faded ones first, because they was waiting waits the longest. And she did take them all up in her arms. And I told her my dog's name was Brave Horatius, and he was a fine dog, and that Thomas Chatterton Jupiter Zeus was a most lovely wood-rat. And I held out his white paw for her to have feels of; but he did pull it back and cuddle his nose up close to my curls. I told her how it was he was shy, too, and when he had knows of her better, he would let her pat his nice white paws.

Then I did take my basket and go goes in a hurry back to get the flowers. I did carry the next most old ones to her, and she was glad for them. She was waiting waits for me on the steps of the house of her aunt of the gray calico dress with the black bow at its neck. She was ready to go back with us to the log where the flowers was, and there was joy-lights in her eyes.

While we did go along, I did tell her more about the little animal and bird folks that do live in the woods, and I did tell her about the great love the man of the long step that whistles most all of the time does have for her. Quietness was upon her, and we did walk on in a slow way. A beetle went across the path, and a salal bush did nod itself to us. The wind made little soft whispers.

And by-and-by, we was come to the log. She did kneel down by it, and she looked looks for a long time at all the bunches of flowers. And I did say a little prayer, and Thomas Chatterton Jupiter Zeus did squeak a little squeak. I made counts of the bunches of flowers, and they were thirty-and-three.

I saw a chipmunk, and I followed him after, to see how many stripes he did have on his back, and where was his home. And on the way, I saw other birds, and I followed them after on tiptoes, to have sees where they were having goes to. And in the bushes, there was a little nest with four eggs in it with speckles on them. I did have thinks there was needs for me to pick out names for the little birds that will hatch out of those eggs. This is a very busy world to live in — there is much needs for picking out names for things.

I am very happy. I have been to the cathedral, to pray again that the angels will bring a baby to Dear Love soon.

# Twenty-three

# The Playing of the Lambs, the Voices of the Earth, Missing Feathers, and Beautiful Blue Water

**M**y legs do feel some tired this eventime. I've been most everywhere today. I so have been going to tell the plant-folks and the flower-folks and the birds about this day being the going-away day of one William Shakespeare, in 1616. Before yet breakfast-time was come, I did go to the cathedral to say prayers of thanks for all the writings he did write. With me did go Brave Horatius and Lars Porsena of Clusium and Thomas Chatterton Jupiter Zeus and Lucian Horace Ovid Virgil.

When we were come again to the house, they did wait waits while I did go to do the morning works. After the morning works were done, I did put pieces of bread and butter in papers in my pockets, for all of us. I put some milk in the bottle for Menander Euripides Theocritus Thucydides.

He was waiting waits for me by the pasture-bars. He is a most woolly lamb. He was glad for his breakfast, and he was glad to have knows about this day. While I was telling them all there what day this is, Plutarch

Demosthenes made a little jump onto a little stump. He looked a look about, and made a jump-off. Sophocles Diogenes came a-following after. They both did make some more jumps. Their ways are ways of playfulness. They are dear lambs.

While I was telling them all, Menander Euripides Theocritus Thucydides did in some way get the nipple off his bottle, and the rest of the milk did spill itself out the bottle. I hid the bottle away by a rock. Menander Euripides Theocritus Thucydides did follow me after. He does follow me, many wheres I do go to.

We went all on. We saw fleurs, and I did stop moments to have talks with them. I looked for other fleurs that I had longs to see — everywhere that we did go, I did look looks for *teverin*, and yellow *éclaire*, and pink *mahonille*, and *mauve*, and *morgeline*. When Brave Horatius had askings in his eyes for what I was looking, I did give to him explanations. He looked looks back at me from his gentle eyes. In his looks, he did say, "They are not hereabout." We went on.

We went to forêt d'Ermenonville, and forêt de Chantilly. We went adown Lounette to where it flows into Nonette, and we went on. Everywhere there were little whisperings of earth-voices — they all did say of the writes of William Shakespeare. And there were more talkings. I lay my ear close to the earth, where the grasses grew close together. I did listen. The wind made ripples on the grass as it went over. There were voices from out the earth. And the things of their saying were the things of gladness of growing. And there was music. And in the music, there was sky-twinkles and earth-tinkles that was come of the joy of living. I have thinks all the grasses growing there did feel glad feels from the tips of their green arms to their toe roots in the ground.

And Brave Horatius and the rest of us didn't get home until after supper-time. The folks was gone to the house of Elsie. I made a hunt for some supper for Brave Horatius. I found some, and I put it in his special dish. Then I came again into the house, to get some bread and milk. There was a jar of blackberry jam on the cook-table — it had interest looks.

Just when I happened to be having all my fingers in the jar of blackberry jam, there was rumblings of distress come from the back yard. I climbed onto the flour-barrel and looked a look out the window. There, near unto my chum's special supper-dish, sat the pet crow, with top-heavy appears. There was reasons for his forlorn looks — for Brave Horatius had advanced to the rear of Lars Porsena of Clusium and pulled out his tail-feathers.

I have had no case like this before. I felt disturbs. I had not knowings what to do for it. I had some bandages and some Mentholatum in my pocket. I took Lars Porsena of Clusium — all that was left of him, with his tail-feathers gone — and I sat down on the steps. First I took some Mentholatum, and put it on a piece of bandage. I put the piece of bandage onto Lars Porsena of Clusium, where his tail-feathers did come out. Then I did take the long white bandage in the middle, and I did wrap it about Lars Porsena of Clusium from back to front — in under his wings, and twice on top, so the bandage would stay in place on the end of him where his tail-feathers came out. Then I did make a start to the hospital. I did have wonders how long the needs would be for Làrs Porsena of Clusium to be there before his tail would grow well again.

I only did have going a little way when I did meet with the man that wears gray neckties and is kind to mice. He looked a look at me, and he looked a look at Lars Porsena of Clusium in my arms. Then he did have askings why was it Lars Porsena was in bandages. I told him explanations all about it. He pondered on the matter. Then he picked me and Lars Porsena up and set us down on a stump. He told me there was no needs for me to have wonders about how long the need would be for Lars Porsena of Clusium to be in the hospital with bandages on him. He did talk on in his gentle way, of how it is birds that do lose their tail-feathers do grow them on again. He so said, and I did have understanding.

Then he did take up Lars Porsena of Clusium in his arms, and he unwrapped him from front to back and back to front. When the bandage was all off him, Lars Porsena of Clusium did give himself a stretch, and his wings a little shake. And I said a little prayer for his getting well, and a new tail soon; and the man that wears gray neckties and is kind to mice said Amen. Then we came home.

Today was dyeing day. The mamma dyed — she dyed clothes, old ones. First she washed them in the tub; then she put them in the boiler on the stove. In the boiler was beautiful blue water. I know, because I climbed on the stove-hearth and peeked in. The mamma didn't make this water blue with balls, like she does the rench water for the clothes on wash-days. She made this water blue with stuff out of an envelope. I had sees of her tear its corner off, and the blue little specks came out of that envelope in a quick way. The specks so did come in a more hurry way when she did give the envelope some shakes. All the clothes the mamma did carry from the wash-tub to the boiler, all those clothes was blue when she took them out. And afterwards, the

blue was yet with them, and they hung upon the line. I
see them quiver blue quivers when the wind blows.

After she did hang them there on the line, the
mamma did leave the boiler of dye-blue water on the
stove. And she is gone goes to the house of her mother,
by the meeting of the roads. She told me to watch the
house, and let the fire go out. It so is gone a long time
ago, and I keep watch.

The blue water in the boiler has cold feels, now — I
stood upon the stove and I put my arm way down in it,
and it was coldness. First I did only touch touches on
the water with my finger. It was warmness, then. That
was just when the mamma did go.

She is hours and hours gone now. I have been keeping watches of the house, like she did say for me to do
when she went away. And in-between times, I have
been reading reads in the books Angel Mother and
Angel Father did write in. I have been screwtineyesing
the spell of words. Now I am going to have dyeing day,
like the mamma did have on this morning. It is so much
of fun to lift things up and down in blue water. On
wash-days, the mamma has me to do it much — she
calls it renching the clothes. When it's blue water in a
boiler, it's dyeing them.

I have been dyeing like the mamma dyed this morning. First I did dye the mamma's bag of blueing balls.
That bag was getting pale looks. Next I did dip in the
mamma's clothes-pin bag. It was brownness before. I
have not sure feels yet what color it is going to be since
it has had its dye. I took all the clothes-pins out first;
then I did give them all a dip. They did bob about in a
funny way. I made whirls in the dye-blue water with
my fingers, so the clothes-pins would make some more
bobs. It was very nice, standing there on top the cook-

stove watching the bobs they made in the boiler.

Then I made a start to dye handles. First I dipped in the butcher-knife handle. Then I did give the dipper-handle a dip. I had carefuls to make it go only halfway. Then I did give the handle of the potato-masher a dip. And I gave the hammer-handle a dip in the dye-blue water.

Clementine came in a walk-up step on the back porch. She looked a look in. She is such a friendly Plymouth Rock hen. She walked right into our house, and came in a hop-up by the dye-blue water. She so does like my blue calico apron. She hops up on my knee when I sit down to talk to the chickens in the chicken park. I had thinks, being as she has likes for my blue calico apron, she would have likes for blue *feathers*. So I did give her a gentle dip in the dye-blue water, and two more. She walked right out our front door, without even a thank chuckle. I never had knows of her to do so before.

*The dye-blue water was waiting waits.*

Next I dipped the Plymouth Rock rooster in. He did object to being dyed blue. He was quite fidgety. I had decides not to coax any more folks from the chicken-yard to get dyed-blue feathers.

I looked looks about the house we live in. I had seeing of a box of matches the mamma did leave on a chair in the bedroom. The mamma has said I mustn't touch a box of matches on the cupboard shelf. And I don't. But she didn't say I mustn't touch them when she leaves them on a *chair*. So I have took the box of matches, and it has had its dip. It has a limp feel. I have put it on the back steps, to get its form again. And all the matches that was in the box have had their dips in the dye-blue water. I have laid them in rows on the grass, to have a dry.

And now I do have thinks how nice it will be on next time when dyeing day is come, if the mamma does have seeing as how I could be helps — being as I now do have so much knowing of the ways of dyeing. I have thinks a big amount of helps I could be.

Now, while the things I have dyed do dry, I am going goes to the cathedral, to have a long service there; for this is the borning day of Saint Louis, in 1215. And many wheres there is needs for me to go, to tell the plant-folk all about this being the day of his borning. And too, it is the borning day of Oliver Cromwell in 1599, and the borning day of Padre Martini in 1706; and it is the going-away day of Torquato Tasso, in 1595. The winds sing of these, and the great pine tree is saying a poem about this day.

# Twenty-four

# A Wish Come True, and a Portrait of Solomon Grundy

In the morning of today, before I did eat my bowl of mush and milk for breakfast, I did go to the cathedral to say thank prayers for the good works of Leonardo da Vinci; for this is the day of his going away, in 1519.

When after-breakfast works was done, the mamma did have me to churn. While I did make the handle with the cross sticks on it go up and down in the churn, I did have hearing of the little glad songs all the fleurs were singing out in the field.

When the butter was come, the mamma did take it out the churn. She put all the little yellow lumps in a wood bowl. Then she gave to them pats, and more pats. When she got through patting the butter into its proper form, the mamma did throw the butter-paddle over on the cook-table. She said she hoped and wished that she would never see that butter-paddle again.

She won't. After I heard her say that, I floated it away in the creek. It made a nice boat. It did sail along in a bobby way. I took Solomon Grundy with me. I just let him dabble his toes. When he is an older pig, he can wade right out into the creek with me. His eyes did look bright today while I was telling him what we was going to do when he got to be a bigger pig.

When I was come back to the house we live in, the mamma did spank me. Then she did send me to get that butter-paddle, in a hurry. It was making bobs by the reeds by the old rail fence, where the singing creek goes under and on. I brought it back to her, and then she did take and spank me again. Now I have wonders about things — the mamma did say she wished she would *never see it again.*

After I did mind the baby and sleeps was come upon it, then I did walk into the garden. I went there to find out how much things had grown since last time I was there. First I pulled up a bean plant. It looked a little more big, the two peek-a-boo leaves did. After I looked close looks at it, I did plant it again. Then I pulled up a radish. It was doing nicely, and I ate it. I forgot to give it close looks before I put it in my mouth, to see how much it did grow since that last time. After I swallowed it, I pulled up another radish to find out. It was doing well. I put it back in the garden again, and I went to the house and got it a drink of buttermilk. I carried it out to it in the papa's shaving-mug. There was more drink than one radish needs, so I did give four onions and two more radishes sips of buttermilk. And I did give to the papa's shaving-mug some washes in the brook, and I put it back in its place on the shelf again. Just then, the mamma had comes into the house, and there was more spanks. The back part of me does feel sore feels.

I have thinks I will go and give geology lectures to

the folks in the nursery, and too I will sing them lullaby songs, and the bird and fleur *chant de fête* [birthday song] *de grandpère*, of *niverolle* and *ortolan* and *verdier* and *étourneau* and *nenufar* and *éclaire* and *ulmaire* and *fraxinelle*.

I so have gone goes, and the folks in the nursery was glad for food and songs. And afterwards I went more on, into the woods. There was little whispers among the leaves, and there was a song in the tall fir-tree-tops; and a pine tree was saying a poem. I listened listens. Then I went goes on.

I saw a man coming. He did take long steps. When he was nearer come, I had seeing it was the man that wears gray neckties and is kind to mice. I did go adown the path in a more quick way. He did have seeing of my coming. Then I did hide behind a tree. He came on. When he was near the tree, he did say, "I thought I saw someone coming. Guess I was mistaken. *I think I'll take these splints for the hospital back to the mill.*"

When I did hear him say that, I ran in a quick way back to the path. He didn't see me — he was looking long looks away. Then I did give his coat-sleeve a gentle pull, and he did whistle. And he did ask me if there was needs for splints at the hospital, and I told him all in one breath how much needs there was. He had me to tell him all over again about the little chicken that did have its leg hurt. And I gave him explanations how it was Sir Francis Bacon did have his leg hurt in a real bad way, and the big folks was going to kill him; but they gave him to me for my very own, because he wasn't any good anymore.

And the man that wears gray neckties and is kind to mice did have understanding, and he went goes with me to the hospital that I do have for little hurt folks at

Saint-Germain-en-Laye. While I did hold little Sir Francis Bacon, the man that wears gray neckties and is kind to mice did fix the splints on his hurt leg in a gentle way. Then I did pray prayers for his getting well soon. Brave Horatius did bark Amen. And one of the most tall pine trees was saying a poem.

After morning's works was done, I was washing out clothes for the baby. I thought what a nice christening robe one of the baby's dresses would make for one of the new baby pigs. The mamma had not thoughts that way.

When the dress was on the line, I did go by the chicken-yard, to have sees how the children of Minerva are growing. Pius VII is getting some tail-feathers. He comes to feed from my hand every day, and he likes to go to school in my little basket. He has not been for a whole week now, because the last time I took him he peeped, and teacher sent us home. Next day, I took Francis Beaumont and John Fletcher, and they was quiet.

Last time I took them to cathedral service, Ben Jonson pecked Sir Walter Raleigh on the head. I said prayers over them for peace between them. Then I put one in a little box on one log, and I put the other one in a little box on the other log. The boxes was alike. Today I had sees of these two drinking out of the water-pan together. Peace was between them. She is a nice mother hen that has got all her children growed up. And little Edmund Spenser was scratching for a worm near his little brown brother Oliver Goldsmith, and all Minerva's family was growing well. I felt satisfaction feels about it.

And I sat down on a log to pick out names for the twins I am going to have when I grow up. I picked out a goodly number of names, but I could not have decides which ones. I had thinks I would wait a little time. And I had remembers it was time for me to be making another portrait of Solomon Grundy, so I went around by the pig-pen to get Solomon Grundy.

I said comfort words to Aphrodite. I told her how it was I was just taking Solomon Grundy to make a portrait of him, and as how I was going to make it in the same way and in the same place as I did make *her* portrait, quite a time ago. She grunted a short grunt, and then a long grunt. Sometimes it is difficult to understand pig talk. But her next grunt, it was very plain — it was just an invitation to make Solomon Grundy's portrait there by her side, and no needs of taking him out of the pig-pen. I told her yes — I would make his portrait right there by her.

And I did bring many brown bracken ferns, after I did have the pig-pen cleaned out. Most every day I do give the pig-pen a rake-out, and bring some clean dirt from the garden. I have thinks pigs do have likes for clean places to live in — it brings more inspirations to their souls. And too, every day Aphrodite does have likes for her feeding-trough to be scrubbed clean all over. And I have planted ferns and fleurs all around her pig-pen. It is a very nice place, with sweet smells of grass and fleurs. And Aphrodite was glad for the brushing I did give her today.

I've got a brush — a nice new brush, a good new brush. It is for to brush my pig friends. They so do need brushings. This new brush the man that wears gray neckties and is kind to mice did get for me last time he did go to the mill town. The pigs do like the feels the new brush does make upon their backs. The clean feels it does give to them are pleasant to their souls.

After I did give her the brushing, I did get moss, and

cover the clean feed-trough with it. That made a nice place to sit and draw Solomon Grundy's portrait, by his mother there. I drew him lying by her side. Then I had him to stand on his feet, and I drew one of him that way. I had it almost done. There was a little noise. It was the step of someone going by. I had not knows who it was. I went on drawing Solomon Grundy's ears, and his curly tail. Then I had knows what it was: It was that chore boy, come to feed the pigs — and he poured all that bucket of swill on top the moss and Solomon Grundy's portrait and me.

The feels I did have — they was drippy ones. And I did have decides to make that other portrait of Solomon Grundy another time.

I said good-bye to Aphrodite. Then I went goes in a quick way to the singing creek where the willows grow, to get the swill-smells off. First I did wade out a little way; then I sat down. The water came in a nice way up to my neck, and it went singing on. I gave my curls wash-offs, and I did listen to the song the creek was singing, as it did go by. It was a song of the hills. Being up to my neck made the water sounds very near to my ears. I had likes for that.

By-and-by, I did have feels that I was clean again. And I did have thinks I better go get some dry clothes on, because sitting there in the singing creek did make my clothes some wet.

When I was come to the house we live in, the mamma was gone to the house of Elsie, so I did go in. First I did give my clothes some wring-outs by the steps so the water would not have drips on the kitchen floor, for the mamma has likes to keep her house very clean.

When I did have dry clothes on me, I did go to hang the wet ones on bushes in the woods to dry. Thomas

Chatterton Jupiter Zeus went with me. Lucian Horace Ovid Virgil rode in one of my apron pockets, and Felix Mendelssohn rode in the other one; and Louis II, le Grand Condé, did have rides in my sleeve. We was all very glad. As we went along, I had seeings the strings I have put on the bushes for the birds was gone.

We went on, and on some more. I did have looks about. I did have seeing of little wood-folks going their ways. I watched their little moves, and I had seeing of what color they was. I made stops to tell them about this being the borning day of Linnaeus in 1707, and the going-away day of Georges Cuvier, in 1832.

We went on. All things was glad. The winds did sing. The leaves did sing. The grasses talked in whispers, all along the way. I have thinks they were saying, "*Petite Françoise — l'été approche, l'été approche.*" ["Summer approaches, summer approaches."] I did have hearings to all they were so saying, as I did go along. And the little birdlings in their cradles were calling for more to eat. And I did make a stop to watch the mother birds and father birds, in their comings and goings. Now are busy times.

# Twenty-five

# Opal and Mathilde Plantagenet visit The Girl Who Has No Seeing

Today I did take Mathilde Plantagenet to visit the girl that has no seeing. I did tell her I would so bring Mathilde Plantagenet, and she did have joy feels when she did have thinks about Mathilde Plantagenet coming to visit her.

Before we did start, I did give Mathilde Plantagenet a good foot-bath, as Sadie McKibben does always take one before she goes a-visiting. Then I did wash the neck and ears of Mathilde Plantagenet in a careful way. It took four Castoria bottles full of water to do so.

I have had a big problem. That's what Sadie McKibben says when she has had a difficulty of managing. My big problem was what to carry water in when I go to makes prepares to give my pets foot-baths and neck-and-ear washes. I have tried thimbles to use for wash-pans when I do wash the hands of my pets, but thimbles hold not enough of water — often and often again there is needs to go for more water, when one does use thimblefuls at a time. Sometimes now, I do use a Mentho-latum jar. It holds more water than does a thimble. But mostly now, I do carry Castoria bottles full of water when I start on my way to wash the neck and ears of my animal friends. Sadie McKibben has gave me advice, and a lard-bucket to carry those Castoria bottles full of water in.

After I so did have Mathilde Plantagenet washed, then I did dry her neck and ears with the soft salt-sack towel that Sadie McKibben has gave to me. After I did have her neck and ears washed, and her hair rubbed down in the way it does go, I did give her a little lump of salt. She liked that. Then I tied the little rope around her neck that I do lead her by, and we made starts to go visit the girl that has no seeing.

When we were come to her gate, I did open it, and Mathilde Plantagenet and I went down the path to her door. Mathilde Plantagenet went around with me to the window where I do tap taps, so she will have knows I am come.

She did rub the nose of Mathilde Plantagenet, and she was so glad to see her. She straightway did go to bring her a salt-lump. But I told her Mathilde Plantagenet did just have a salt-lump after her foot-bath. And I did give her explainings as how I thought one salt-lump a day is enough for Mathilde Plantagenet while she is yet so young — when she is older grown, she may have *two* salt-lumps in one day. Then the girl that has no seeing did give me the salt-lump for her to have tomorrow. She has thinks like my thinks, that there is music in the moos of Mathilde Plantagenet.

And she had asks how was the dear baby of Elsie's. And I told her as how I thought it would have two tooths soon. And she said that would be interest. I had thinks so, too. I told her the mamma's nice baby has a lot of tooths — it's had them quite a time long. And so has Thomas Chatterton Jupiter Zeus.

Then we all did go for a walk. With my right hand,

I did lead the girl who has no seeing; with my left hand, I did lead Mathilde Plantagenet. And Brave Horatius came a-following after. As we did go along, we did have listens to the voices of the trees and grass. The girl that has no seeing is learning to have hearing of what the grasses say, and of the waters of the brooks that tell the hill songs. Too, she is learning to see things. She shuts her eyes when I shut mine. We go on journeys together. We ride in a cloud — in a fleecy white one that does sail away, over the hills. We look down on beautiful earth, and we see Nonette, and Iraouaddy, and Launette, and forêt d'Ermenonville, and Aunette, and forêt de Chantilly, and Saint Firmin.

Today, after we did have our eyes shut for quite a time long, I did open mine just a little bit, to have seeing how big that bee was that was making such a buzz. He was quite a big bee, and he was in a hurry.

When he did go on, the girl who has no seeing did have asks when was I going to bring Menander Euripides Theocritus Thucydides to visit her. She said she had thinks he must be a bigger lamb now, with me giving him his bottle of milk morning and eventime. I said he was growing more big — a little bit. He is a very dear lamb. Then she had askings when was Thomas Chatterton Jupiter Zeus and Lucian Horace Ovid Virgil coming to visit her. And she had wants to know when was Lars Porsena of Clusium coming again. I did have thinks about it, and I did tell her we would all come to visit her on the fourth day from the day that is now. And I did sing her the song of fleurs of *tante* [aunt], of *myosotis, aubépine, romarin, gentiane, ulmaire, églantier, rosagine, iris, tulipe*, and *éclaire*.

And we came home. And before we were yet to the house we live in, we did make a stop at the cathedral for prayers, and "*Hosanna in excelsis.*"

Twenty-six

# Why The Girl Who Has No Seeing was not At Home when Opal and her Friends came Visiting

Now is the fourth day come, and we are going goes to the house of the girl who has no seeing. All the morning hours, there was works to do, to help the mamma. Afternoon is now come, and we go.

We did. First I did make begins to get us all together. Brave Horatius was waiting by the back steps. Lars Porsena of Clusium was near unto him. Lucian Horace Ovid Virgil was under the front doorstep. Thomas Chatterton Jupiter Zeus was back of the house, in his home of sticks that he does have likes for. I did help Thomas Chatterton Jupiter Zeus to build that home. I had sees in the woods of how other wood-rats do have their houses builded of sticks, and some sticks, and some more sticks. Today when I did squeak calls for Thomas Chatterton Jupiter Zeus to come out of his house, he did come out, and he did crawl up on my shoulder and cuddle his nose up close to my curls.

We made a start. We went by the nursery, to get Nannerl Mozart. We went on. Menander Euripides

Theocritus Thucydides was playing close by the pasture-bars. He is a very jumpy lamb. He did jump a long jump to meet us today, and his tail did wiggle more wiggles. We went adown the lane. We made a stop to get Solomon Grundy and his little sister Anthonya Mundy, that has not got as much curl in her tail as Solomon Grundy.

We went out along the road. They were a sweet picture. I made a stop to look at them all — some running ahead, and some behind. They all did wear their pink ribbons that the fairies did bring. Solomon Grundy and Anthonya Mundy and Menander Euripides Theocritus Thucydides all did wear divides of the ribbon that was the ribbon that dear William Shakespeare used to wear. And they all did have joy feels, as they had knows they were going on a visit to visit the girl that has no seeing. She has love for them. And we did go in a hurry on. I did feel a big amount of satisfaction that I have such a nice family.

Lars Porsena of Clusium did ride most of the way on the back of Brave Horatius. His appears are not what they were before he did lose his tail-feathers. I am praying prayers every day for him to get a new tail soon.

When we were all come near to the house of the girl that has no seeing, we did walk right up to the door. And I stepped three steps back, and three hops over, and three steps up to the door, so she would have knows we was come. We had knows only she would be there, because this day is the going-to-town day of her people.

I stepped more steps. Brave Horatius barked more barks for her coming, and Solomon Grundy squealed his most nice baby-pig squeal. We did listen listens. She had not coming to the door. I sat on the steps, to wait waits. I so did for some time long.

While we did have waits, I did sing to Brave Horatius and Solomon Grundy and all of them songs of Nonette and Iraouaddy, and more songs Angel Father did teach me to sing, of birds of *oncle* [uncle] what did have going away — of *roitelet, ortolan, bruant, épervier, rousserolle, tourterelle, farlouse, ramier, aigle, nonnette, chardonneret, orfraie, ibis, rossignol, loriot, ortolan, ibis, sansonnet, pinson, hirondelle, ibis, lanier, ibis, pic, pivoine, épeiche, faisan, étourneau, roitelet, draine, ibis, nonnette, aigle, niverolle, durbec, aigle, roitelet, ibis, étourneau, draine, ortolan, roitelet, loriot, émerillon, aigle, niverolle, sarcelle.* All my pets do have likes for those songs. Today Brave Horatius did bark a bark when I was done, and Solomon Grundy did squeal his baby-pig squeal again. I had wonders why she did not come.

After by-and-by, I did go sit on the gate-post, to wait waits. It was a long time. A man on a horse went by. Another man went by — he had asks what for was I sitting on the gate-post. I did tell him I was waiting waits for the coming of the girl that has no seeing. He did look away, off to the hills. Then he started to say something, but he swallowed it. He looked off to the hills, again. Then he did say, "Child, she won't come back. She is gone to the graveyard."

I did smile a sorry smile upon him, because I had knows he didn't know what he was talking about when he did say she won't come back. It is not often she goes anywhere, and when she does, she always does come back. I told him I knew she would come back.

I waited some more waits. Then it was time for my pets to be going back, because it would not do for the chore boy not to find Solomon Grundy and Anthonya Mundy in the pig-pen. I will go goes again tomorrow to see the girl that has no seeing, for I have knows she will come again home tonight in starlight-time.

When Solomon Grundy and Anthonya Mundy did have their pink ribbons off and was again in the pig-pen, the rest of us did have going to the cathedral, for songs and prayers. I did pray that the girl that has no seeing may not stub her toe and fall when she comes home tonight by starlight-time. And Brave Horatius did bark Amen.

Early on this morning, I went again to the house of the girl who has no seeing. There were little singings everywhere, sky and hills; and the willows were whispering little whispers by Nonette.

I went in a quick way down along the lane and in along the fields, until I was come near unto her house. I cuddled Thomas Chatterton Jupiter Zeus more close in my arms, and I tiptoed on the grass. Menander Euripides Theocritus Thucydides did make little jumps beside me, and Brave Horatius came a-following after.

I made a stop by the window that I always do make stops by, and I rapped six raps on the window-pane. Six raps means, *"Come — on — out! We — are — come!"* I had no hears of her steps a-coming, like they always do. I put my hands above my eyes, so I could see inside the window. She was not there. Nobody was. I did tap six more raps. She did not come.

I went on around by the lilac bush. I crawled in under it, to wait waits for her coming. Two men were talking by the fence. One did say, "It is better so." I had wonders — what did he mean? The other man did say, "A pity it was she couldn't have had a little sight, to see that brush-fire ahead." And I had hears of the other one say, "Probably the smell of the smoke caused her worry about the fire coming to the house, and probably she was trying to find out where it was, when she walked right into it." And the other man did have asks if she was conchus after. And the other one did say, "Yes."

I listened more listens to their queer talk. I had wonders — what did it all mean? Another man did come in the gate. He came to where they was. He put his hand on a fence-post. There was a green caterpillar close by him on a bush, but he had not seeing of it. He did begin to talk. First thing he said was, "When Jim went by here last even, that child was sitting on the gate-post. She was waiting for her to come back." He said more. He said, "Jim told her she was gone to the graveyard, but she said she knew she would come back." Why, that was what I told that man. It all did sound queer.

I heard them say some more. Then I had understanding. I had knows then it was the girl that has no seeing they was having talks about, because I was waiting waits for her on yesterday when the man did tell me that. I felt queerness in my throat, and I couldn't see, either. I couldn't see the green caterpillar on the leaf by the man that said it. And Thomas Chatterton Jupiter Zeus had looks like a gray cloud in my arms.

More the men said. They talked it all over again. They said she smelled the smoke of the brush-fire, and not having sees of it, she did walk right into it, and all her clothes did have fire — and then she ran, and her running did make the fire to burn her more; and she stubbed her toe and fell. She fell in a place where there was mud and water. She was rolling in it when they found her. And all the fire-pains that was did make her moan moans until hours after, when she died. They say she died. And I couldn't see Thomas Chatterton Jupiter Zeus or Brave Horatius or anything, then.

When after a while I did come again the way that goes to the house we live in, I did have sees of the little fleurs along the way that she so did love. I have thinks they were having longings for her presence. And I so was, too. But I do have thinks her soul will come again to the woods, and she will have sees of the blooming of the fleurs in the field she has loves for.

I go now to write a message on a leaf for her, like I do to Angel Father and Angel Mother. I will put one by the ferns, and I will tie one to a branch of the singing fir tree. And I will pray that the angels may find them when they come a-walking in the woods. Then they will carry them up to her in heaven, there.

Twenty-seven

Cathedral Service in the
Pig-Pen; a New Friend,
with Big Eyes and a Velvet
Nose; a Leaf for The Girl
Who Has No Seeing

In the morning of today, being as I could not
get the fence down about the pig-pen so Aphrodite
could get out to go to service in the cathedral, I did have
decides to have cathedral service in the pig-pen.

I brought large pieces of moss, and lovely ferns. I got
a wood box, so Brave Horatius could get in. After he
was in the pig-pen, I did use the box for an altar. I lay
moss upon it, and ferns about it. While I was fixing it,
Lars Porsena did perch on my shoulder, and he stayed
there for service. Thomas Chatterton Jupiter Zeus
nestled by my side. Solomon Grundy and Anthonya
Mundy, who hasn't as much curl in her tail as Solomon
Grundy, these lay by their mother Aphrodite and me
and all the other little pigs. I sat on a board, and
Clementine did perch on the edge of the feeding-trough.
In its middle was her sister hen, Andromeda. Felix
Mendelssohn did snuggle up in my right apron pocket,

and in the left apron pocket was that lovely toad, Lucian Horace Ovid Virgil.

After some long time, when we all did get settled down to quietness, I did start service. It took a long time to get quietness, because the dear folks weren't used to having cathedral service in the pig-pen.

After the third hymn, I did preach the morning sermon. I did choose for my text, "*I will lift up mine eyes unto the hills.*" I had to peek through the pig-pen fence to do it, for it did have more tallness than *I* did have. I lifted most all the congregation up to have a peek. I did lift them one at a time. And so they saw, and lifted up their eyes unto the hills. But most of them didn't. They looked in different ways. Some saw God's goodness in the grass, and some did see it in the trees. And Thomas Chatterton Jupiter Zeus did not have seeing for more than for the piece of cheese I did have hid in my sleeve for him. He gave his cheese squeak. I gave him a nibble. Then we had prayers.

Rain is come some more. It came all night. And earth is damp again, and things grow more in the garden. Some things grow very fast. Weeds so do.

When the rain did stop having come-downs on this morning, then the mamma did have me to hoe in-between the rows of things that do grow in the garden. As I did go along, I did have talks with these folks that grow in the garden, there. I did tell them little poems, and I did sing to them little songs. As I did go along between the rows, Brave Horatius did follow after. I had thinks about the things growing there. I wonder if I would get roots like the plants in the garden, if I planted my feet some inches in the soil and did keep still quite a time long. I have thinks I will try it some day and find out.

As I did go on, I did have sees there were earthworms on the window-panes over the young cabbage plants. The grownups say the earthworms rained down. They are mistaken. Those earthworms crawled up — I've watched them do it. They were about in many places. I have been learning things about earthworms. I think being an earthworm must be an interesting life. I wonder how it feels to stretch out long, and then get short again.

I went goes on, to pull weeds by the bean-folks. I went back some steps to look looks at them. Those bean-folks in the garden are such climbers. Their thoughts reach up toward the sky, and they climb up on the poles we put in the garden, there.

By-and-by, I saw another earthworm. He was alone. I did have sees of his movements. I always do see more earthworms after rain. This one was making himself very long. Lucian Horace Ovid Virgil too did have seeing of that earthworm. I made a stop to see what he was going to do about it. I did see. He did walk walks around that earthworm. Then he did take it in a quick way. It was a very big earthworm, and Lucian Horace Ovid Virgil did have needs to use his hands to stuff it down his throat. The earthworm made wiggles, and Lucian Horace Ovid Virgil gave it pushes down his throat.

In afternoon-time, when other works was done, I did take Thomas Chatterton Jupiter Zeus and Felix Mendelssohn and Lucian Horace Ovid Virgil with me; and Louis II, le Grand Condé, did have rides in my sleeve. We went goes to the barn. I made a stop to talk with Michael Angelo Sanzio Raphael. Then I did go in to play on the hay.

I had hearing of sounds in the stall below. I slid a slide-down into the manger of that stall. There was someone I have never had sees of before — he had big eyes and a velvet nose, and he was brownish. When I did land in his manger there, he did look afraid looks. But I just sat quiet in the corner of the manger, and reached out handfuls of hay to him. I have knows he is that new saw rel horse I have heard the grandpa at the ranch house say he was going to get. And now he is got. I have likes for him.

I told him a poem, and I did sing him a song of *fleurs de tante*, of *myosotis et anemone et romarin et iris et éclaire*. He did have likes for that song, and the bunches of hay I did hold out to him. And this being the going-away day of Savonarola in 1498, I have give this new saw rel horse for name Girolamo Savonarola. I did tell him his name while I did give him more pats on his velvet nose. I have likes for him.

On yesterday, the coffee-pot tipped over on Harold [Elsie's first child]. He had pains — worse than when the baby has colic. Elsie puts oil on him. When she puts the oil on him, some of his cries go under the floor, and we do not hear them any more. I feel I have needs of that oil in my hospital. Three times on this morning I have been on goes to the house of Elsie, to have asks if he is growing well. She says his feels are better — the oil does make them so. And I yet have more thinks then there is needs of oil like that oil, in my hospital.

When I was coming back from the house of Elsie, I did look looks about as I did go along. I saw a piece of bark. I did turn it over with care. There were ants. I made a set-down to watch them. Some ants did carry bundles with queer looks. Big Jud at school says they are ant eggs. I have not thinks so — they be too big for ant eggs. And I have remembers that Angel Father did call them *nymphes de fourmis* [pupas of ants].

When I was come to the house we live in, there was

Lars Porsena of Clusium walking about on the clean tablecloth that has been put on for company. And there he was, tracking crow-tracks in jam all over it. I picked him up, and the mamma picked *me* up; and right away, she did spank me for his doing it.

The time it did take to wash that tablecloth was quite a time long. I made little rubs on it where was the jam-tracks of Lars Porsena of Clusium. When they was all come out and it had clean looks that did suit the needs of the mamma, then she did tell us to get out of her way.

We did — we went to the woods, and Thomas Chatterton Jupiter Zeus went with us. When we were come to the great fir tree, I did say a prayer. We went on. A little way we went. Then I made a stop to print a message on a leaf, for the soul of the girl that has no seeing. I had wants to tie it on a limb of a tree that I could not reach up to, and there was no tree fallen against it.

While I did stand close by it, the man that wears gray neckties and is kind to mice did come that way by. When he saw me in meditation by that tree, he did ask me what I wanted. I told him I did have needs of being up in that tree. He did set me on his shoulder. From there, I could reach the tree-arm that was most near earth.

But before I did climb onto the limb from his shoulder, I did take long looks about, in three straight ways and four corner ways. One does get such a good view of life from a man's shoulder — one feels so much more tall. I saw a mouse run under a log. I saw a mother bird come to her babies. I saw a toad by an old gray rock. I saw a caterpillar on a bush close by. I saw a squirrel on a tree beyond the next bush.

Then I did climb up into the tree, and I tied the leaf

with the message on it out far on a limb high up, so the angels would have sees of it when they went flying by, and carry it up to her in heaven, there.

Afterwards, I did go to the house of Sadie McKibben. Lars Porsena of Clusium and Thomas Chatterton Jupiter Zeus went goes with me.

Sadie McKibben has a new back-comb. She did have me put it in her hair for the first time. It so is in. It has crinkles on its back, and it does hold her hair up from her neck in a nice way.

Sometimes Sadie McKibben does let me help her to do up her hair. I have satisfaction feels that I can be of helps. I do roll her hair in a roll on top of her head. It makes loop-looks where some hairs want not to be in the roll on top of her head. Then I do put the hairpins in, to make them look like a water-wheel that the chore boy docs build in the brook. But all the times I do put Sadie McKibben's hairpins in like a water-wheel, her hair, it does not stay up long. Then she does smile a smile, and give her hair a quick roll. She sticks the hairpins in tight. Her hair, it does stay up. She so did today. And when we came away, she did give me a kiss on both my cheeks, and one on my nose. I have glad feels that she does remember about the nose.

After I was come home, I did bring the wood in and set the table. Then I made a start to go to the ranch house, to get the milk. On the way along, I heard a little lamb bleating. It was crying for its mother. I went to look for it.

I left the path. I went to the pasture, up by the woods. When I got there, the little lamb seemed to be away back in the woods. I set the milk-pail down and ran. I ran quick. There were long gray shadows in the woods. I felt their soft fingers touch my cheeks. I ran on. The little lamb had stopped crying. I heard it bleat no more. Where last time it did cry, there was only the husband of Sadie McKibben, sitting on a log. I have thinks the wee lamb did find its mother, so I came back again. And the time was not long until I did have the milk brought to the house we live in.

Afterwards, in graylight-time, I did go to the cathedral. And with me went Brave Horatius and most all the others. We did have service, and I did sing and say thank prayers for the goodness of Grégoire VII. It was on this day in 1085, it was then he did have going away. And this eventime, there was a song in the tree-tops at the cathedral. I have thinks it was a song of his goodness.

# Twenty-eight

## A Visit with Dear Love, Sunbeams in the Far Woods, and the Voices along the Dim Trail

Very early in the morning of today, I did get out of my bed and I did get dressed in a quick way. Then I climbed out the window of the house we live in. The sun was up, and the birds were singing. I went my way. As I did go, I did have hearing of many voices — they were the voices of earth, glad for the spring. They did say what they had to say in the growing grass, and in the leaves growing out from tips of branches. The birds did have knowing, and sang what the grasses and leaves did say of the gladness of living. I too did feel glad feels, from my toes to my curls.

I went down by the swamp. I went there to get reeds. There I saw a black bird with red upon his wings. He was going in among the rushes. I made a stop to watch him. I have thinks tomorrow I must be going in among the rushes, where he did go. I shall pull off my shoes and stockings first, for mud is there, and there is water. I like to go in among the rushes where the black birds with red upon their wings do go. I like to touch finger-tips with the rushes. I like to listen to the voices that whisper in the swamp. And I do so like to feel the mud ooze up between my toes. Mud has so much of interest in it — slippery feels, and sometimes little seeds that someday will grow into plant-folk, if they do get the right chance. And some were so growing this morning, and more were making begins — I did have seeing of them while I was looking looks about for reeds.

With the reeds I did find there, I did go a-piping. I went adown the creek, and out across the field, and in along the lane. Every stump I did come to, I did climb upon.

By-and-by, I was come near unto the house we live in. I thought it would be nice to go adown the path and pipe a forest song to the mamma of the gladness of the spring. When the mamma met me piping in the path, she did turn me about to the way that does lead to the house we live in — she so did with switches. She made me to stop piping the song of the forest. But it didn't go out of my heart.

When we was come into the house, the mamma did tell me works to do. And then she went with the little girl and the baby, and some lace she was making for a skirt for the baby, all to the house of Elsie. I did make begins on the works. I like to be helps to the mamma. I like to sing while I have works to do — it does so help.

After I did scrub the steps and empty the ashes and fill the wood-box and give the baby's clothes some washes, all as the mamma did say for me to do, then I made prepares to take Thomas Chatterton Jupiter Zeus to visit Dear Love. She has kind thoughts of him, and it is four whole days since she has seen him.

First I brought out his nice pink ribbon that the

fairies did bring to him. I hung it on a branch of willow. Then I did sit down. I had only a half a Castoria bottle full of warm water, so I did have needs to be careful in the use of it. First I did wash his beautiful white paws. I dried them on my apron, as I did forget to bring his little towel. Dear Love made that little towel for him. It is like her big bath-towel. And she marked his initials on it with red ink, like Big Jud has a bottle of at school. She put a dot after each letter — it is T.C.J.Z. on his bath-towel. When I do have thinks about that nice little bath-towel of his, I do give his paws a wash; and if I have not the towel with me, I do dry them with my apron. So I did today.

And we did go our way to the little house of Dear Love, by the mill by the far woods. In our going, we went among the great trees, along little paths between tall ferns; and we went over logs.

When we were come near unto the house of Dear Love, she did come to meet us. She gave me two kisses — one on each cheek — and one on the nose. She so does every time now, since that day when she did give me one on each cheek and I did tell her Sadie McKibben does give me one on the nose, too. She was so glad to see Thomas Chatterton Jupiter Zeus.

We had a very nice visit. We did sit on an old log under a big tree. And there was some vines growing by that log. And we did have talks. I did tell her how I was praying on every day for her baby to come real soon. And we did see a chipmunk that had some nice stripes on its back. And I told her I was putting it into my prayer for the angels to bring a baby brush with blue fleurs on it and a cradle-quilt with a blue bow on it when they do bring her baby, because I did have thinks a blue fleur on its baby brush and a blue bow on its cradle-quilt would look nicer with its red hair than pink ones would look. And she had thinks like my thinks. And we saw a caterpillar. Some caterpillars grow into butterflies. All caterpillars do not. Some grow into moths.

When I was coming my way home through the far woods from the house of Dear Love, I saw more chipmunks, and I saw her husband. He was fixing a log. His hat, it was not on him. It was on a stump, a little way away. He was most busy. His sleeves were up in a roll unto his arms's middle. He made bends-over as he did work at that log. A little fern by his foot had its growing up to the fringes on the legs of his overalls. The sun did come in between the grand trees, and it did shine upon his head. I so do like to see the sun shine upon the hair of the husband of Dear Love. I kept most still as I did go along, and I did look looks back. The sunbeams yet did shine upon his head.

When I did come more near unto the house we do live in, I did see a squirrel in a chêne tree. He was a lovely gray squirrel. I came more near unto the tree. I looked more looks at that gray squirrel sitting out on a limb. His tail was very bushy — it had many, many hairs on it. I did look at his tail, and I did look at the tail of my beautiful Thomas Chatterton Jupiter Zeus. The hairs he does have on *his* tail, they are not so many as are the hairs on the tail of that big gray squirrel. When I did look looks from his tail to the tail of my dear Thomas Chatterton Jupiter Zeus, I did have some wishes that there was as many hairs on *his* tail as are on the tail of that gray squirrel. While I so did think, Thomas Chatterton Jupiter Zeus did nestle more close in my arms. And I was glad for him as he is. He is so lovely, and his ways are ways of gentleness.

We went on along the dim trail. There by the dim

trail grow the honeysuckles. I nod to them as I go that way. In the daytime, I hear them talk with sunbeams and the wind. They talk in shadows with the little people of the sun. And this I have learned: Grownups do not know the language of shadows. Angel Mother and Angel Father did know, and they taught me. I wish they were here now, here to listen with me. I do so want them. Sometimes they do seem near. I have thinks sometimes kind God just opens the gates of heaven and lets them come out to be guardian angels for a little while.

I wonder if honeysuckles grow about the gates of heaven. I've heard they are made of precious jewels. I have thinks there will be flowers growing all about. Probably God brought the seed from heaven when he did plant the flowers here on earth. Too, I do think when angels bring babies from heaven to folks that live here below, they do also bring seeds of flowers, and do scatter them about. I have thinks that they do this so the babies may hear the voices of the loving flowers, and grow in the way of God.

# Twenty-nine

# Opal draws Portraits of her Friends, and looks for Thoughts among the Flowers

Today I didn't get to finish the exploration trip over the river, because just as I was starting around the house-corner after I did do my morning work early, the mamma grabbed me. She did tie me to the wood-shed corner with a piece of clothes-line. So we couldn't play together, she did tie to another corner that very wise crow, Lars Porsena of Clusium. To the corner beyond the next corner, to the corner that was the most longways off, she did tie him. But we played peek-a-boo around the middle corner. I'd lean just as far over as I could, with the rope a-pulling back my arms. Real quick, I'd stretch my neck, and peek and nod to Lars Porsena of Clusium. Then he of Clusium would flutter and say, "*How-do-you-do*," in squeaky crow-tones.

The day was growing warm. When it grew awful hot, my arms did have feelings too sore to lean over any more. I sat down by the wood-shed wall, and I did watch the passers-by. First went along Clementine, the Plymouth Rock hen. Then along stepped Napoleon, the Rhode Island rooster. By-and-by, I did hear Solomon Grundy squealing in the pig-pen. Then a butterfly did rest on the handle of the pump, where I did have longings to be. The wee mother hummingbird never left her nest on the lower oak limb — I could see her bill. I did have hopes Brave Horatius would come marching by. I called, and I did hear his whine, afar off. Then I knew he was tied up, too.

Another Plymouth Rock hen came walking by. Over in the shade by the old root was a *canard*. He did have a sleepy look. And I did have a sleepy feel. I looked a short look at the sky. A *merle* was flying over. I looked looks afar off; then I did look near. The old black cat sat on the doorstep. He had a saucer of milk, and then he did wash his face. I would have been partly glad if he did come over to see me. But I haven't made up with him since he did catch the baby robin. I forgot the cat when a snake did crawl around the stump — one with stripes on it. I did have thinks it might at least have come nearer, that I might count the stripes on its back; but it did go under the house. A grasshopper came hopping along. I stuck out my foot, and he did hop over it. Through the slats of the chicken-coop, I could see the mother hen with her young ducklings. I did have longings to cuddle them in my apron, and I did want to take them down to the brook. I was having very sad feels.

The sun got hotter and hotter. And pretty soon, I did have queer feels in the head and the middle. Then my nose did begin to bleed. I felt all choked-up and sticky. And every time I gave my head a shake to get a good breath, my curls did get mixed up with the nose-bleed. Pretty soon, the mamma passing by did see my apron with blood upon it, and she untied me. After she did souse me in the tub under the pump, I felt better. My arms did tingle where the rope was tied. After that, I went to bed.

And near suppertime, the mamma did call me to wash the stockings of the baby, and the stockings of the other little girl. I had needs to climb upon a stump to hang the stockings out to dry. Then I set the table. While I was carrying in the wood, I did crawl under the house to find the snake with the stripes on his back. But he wasn't there, so I don't know how many stripes he did have on his back.

When the wood was all stacked up in the wood-box, and the kindling under the stove, the mamma did say I might take the ducklings to the brook. That did make me very happy. All the way to the brook, I did sing, *"Sanctus, sanctus, sanctus, Dominus Deus, Te Deum laudamus."*

There was *rosée* [dew] on the verdure everywhere this morning, and the sunbeams made all the drops to shine. And there was glory and gladness everywhere. When I did look upon it, I did have thinks to go explores down along Nonette, and into the forêt de Chantilly. But the mamma had not thinks like my thinks. She did tell me of the many works she did have for me to do, and I did go to do them. But as I did go about to do them, I did have thinks about the appears with rosée on them of the things that grow where Nonette flows.

After the morning works was done, the mamma did have me to mind the baby, while she was making it a dress. While I did mind the baby, and while the mamma was making a dress for the baby, I made out of the piece that was left a christening robe. I made it for a young rooster. It isn't the first one I have made for him. But all the others he has got too big to wear, and I haven't been able to catch him yet.

A little time before I did eat my bowl of bread and milk — it was a little time before noontime — the mamma did take the little girl and the baby and the dress she was making for the baby, and they all did go to the house of her mother. She did have me to help her to take them. And when they were come to the door of the house of her mother, I did come again home.

When I did eat my bowl of bread and milk, I did have thinks I would make portraits of the folks in the pasture and pig-pen this afternoon. I did have decides to begin their portraits, and afterwards on other days, I will do more works on them.

I did make ready to go. I put more wood in the wood-box, so it would be full when the mamma came home. Then I put four white poker-chips in my apron pocket. One is for the portrait of the gentle Jersey cow. I will have to draw her head in a small way, so the horns can go in the picture, too. I have thinks that the people who made poker-chips ought to have made them with more bigness, so there would be more room to put horns on the cows's pictures that one does draw on poker-chips. One of the other three poker-chips I did put into my apron pocket is to draw Aphrodite's portrait on. And one of them is to draw Elizabeth Barrett Browning's picture on. And one is for someone else that does live in the pasture. Now I go.

When I did get these pictures made, I did take them to a log in the near woods that has got a hollow place in it. There is room in this log for me to take naps in on rainy days, and in this log I do keep the white poker-chips with pictures on them. In this log, I do have a goodly number of white poker-chips in rows, with por-

traits on them of the animal folks that do dwell hereabout. All my chums's pictures are there. There are five
of Mathilde Plantagenet, on three poker-chips. And
there are seven of William Shakespeare that I did draw
in *automne* and *hiver* time. And too, there are six of
dear Peter Paul Rubens that was. And now, four more
portraits did go in the rows today.

There are nine more white poker-chips in a little pile
under the root of a stump, close by the old log. These
nine white poker-chips are waiting waits to have portraits made on them. When I do get portraits made on
most all the white poker-chips I do have, then one of
the logging men at the mill by the far woods does give
me more white poker-chips, to draw more pictures of
Aphrodite and Elizabeth Barrett Browning and all of
us on.

The chore boy does have objects to my drawing pictures on his poker-chips that he does hide in the barn.
It was one day when I was walking around exploring in
the barn, and singing songs to William Shakespeare and
the gentle Jersey cow — on *that* day — and then I did
find the poker-chips of the chore boy, where he did hide
them away. I had not knows whose they were. But the
white ones all did lay there in a heap, having askings
for pictures to be drawn on them. So I did take some of
them, and I did make portraits of Thomas Chatterton
Jupiter Zeus, and Louis II, le Grand Condé, and Brave
Horatius. Then I did put them back in their places
again.

The day that was after that, I did take some more,
and I did make portraits on them. On them, I did make
portraits of Lars Porsena of Clusium, and Lucian Horace
Ovid Virgil, and Nannerl Mozart, and Felix Mendelssohn. Then I did carry them back to their place in

the barn. They did look satisfaction looks there in that corner, with portraits on them.

Then next day, when I was going down our lane by the barn, the chore boy did come by the gate. When I came through, he did give my curls a pull. He did say in a cross way, "What for did you mark up my nice poker-chips with your old pictures?" Then I did have knows they were *his* poker-chips, there in the barn. I did tell him the white ones had wants to have portraits on them, and it was to give them what they had wants for. I told him he better draw pictures on what white ones was left that did not have pictures on. I had thinks they would be lonesome.

But the chore boy did not have thinks like my thinks. He said he had more knows what poker-chips want than I have thinks. He says poker-chips want to be on a table in a game with men. I have thinks he has not knows what he is talking about. I have knows white poker-chips do have wants for portraits to be drawn on them — portraits of Thomas Chatterton Jupiter Zeus, and Brave Horatius, and Lars Porsena of Clusium, and all the rest.

After I did put the four new portraits in the old log, I did follow a path that leads to a path that leads to a path that goes to the house of Elsie. I so went because I did have a little longing to rock again the baby's cradle.

Elsie was making for her young husband a whipped-cream cake. He has such a fondness for them. And she does make them for him as often as there is cream enough. She was stirring things together in the most big yellow bowl. She did stir them in a quick way.

While she so did, the baby did have a wake-up. She said I might rock it in its cradle. I went in a quick way to do so. I did give its cradle little touches on its corner with my fingers, and it did rock in a gentle way. As the cradle so did rock back and forth in that gentle way, I did sing to the dear baby in it a little song. I did sing to it *le chant de fleurs* that Angel Father did teach me to sing, of *hyacinthe, éclaire, nenufar, rose, iris, et dauphin-elle, et oléandre, et romarin, lis, églantier, anemone, narcisse, et souci*. I did sing it four times over, and the baby did go to sleeps again. I do so love to watch it in its cradle.

Afterwards, I went to look for thoughts. Every day now, I do look for thoughts in flowers. Sometimes they are hidden away in the flower-bell, and sometimes I find them on a wild rose, and sometimes they are among the ferns; and sometimes I climb away up in the trees to look looks for them. So many thoughts do abide near unto us. They come from heaven, and live among the flowers and the ferns; and often I find them in the trees. I do so love to go on searches for the thoughts that do dwell near about.

# Thirty

# The Boxes in the Wood-Shed, the Ferns in the Woods, and the Little Bird in the Nest at the House of Dear Love

When I was come home from school this afternoon, first I did go to the wood-shed, to carry in wood. I saw there was some new bran in the bran sack box. That box is a big box. I make climb-ups on it sometimes, to have thinks. And Thomas Chatterton Jupiter Zeus makes a climb-up, too. Then I get down and make a pile of wood high enough so Brave Horatius can make a jump-climb up. We have likes for that big bran-sack box. Jenny Strong says why we do have likes for that box is because it is a hard box to get up on. But we do get up on it often. Sometimes I do eat my bowl of bread and milk for supper there on the bran-sack box.

There is another box in the wood-shed. In that other box is a sack of wheat. In morningtime, a little bit of it goes with the scraps to feed the chickens. In evening before graylight-time, more wheat from that sack goes to feed the chickens. And the chickens do have likes for that wheat from that sack in that box. I strew it on the ground for them in swings — I swing my arm a long swing, and then a short swing. When I do swing it a long swing, the wheat goes far; when I swing it a short swing, it goes not so — it goes only a little ways. Today I did swing my arm four long swings, and three short swings, and two more long swings. The chickens were glad to have it so. They did pick up that wheat in a hurry way.

Then I went into the kitchen to get the egg-turner, to pat the dirt down good around that tomato plant that's been dabbling its toes in the brook, and is now planted again. Just when I got it most patted down right, so it looked real proper, just then the mamma stepped behind me. She turned me over her knee. She wouldn't listen to explanations. She just applied that egg-turner to the back part of me. Now I feel too much sore to sit down, so I lean over a stump to print this. I have thinks I will go goes to the house of Dear Love.

I so did. I went through the near woods, and into the far woods. In my going, I went by where the man of the long step that whistles most all of the time does gather ferns for the *pensée* girl with the far-away look in her eyes. There, little ferns grow tall, and big ferns grow very tall, and sunbeams and shadows are among them before graylight-time. It is the same place where the man that wears gray neckties and is kind to mice did dig up little ferns to make fern wishes to the fairies, when I put letters in the moss-box by the old log. But now we dig not up little ferns here — we find them in another place. We have feels the fairies would like it, and these ferns grow there for the *pensée* girl with the far-away look in her eyes. Often it is now she is come to visit her aunt of the gray calico dress with a black bow at its neck.

After I did say a little prayer at the growing-place of the little tall ferns and the very tall ferns, I did go on. I went on along a winding path that goes in-between old logs. I went a little way. I did hear a little squeal. I did look looks about. There was Solomon Grundy coming after me, just as quick as he could come! His little legs did bring him in a quick way. I made a stop to wait for him. He was joys all over, when he did come up by me. He did jump upon me, and his squeals were squeals of gladness. Then we did go on together.

We went on. As we so did, I did sing to him one of the songs Angel Father did teach me to sing. Every day, I do sing him one of them. Today I did sing him *un chant des fleurs de fête d'oncle*, of *souci, et églantine, et pensée, et tulipe, et quintefeuille, et ulmaire, et apalachine, et tournesol, et romarin, et éclaire.* He did grunt grunts, in-between times.

When we were come to the house of Dear Love, they were standing by the steps. The husband of Dear Love did bring to her a little nest that was in a tree that they did fall in the far woods today. The nest, it was a long nest — its longness was very long. I have thinks when the wind did go through the woods, sometimes this cradle did swing, its largeness was so long. The husband of Dear Love did think these little birds were most ready to fly from the nest when the tree did fall today. All the six little birds but one did get death as the tree did fall.

They were such little things, when we did take them out. The one live one was hungry, and we did feed him. We did feed him little bits at a time. A little bit of egg that was left in the dinner-pail of the husband of Dear Love did give to this little bird some satisfaction feels.

Dear Love did cuddle it warm in her hands, and her husband did make the piece of egg into little divides, for me to give to it. It did open its mouth most wide.

When I so did see it do, I did open my mouth too, like it did. The husband of Dear Love did laugh. I did have asking of him why he did laugh, for it was not thoughtful to laugh at the little hungry bird that did have so hungry feels, and lonesome ones. He did say in his gentle way that it was not at the little bird he did laugh. He did say he just did laugh sometimes, when he had thinks about things at work.

I told him it was nice he had thoughtfuls of the nest that they saw in the tree after it did fall. He said he thought of me, and that made him think it would be nice to bring the nest home. And he broke off another piece of egg for the little bird. And more he so did. And every time I did drop a piece of egg into the mouth of the little bird, I did open my mouth wide too, from seeing the bird do it.

When it was full of satisfaction feels, Dear Love did fix it all up nice, in a warm little box. She is going to give it careful cares, so it will grow up. She has asked me to pick out a name for it. I am so going to do. And tomorrow, I am going to have the funerals of the other five little birds that did get death as the tree did fall. Dear Love gave me white soft pieces to wrap them in, and the husband of Dear Love says he will make the tombstones for their graves. I am going to bury them at Dreux, by Blaise. There will they rest. On tomorrow it so will be.

Tonight when I was come home, I took the pillow from my bed to sit on at the supper-table, because the back part of me did feel so sore from that spanking the mamma gave me with the egg-turner, out in the garden today.

After supper-time, I did have seeing out the window of the night. It was calling, *"Petite Françoise — come, petite Françoise."* I went. Brave Horatius followed after.

We went adown the path. A big silver yellow ball was coming up over the hill. We made a stop. I did climb on a rock, to watch its coming. Brave Horatius put his nose by my hand. I gave him pats. He looked up at me. I told him, *"C'est la pleine lune."* ["It's the full moon."] We went on — we went on to the hill where its coming was.

# Thirty-one

## Lola wears her White Silk Dress

Lola has got her white silk dress that she did have so much wants for. And it has a little ruffle around the neck, and one around each sleeve, like she had wants for it to have. It is nice she is a great lady, now.

She so did say at school she would be a great lady when she did have her white silk dress on. And too at school, she did say the children would gather around her and sing. And they did. And she did say at school, when the children would gather around her and sing, when she does have her white silk dress on — she did say then she would stand up and stretch out her arms and bestow her blessing on all of them, like the deacon does to the people in the church in the mill town. But she didn't. She didn't even raise up her hands. She stayed asleep in that long box, the whole time the children was marching around her and singing "Nearer My God to Thee," and more songs. She did just lay there in that long box, with her white silk dress on and her eyes shut and her hands folded; and she was very still, all the time.

Her sister did cry. I did walk up to her and touch her hand, where she did sit in the rocking-chair. I did have asks if it was a white silk dress she was having wants for, too. And she patted my hand. And I told her maybe she would get a white silk dress soon, too, and how nice it was Lola did have hers, what she had wants for — and the ruffles in its neck and sleeves. And Lola's sister did pat me on the head, and went out to her kitchen. And I did go out of doors again.

And there was Brave Horatius by the steps; and I saw a yellow butterfly. And a little way away, there was a mud-puddle. By the mud-puddle was a *guêpe* [wasp]. She came; she went. Every time she did come, she did take a bit of mud. I did watch. When she was gone away, a little hole was, where she did take the mud. She did make comes again. It was for mud she did come, every time. Last time, I did follow after. It was a difficulty, the following after — she was so little a person, and the way she did go, it was a quick way. And I had seeing she was making a cradle of mud, for a baby-guêpe-to-be.

Then I went a little way back. I saw a white butterfly. I have wonders if Lola will wear her white silk dress to school, when falltime is come. I saw one more white butterfly. I looked more looks about.

Among the grasses on a little bush, there was a katydid, and its green was a pretty greenness. Its wings, they were folded close, and it was washing its front feet. I have thinks katydids do keep their feet most clean — they do wash them again, and more times. I do so like to keep watches of the way the katydid does clean its face with its front foot. I have thinks to be a katydid would be an interest life.

Brave Horatius and me looked looks away. We did see the little pond. We went goes to it. Little white fleurs were along the way. I have wonders if Lola will wear her white silk dress when at school they do play "London Bridge Is Falling Down."

When we was come to the little pond, I lay myself down close to its edge. I did look looks into the pond. I saw things there. There were sky-clouds in the water. I saw a crayfish come from under a rock. I saw minnows all about. First they were still; then they made moves about. I saw a little cradle of tiny stones — it was about an inch long. While I did look looks at it, it walked off. Then me and Brave Horatius did go on explores to the near woods.

Thirty-two

# The Folks in the Garden, the Writing of the Fairies, and the Glad Song of the Brook

When morning works was done, then I did go calling on the folks that wear sun-bonnets. I thought I better keep my sun-bonnet on my head, being as I was going calling on sun-bonnet folks.

First I went to the garden to visit the pea family. I shook hands all down the row, and back up the other row. Then I went to call on their neighbors, the beans. And I saw a rabbit in the garden, near unto the cabbages. I went a little nearer — I went to see who it was. It was Madame Lapine [Mrs. Rabbit]. She is a gentle woman, and her ways are quiet ways; and she does have a fondness for bits of apple. Whenever I do have an apple, I do save bits for her. Too, she likes cabbage, and I have showed her the way into the garden to get it, when I am not there to get it for her.

Today, after I did have talks with most all the folks in the garden, I did tell them about this day being the crowning day of Louis XIV in 1654, and the going-away day of Robert de Bruce, in 1329. Then I did go out

283

across the fields, to have talks with Aphrodite and Solomon Grundy and Michael Angelo Sanzio Raphael.

Then it was I saw the chore boy, near unto the barn. He had a long stick. He was knocking down the homes of the swallows. There were broken cradles on the ground, and there were grown-up swallows about, with distresses in their flying. That did make me to have so sad feels. I did tell him how dear are swallows, but he would have no listens.

Afterwards, I did go goes to the house of Sadie Mc-Kibben. As I did go along, I did have seeing of a little thing in the road ahead. It was a very little thing, and it made little moves. They were only flutterings. It went not away from where it was. I did go in a hurry on. When I was come to it, I did have seeing it was a little bird — it was a little bird that was hurt by the step of a cow. I have thinks it was making a try to make a go across the road. I cuddled it up, and I felt feels in my apron pocket, and there was some Mentholatum. And I give it some applys, and we went to the hospital. And I put it there on moss, in a little soap-box room, where nothing can come and bring it more hurts. And it did have likes for the water I gave it to drink in a thimble, and more likes it did have for the food I gave it to eat. I named it William Makepeace Thackeray.

Then I did go goes on to the house of Sadie Mc-Kibben, and Brave Horatius and Lars Porsena of Clusium went goes with me. Lars Porsena of Clusium did ride part ways on the back of Brave Horatius.

When we was come to the house of Sadie McKibben, she was having troubles. Just when she did have her clothes all hung out, then the clothes-line did break, and they all had falls on the ground. While she did gather them up, she did have talks to herself. She did say, " 'Tis a folly to fret. *Grief's* no comfort." When her bread gets burns in the oven, and the chickens bother on the porch, and the clothes boil over on the stove, and everything seems to go wrong, Sadie McKibben has a way of saying, " 'Tis a folly to fret. *Grief's* no comfort."

While she was giving more wash-outs to them clothes that did have a fall while the clothes-line did break, she did sing. She sings on days when sunshine is. She sings on days when rain is. Sadie McKibben always sings before the summer rain, as does the robin.

Today when she did have them clothes part hung on the line again, then it was the man that wears gray neck-ties did come by, on his way to the mill town. He had asks if there was any things she was having needs of that he could bring back. And she did say bacon, and some soda, and some more things what she had needs of for to cook with.

While she told him, he did write it down. I breathed a big breathe when I did see him write it down — for he does write in the way that the fairies write! I said, *"Oh!"* He did turn himself around. He did say, "What is it, little one?" And I did tell him, all in one breath — I did tell him, "Oh, it's that you write in the way the fairies write, that do put things for me by the old log where the moss-box is!"

Then he did smile, and he looked a long look out the door. I have thinks he was thinking of the long-ago time when the fairies did teach him to write their way.

When he did start to go, I heard him say to Sadie McKibben, *"I guess I will have to change my writing."* I most slipped off the chair I was setting on the edge of. I had feels I better speak to him about it. I had feels of the sorry feels the fairies would feel, when they had knowing he was not going to write in the way they did teach him to write.

When he did tell me good-bye, I did say, "Please don't

change your writing because you write the way the fairies do. I have thinks the way they write is lovely." And he did smile his gentle smile. Then I did tell him how sorry I knew the fairies would feel, if he wrote not on in their way. Then he did say he guessed it would be a pretty hard thing, trying to write another way from what the fairies did teach him to write. I have thinks it would so be.

And tonight in my prayers, I will thank God the fairies did teach the man that wears gray neckties and is kind to mice to write in their way. It is a very beautiful way. Some of the letters are like ripples on the water. I have longings to write as the fairies write.

First thing I did do on the morning of today was to go to prayers in the cathedral. When I was come again to the house we live in, I did eat my breakfast. (For breakfast, I do eat a bowl of bread and milk.) Then I did give the back porch a sweep-off. That made its appears better. Then I did go to feed the chickens. And after that, I did go to feed the folks in the nursery.

The caterpillars do eat so much — they do get hungry feels inside them most often. When I did have them well fed on this morning, I did make tries to get some of them into their christening robes, so that they can be christened before they do grow more old, and before they do grow too big to wear their little christening robes.

The matter of making christening robes for caterpillars, it is not a difficult one; the difficulty is to get a frisky caterpillar to keep still while one is putting on his christening robe. And then it is a problem to *keep* it on, after one does *get* it on. I do have much troubles with caterpillars crawling out of their christening robes after I do get them on.

Before I did get five caterpillars into their christening robes, I did hear the mamma calling. She did have needs of me. I ran a quick run to the house.

When I did walk in the door, I did hold up my dress. Now the mamma makes me raise up my dress when I come into the house, so she can get a good look at my underskirt all around. She does it to see if I have any animals about me, in the pockets I pin on my underskirts. The mamma objects to my bringing animals into the house. In the days of now, I am real careful not to be bringing in my friends in these pockets when the mamma is at home. This morning, she did look satisfaction looks when she saw not an animal in the pockets I have pinned onto my underskirt.

When I was walked in, she did send me again to get wood. She did want the wood-box filled with wood. Sometimes it takes an awful long time to fill the wood-box. The longest time is when I am in a hurry to go on exploration trips. While I did pile the wood in, I did whisper my feels about it all to Felix Mendelssohn, that was hiding up my sleeve. Then the mamma said if I was born her child, I wouldn't have had this longing to go on exploration trips. Then she did send me to pick elderberries. She did tell me to scoot up the tree in a hurry.

I did so. When I was up in the tree, I did not hurry so to get the berries. I took looks about. I looked to the divides in the road, and away to the blue hills. Then I sat on another limb, and looked looks more near.

I did watch the little pond. In the pond is a lily. The lily is a yellow lily, and it floats upon the water. It does float upon the water like a little sky-star. Maybe it was a little one that did have longings to cuddle in among the raindrops that do come together in the pond. I wonder how it came to be. I would like to know.

In the pasture by the pond, I did see a mother sheep. I think it must be nice to be a sheep — to be a mother sheep, and have a little lamb. Children are such a blessing. When I did have my pail half full of berries, I did stop to pick out names for the twins I am going to have when I grow up. I did pick out sixteen names. And then, being as I could not make decides between them, I did have decides to pick out names for them some other day. And I did begin at once to get that pail all full of elderberries.

When that was come to pass, I set the pail on a little stump. Brave Horatius stayed to guard it, and I did go the way that leads to the hill-top. I did have longings to dance. Most every day, I do dance. I dance with the leaves and the grass. I feel thrills from my toes to my curls. I feel like a bird, sometimes. Then I spread my arms for wings, and I go my way from stump to stump, and on adown the hill. Sometimes I am a demoiselle, flitting near unto the water. Then I nod unto the willows, and they nod unto me. They wave their arms, and I wave mine. They wiggle their toes in the water a bit, and I do so, too. And every time we wiggle our toes, we do drink into our souls the song of the brook — the glad song it is always singing. And the joy-song does sing on in our hearts. So did it today.

And afterwards, when I did go to get my pail of elderberries, they were gone. They were gone only a little way. Brave Horatius did have feelings those elderberries ought to be going to the house we live in, so he did make starts with them. When I did catch up with him, he did have the pail-handle in his mouth. He was going in a slow way, and only a few elderberries did spill out. I have thinks they did roll out when he took the bucket off the stump.

# Thirty-three

# The Death of
# Lars Porsena of Clusium

The waters of the brook lap and lap. They come in little ripples, over gray stones. They are rippling a song. It is a gentle song. It is a good-bye song to Lars Porsena of Clusium. The time now is when there is no Lars Porsena of Clusium.

It was only on yesterday. It was near eventime, when the mamma was gone to the house of her mother. I was making a go across the cornfield, to see the tree-folks in the lane. Brave Horatius did follow after me. Lars Porsena of Clusium was going on a way ahead. His movements did look queer, with his tail-feathers not growed out yet. He went on; he came a little way back, to see if we were coming; then he started on in a hurry way. I was watching him with joy feels in my heart. I was having thinks how nice it would be when he does get his new tail-feathers all growed out.

Brave Horatius did give a queer bark, and he pulled the corner of my apron. I looked looks about — there the chore boy was, in a corner of the cornfield, with a gun. He was pointing it out on the field. I had thinks he had not seeing of my dear Lars Porsena out there. I ran a quick run, to keep him from pulling that thing on the gun that makes the noise and pains. I hollered hollers at him about Lars Porsena of Clusium crossing the cornfield. When I was come to where the chore boy was, I did tell him he must not shoot that old gun — a ball in it might go as far as my dear Lars Porsena of Clusium.

He just laughed a laugh. And he said, he did, that Lars Porsena was nothing but a crow. And then he pointed that gun right at my own dear Lars Porsena of Clusium. The noise was a big awful calamity. I had feels I was killed dead, when I saw him fall. I ran a quick run. When I was come to him, I found he was making little flutterings. When I did go to pick him up, he was wet with much blood. I felt the shivers of his pains. I wrapped my apron around him, so he would not have cold feels. There was much wetness upon my apron as I did go along — it was wetness of blood. The sky was more gray, and before I was come to the house we live in, the raindrops were coming down in a slow, sad way. I have thinks the sky was crying tears for the hurts of Lars Porsena of Clusium. And I was, too.

I had longs for the man that wears gray neckties and is kind to mice to be come back again. He and other mill folks and Dear Love and her husband and Sadie Mc-Kibben and her husband are all away gone until tomorrow eventime. I had not knows what to do for Lars Porsena of Clusium. This was not like that time he lost his tail. I did cuddle him up close in my arms, and I washed off some of the blood. But more and more came, and sleepy feels were upon him. I wrapped my apron more close around him, and I did sing songs to him about *Ave Maria,* and *Sanctus, sanctus, sanctus, Dominus Deus.*

After the mamma was gone to bed and sleeps, I did take Lars Porsena of Clusium to bed with me. He was so sleepy. I cuddled him up in my arms and we both did go to sleep, for tired feels was upon us. When I had wake-ups early on this morning, my own dear Lars Porsena was very cold, and he was very dead, and stiffness was upon him. I did have queer feels in my throat, and pain feels all up and down me. I so did want him alive again, to go explores.

When the mamma was most awake, I climbed out the bedroom window with him in a quick way. I went on. I did go until I was come to the lane. And I did go on down our lane until I was come to the tall fir tree, Good King Edward I. I lay Lars Porsena of Clusium near unto Good King Edward I, and I said a little prayer, and I covered him over with moss.

I now go to have his funeral, at Dreux. Brave Horatius too does wait waits, and quiet is upon him. He has longs for Lars Porsena of Clusium to come perch on his back. And the winds are calling; and between the callings of the wind, the willows do call, down by the creek. They beckon and call to the soul of Lars Porsena of Clusium.

The clouds go slow across the sky. The water goes slow in the brook. No one seems to be in a hurry. Even the wind walks slow. I think she wears a silk robe today — I can hear its faint rustle. I think the wind is dreaming, too. With the whispering leaves, she sings a dream-song. This is a dream-day.

I stopped in the dusty road, and looked a long while at the sun. It was round and abright-shining. Then for a little time afterwards, everywhere I looked I saw a tiny, bright shining; and there was a queer feeling in my head.

When I was come to the field, Savonarola did look like the flies were giving him some bothers. I took my apron and shooed some of them off. I could only reach a little way up. I have thinks it did help some. The chore boy did not come for some long time. While Savonarola waited his coming, I did give him some more fans with my apron. I had longings for the papa's news-paper — I had thinks I could make that go more far up than I could make my apron go. First I did stand on one side of Savonarola and shake my apron at the flies; then I did stand on the other side of him. Those flies were most lazy — they didn't want to make moves at all.

While I did make tries to make the flies make moves away, I did sing a song of fleurs of grandmère — of *fraxinelle, romarin, anemone, narcisse, cornope, olé-andre, iris, souci, églantier, marguerite, aubépine, renon-cule, immortelle, éclaire, anemone, myosotis, églantier, lis, iris, éclaire, dauphinelle, ornithogale, romarin, lis, églantier, anemone, narcisse, souci* — to Savonarola. Then I went to get him a drink in my little bucket that I do hide by the willows. He had likes for that drink of cold water, and some more. When that chore boy was most come, I did give Savonarola good-bye pats on his velvet nose.

Afterwards, I did go goes down by Launette, and on to Nonette, where the willows grow. I did print a mes-sage on a leaf. It was for the soul of Lars Porsena of Clusium. I left it on a willow branch, with a little prayer that his soul would have finding of it.

Then I did make begins to get ready for Aphrodite's foot-bath. She has needs for one most every day. And most days, she does get it. I do fill seven Castoria bottles full of water; then I put their corks in. And all of them that will go into the lard-pail, I do so put in. Too, I have a little brush to brush her feet with, while I do give them splash-water baths out of the Castoria bottles. Aphrodite has likes for foot-baths, and some days she does have likes for the shower-baths I do give to her out of the little flower-sprinkler. I give her back brushes, and then some more showers from the flower-sprinkler.

That flower-sprinkler I did write to the fairies for. I put the letter in the moss-box by the old log, where I do put other letters for the fairies. The time it was not long until the fairies did leave this flower-sprinkler for it. I water the wildflowers after warm days, and I water the plants that do grow in the garden. I can almost hear the tomato plants say, *"We were waiting for you!"* every time I do give them sprinkles. And the cabbage plants have likes for them, too.

Today, after I did give shower-baths to Aphrodite and Solomon Grundy and his sister Anthonya Mundy that has not got as much curl in her tail as has Solomon Grundy, then I did give shower-baths to some other folks.

Afterwards, I went to the cathedral, to have service there; for this is the going-away day of Good King Edward I, in 1307. Brave Horatius went with me, and so did Minerva. She wore her cap with ruffles on it, like the morning-cap of Jenny Strong. Menander Euripides Theocritus Thucydides walked by my side. And too, Sir Francis Bacon went with us. His leg has well feels a long time now, but he walks not as other chickens walk. He has likes to go to cathedral service. And so has Thomas Chatterton Jupiter Zeus.

Today, after I did sing, *"Sanctus, sanctus, sanctus, Dominus Deus,"* then we all did go goes to the house of Sadie McKibben.

When we was come near unto it, there was Sadie

McKibben on the big gray rock under the old fir tree. Her hands made quick moves with needles, the kind that knit. She was knitting socks for the man that is her husband and does live at her house. I sat down on the ground beside her. She had on her blue gingham apron with the cross-stitches on it. I did make counts of thirty cross-stitches on that apron, today. Someday I will count them all. There were some grasses growing close to the gray rock, and their little fingers did touch the cross-stitches on the blue gingham apron of Sadie McKibben. I have thinks they too would like to cuddle up to Sadie McKibben.

# Thirty-four

# The Death-Song of the Great Fir Tree, the Yellow Flowers along the Road, and the Rescue and Naming of Geoffroi Chaucer

Today was a long work-day. When afternoon-time was come, the mamma was worried because the cream wasn't sour enough to churn, and she wanted to get it churned before supper-time. I wanted to help her. I feel so sorry for her when the worry lines come on her face. They make her look tired.

While she was taking a nap by the baby on the bed, I tried to think how I could help her. By-and-by, after a time not very long, I thought of a way. I got a lemon, and cut it in two with the butcher-knife. Then I took the lid off the big churn. I squeezed those lemons lots of times into the cream. Then, when they wouldn't leak any more juice out, I put the rinds in for a finishing touch, just like the mamma puts them into the lemonade after she has squeezed all the squeeze out. I feel better now. I know when the mamma awakes, joy will be hers when she sees the cream is sour enough to churn.

But the feels the mamma did have when she had wake-ups — they was not joy feels. And the feels I now have are sore feels, on the back part of me.

While I did mind the baby, there was an odd sound — like someone crying, a great way off. The mamma says, "I wonder what it is." I know it is the death-song of that gray fir tree they are falling this afternoon. Sleeps is come upon the baby. The mamma says for me to get out of her way. I go now goes to the woods.

I did. I went on to where its growing was. It reaches up and up — most away to the clouds. Days have been when I did sit by it to have thinks. And Thomas Chatterton Jupiter Zeus has gone goes there with me, and Brave Horatius has waited waits while I did say prayers by that great tree. And I have told it all the things I am going to do when I grow up. I have told it about the books I am going to write about wood-folks and them of the field, and about the twins I want when I grow up, and the eight other children. And always I have read to this great fir tree the letters I have wrote and put in the big log for the fairies to take to grandmère and grandpère. And night-times I have heard the little windsong among its arms most near to the sky, and I have almost touched the big gray shadow with velvet fingers that stays close by it at night-time.

And today there, I did watch and I did hear its moans, as the saw went through it. And I sat down on the ground. There was a queer feel in my throat, and I couldn't stand up. All the woods seemed a still sound, except the pain-sound of the saw. It seemed like a little voice was calling from the cliffs. And then it was many voices. They were all little voices calling as one silver voice come together. The saw, it didn't stop — it went on sawing. Then I did have thinks the silver voice was calling to the soul of the big fir tree. The saw did stop. There was a stillness. There was a queer, sad sound. The big tree did quiver. It did sway. It crashed to the earth.

Yesterday was the day of the funeral of Aristotle. He died of eating too many mosquitoes. Now I have not three pet bats; I only have two pet bats, Plato and Pliny. And they are like mice with angel wings. I have likes to watch Pliny scratch his head with his hind-foot, and he does use a part of his wonderful stretchy wing for a wash-cloth. I have lonesome feels about Aristotle being gone. I go now goes to the garden, to get turnips for supper.

I did, and I give to them washes in the brook. When I did take them in to put them on the cook-table, the mamma and the grandma was talking about the garden. The mamma did wonder where that third cabbage-head was gone. I didn't. I know. It is up the brook a ways, dabbling its toes in the water. I dug it up this morning, and put it there. Tonight I shall plant it again in the garden. It will have had a glad day, dabbling its toes in the brook. That does give one such a nice feel.

I have been sitting on a high stump, looking looks to where is the road. Now the sun shines yellow, and many flowers bloom yellow along the road. When I grow up, I'm going to write a book about the folks that wear the sunshine color. I have printed some prints for its begins.

When I was coming back from the stump, I saw a spider. I stopped to watch him. He walked on his web. There was a mosquito in the web. I thought I would take that mosquito to Pliny, to eat. Before I could get to it, that spider ate that mosquito up.

I came a come near unto the chêne trees. I saw the black cat coming in a creep-along. He was coming more near unto the little squirrel that had no seeing of his coming. I ran a more quick run; I hollered a little holler. The little squirrel did make a start to make a run. The cat did make a jump. I so did, too. The cat did begin to make a quick run. I so did, too. I fell over a little root. That helped some, because when I fell, I did catch the tail of that old black cat. I pulled it most hard. He did drop the little squirrel, and made objects to my pulling his tail so.

Then I did get the baby squirrel. It was most killed, but it was not killed dead. I did cuddle it up in my hands, and we did go the way that does go to the hospital. I have Mentholatumed it, and named it Geoffroi Chaucer. And I have told it about this being the day of the going-away of Innocent III, in 1216.

Now I go goes to the cathedral, to say thanks for his borning and all the good he did do, and to pray for the angels to bring a new baby to the mamma and the papa when comes Easter-time.

# Thirty-five

## Other Folks visit the Moss-Box by the Old Log

One of my tooths is loose, and a queer feel. This morning, after I did come back from prayers in the cathedral with Thomas Chatterton Jupiter Zeus, it was then I did have feels of that tooth. It was funny feels, its being loose.

After I did eat some of my mush, I did go to the string-box, and I pulled out a string. It was a white one. There was lots of white strings in that box, and a pink one and a green one. I put the white string back, and I pulled out the green one. It was long, very long — *feets* long. I did tie one part of it around my tooth, with carefuls. Then I did come a walk-over to where the broom stands, behind the back door. I did tie the other end of the long green string to the broom-handle. And I kept hold of the middle of the string in my hand, so when the broom had falls, it wouldn't give a bump to my tooth when it did pull it out. I went a walk-off. The tooth didn't come out. The green string did just have a slip off the broom-handle.

I carried the string in a careful way while I did go to bring in the wood and other morning works the mamma did want done, when she went away to the grandma's house. When the works was done, then I tied that string to the door-knob. I started to walk off. Then I came back a ways. I decided to wait a little while. I walked off again. I got most far enough to get it jerked out. Then I thought I'd wait until after dinner. I took the string off my tooth, but I left it on the door-knob, to remind me to do it after dinner. Now I go.

And I went goes to the woods, with Lucian Horace Ovid Virgil and Louis II, le Grand Condé. And there I met a glad surprise. Today the fairies did bring more color pencils to the moss-box by the old log! I had finding of them in the afternoon of today. There was a blue one, and a green one, and a yellow one, and a purple one. And more there was, too. I looked looks at them.

And I climbed up into the tree that is close by the old log. I climbed up to be more near the sky. There was songs in the tree-tops, and I did make a stop way below to have listens. And I did look looks down on where is the moss-box and the fleurs I have planted near unto it, and the ferns and the vines that do have growing over the old log.

And while I did have watches of the plant-folks that dwell about the moss-box, and while I did have listens of the songs in the tree-tops, then it was the *pensée* girl with the far-away look in her eyes and the man of the long step that whistles most all of the time did come walking through the woods. It is often now they so come, and he does gather ferns for her, and they have listens to what the brook sings. Today they didn't make a stop by the brook; they came right on and on. They so did until they was come right up to where the plant-folks dwell by the moss-box.

First I did have thinks they was coming comes to leave a letter for the fairies. But they came and they stood there — they did not go goes away. Then I had knows they didn't even *see* the moss-box where I do leave the letters for the fairies. They did almost step on it. I had sees there was joy-lights in her eyes, and the looks he looked at her was like the looks the young husband of Dear Love does look at her when he is come home from work at eventime. And I did reach out my arms above them, for blessings to come.

They had not knows of my reaching out my arms above them. Only God had knows. They did just have sees for one another. I have sure feels they didn't see that green caterpillar having sleeps under the green hazel leaf.

He most stepped on the moss-box. I most hollered. My loose tooth was queer feels. He is a most strong man. He put his arms around the *pensée* girl, and he most lifted her off the ground. I had fears he would drop her on the moss-box. I most did have losing of my balance on the tree-arm.

And I had sees of a chipmunk on a stump. He was very saucy, and had nice stripes on his back, and he did sit up and talk chipmunk talk to another chipmunk. I had hears of him and sees of him. But the man of the long step and the *pensée* girl didn't have sees of the chipmunk.

He did take out a ring of gold, and he did tell her that was his mother's wedding-ring. And the caterpillar that was asleep did have wake-ups, and he crawled a little more under the hazel leaf. And a butterfly went by — it was a cream one, with a nice ribbon at its wing-edge, and pinkish spots. I had thinks about how nice it would be to be a butterfly, and come out of a little egg, and be a caterpillar first and have a lot of legs, instead of just two legs like I have got now. And I looked more looks at the fat green caterpillar. I have more like him in the nursery.

He did kiss her again. Last year, I had more green caterpillars like unto this one. And they did grow and change, and they was very big brown moths, with velvet wings and velvet feet. And he did say, "I want to help you to have all the love-joy in the world." And I put more in my prayer: *A baby soon.* And the fat green caterpillar fell off the leaf, away down on the ground; but he fell on some moss I have put about where is the moss-box.

And after his arm did touch the hazel bush, he did step over two steps. I breathed a big breathe of reliefs about the moss-box not having steps on. And he kissed her again. And the green caterpillar made begins to crawl back up the hazel bush. And I felt a big amount of satisfaction feels, that they was so happy. And I did whisper another prayer for the angels to bring them a baby real soon, with pink fleurs on its baby brush and a pink bow on its cradle-quilt.

And in the bushes there was a little bird, and restless was upon him. The color of him was blue-gray, and there were streaks underneath, and there was a bit of yellow on his throat, and so on top of his head. He did move in a quick way. I so did, so I could see him more.

As I did go along, a-following him after, I did have sees of the tracks of the comings and goings of little wood-folks. And a way away was a soft-eyed *faon*. (When it's with its mother, then it is a *daine*.) There was whispers in the ferns, and more songs in the tree-tops. And my tooth had some more queer feels, and I had remembers about the green string tied to the door-knob.

I went a walk back. It was still there when I was come to the house we live in. Brave Horatius was by the steps. He did have watches of me while I did tie the other end of the long green string around my tooth. Then I went a quick walk to the other door, by step-backs. I made a reach-out for the green string — but it wasn't. It was on the floor, and my tooth was. After I did throw it away, then I did do the green string up in a roll. I am going to keep it.

I went goes to the garden, to get the beets the mamma did want for supper. While I did get them, I did have seeing that the green dresses of the turnip-folk are getting faded and old. I thought they might like to have new white dresses. I went again to the kitchen. I lifted the flour-sifter from the flour-drawer in the cook-table. I did go back to the garden. There I sifted flour on the turnip-folks. It came down in sprinkles, like snowflakes. That gave them the proper look. When the wind came along, they nodded appreciation, and some of the flour slid off to the ground.

And Brave Horatius and I went to prayers in the cathedral, and so went Thomas Chatterton Jupiter Zeus and Menander Euripides Theocritus Thucydides. And Mathilde Plantagenet did wait waits at the pasture-bars.

# Thirty-six

# Taking-Egg Day

Today was taking-egg day. Taking-egg day comes mostly one time a week. It is the day the mamma does send me straight to take eggs to the folks hereabout and yonder. First she does send me to take them yonder, before she does send me to take them hereabout. This she does because she knows if she sends me first to take them to the folks that live hereabout, I do stay so long with the folks that live in the nursery and hospital that there isn't time enough left to take eggs unto the people that live yonder.

As quick as I did eat my breakfast, the mamma did set out the lard-pail on the wash-bench, with a dozen eggs in it. As quick as she did so, I put on my sunbonnet. It is blue, and has a ruffle on it. Sometimes I wear it on my head, but most times it hangs back over my shoulders. And often I carry it over my arm, with things in it — earthworms for baby birds, bandages for the folks that get hurt, and Mentholatum in quinine boxes. Then too, on exploration trips, my chums ride in it. Sometimes it's a mouse, and sometimes it's a beetle. Very often, it is toads and caterpillars — only they don't ride in the sun-bonnet at the same time, because I have learned toads like to eat caterpillars for breakfast. Sometimes Thomas Chatterton Jupiter Zeus, that most dear velvety wood-rat, snuggles up in my sun-bonnet. He most fills it up. A sun-bonnet is a very useful garment.

After I did tie my bonnet-strings under my chin in the proper way the mamma thinks they ought to be tied, I walked over to the wash-bench in hippity-hops, to get that bucket of eggs. Before I took up the bucket, I did look long looks at those eggs. They were so plump, and so white, and they did have so nice a feel. I think being a hen must be a very interesting life. How thrilling it must be to cackle after one lays an egg! And then it must be a big amount of satisfaction to have a large number of children hatch out at the same time, and follow one about. I think I would like to be a hen — in the daytime. But I wouldn't like to roost in the chicken-house at night.

When the mamma saw me looking long looks at those eggs, she gave to me a shoulder-shake and told me to get a hurry on me, and take those eggs straight to Mrs. Limberger yonder. That Mrs. Limberger is the quite plump wife of that quite big man that lives in a quite big house that is nice, but isn't as nice as his lane. I thought I'd go straight to Mrs. Limberger's in along that lane from out along the field. But first I did go by to get Felix Mendelssohn.

When I got to where he was, it was very near unto the altar of Good King Edward I; and being as this was the day of his crowning in 1274, I thought I would just go a little farther, to see if the crown I planted in little plants there on the altar were growing in a nice way.

They were. When I planted them there from the woods in spring-days, I did hope they would burst into bloom on this his crowning day, and make a crown of flowers on his altar. But the dear little things got in a hurry, and did bloom more than a month ago. But they were saying today beautiful things with their leaves — I heard them as I did kneel to pray to thank God for Good King Edward I.

After I did pray quite a long time, and Felix Mendelssohn got a little fidgety, I started on to take the eleven eggs that were left straight to Mrs. Limberger. The other egg I could not take because, when I did kneel to pray, in some way it did roll out of the bucket; and before I was through my prayers, a little gray rock by my hand just rolled off the altar and met the egg. There are a lot of little gray rocks on the altar. It is mostly made up of little rocks, and some big ones. While I was making that altar, the man that works at the mill and wears gray neckties and is kind to mice came along. And the big rocks that were too big, he did lift and place on the altar, there. And then he did help me to plant mosses in-between some of the rocks. That made me happy. Men are such a blessing to have about.

Today I did go from the altar to the field. Along the way, I stopped to talk to the trees, and to watch the birds, and to get berries for the nursery. I put them in the bucket with the eggs. I most lost my bonnet climbing over the fence, and I did lose three more of those eggs, and some of the berries for the nursery. I picked up the berries and put them back in the lard-pail, but the eggs I could not pick up. I didn't put my sun-bonnet back on my head again, but I did give the strings a little tie in front, so it wouldn't come off.

Very soon after, I saw a little snake. He was crawling

along. When I see snakes, I like to stop and watch them. The dresses they wear fit them tight — they can't fluff out their clothes like birds can. But snakes are quick people. They move in such a pretty way. Their eyes are bright, and their tongues are slim.

When that snake crawled away where I couldn't see him any more, I walked over to talk to a flower. After we did have conversation for some time, I happened to think the mamma did say to hurry; so I said good-bye. And when I did, I put my nose to the flower to smell it. It had a pleasant odor. I went on. Pretty soon, I felt something on my nose. I wiped it off — it was pollen from that flower. I put it on an egg in the lard-pail. That gave that egg a flowery look. I showed it to an ear of corn. And then as I did go along, I stopped to take the clods away from the roots of some of the corn plants, so the toes of their roots could have some fresh air. They quivered appreciations. And some did bow down most to the ground to thank me, after I was done.

I proceeded. The day was most warm. When I did cross the creek, I looked down it and up it. There were fairy demoiselles near unto the water — their wings did shimmer in the sunlight. All along its edges, the willows were dabbling their toes. Some had waded in a little bit — about enough to get their ankles wet. I looked long looks at them. I knew just how they did feel inside, while they were dabbling their toes in the water. It is such a nice feel to have.

I started on. I looked back. I started on. I turned and came back a little ways — just to take a good-bye look. The willows waved their hands to me. They called to me, *"Petite Françoise! Petite Françoise!"* I hurried on with the eggs. I had got twice as far as I did get before — then I started back to the creek. I ran all the way.

When I arrived, I took off my shoes. I hung my stockings on a willow branch. Then I sat on the edge of the bank, and dabbled my toes. One drinks in so much inspiration while one is dabbling one's toes in a willow creek. And one does hear the talkings of plants that dwell near unto the water.

While I was dabbling my toes, my legs did have longings to go in wading. But I went not in. Something might have happened to what was left of that dozen eggs the mamma was sending straight to Mrs. Limberger. And that was why I did not go. And I did not take Felix Mendelssohn out of the pocket he was riding in, that he might dabble his toes. I took him not out, for he has no longings to dabble his toes in a brook. He has prefers to dabble his toes in *cheese*. (Though I do feel most certain one doesn't get near so much inspirations when one dabbles one's toes in cheese as one gets when one dabbles one's toes in waters that sing.)

After I did take in a goodly amount of inspirations, I drew my toes away from the water and let the sun dry my feet, so I could put my stockings on. While I was lacing my shoes up, I looked looks around, to see what was near about. A little way distant was a haystack.

When I did have my shoes most laced up to the top, I gave the strings a tuck-in and started on. I saw a *bourdon* [bumblebee]. He was plump in body, and he did give a plump buzz. I did halt to screwtineyes him, and to listen to more of those plump buzzings of his. They were cool sounds — what ones I did hear were so. He was a bourdon in a hurry, and he went on in a quick way.

And I went on in a slow way. The sun was so hot it made me squint my eyes, so I put my bonnet on. That made things better.

Pretty soon, I met Elizabeth Barrett Browning. Then we went walking across the field. I took off my sunbonnet and tied it on Elizabeth Barrett Browning, so the sun wouldn't bother her eyes. And she did go her way, and I did go mine. We shall meet again at the pasture-bars, when comes eventime.

When I did say good-bye to Elizabeth Barrett Browning, I went the way that leads to this haystack. And here I have stopped. A haystack is such an interesting place. It's a nice place to explore. *I* think so; *mice* think so. Sometimes — quite often — when I am crawling back in a haystack I do meet a mouse, which is very nice, for mice are nice folks to know.

And now today, when I did crawl back away under the straw, I did feel something. What I did find made me feel gratitudes from my curls to my toes. It was a nest full of eggs, and nobody had used an egg from it! There are — there were — just fifteen eggs under the hay. They are not near so white as are those eight eggs the mamma is sending straight to Mrs. Limberger, but they do have more smooth feels. Oh, such satin feels! They are so slick they came most slipping right out of my hands, but they didn't.

Four and two I have took. I have put them here in the pail. I do know Mrs. Limberger does so like to have things with satin feels about her. I have heard her expressions so, when I was taking eggs to her before. Now I think she will beam delights all over her plumpness when she does see the satin-feel eggs in this pail. I have placed them on top, so she will see them first of all. Too, I think her eyes will kink when she finds she has got a dozen eggs and two. I wonder what she will be doing with those two extra eggs. Now I'll just get a hurry on me, and take them straight to her. And I will hide these printings of today in a little box here in the haystack, until comes eventime. And I will come back again for them when I come to meet Elizabeth Barrett Browning at the pasture-bars.

I'm back again. I did go straight from this haystack with the two and dozen eggs to the door of the house of Mrs. Limberger. When I did get there, she was talking with a woman. The woman was the beautiful Sadie McKibben, and she wore upon her a new dress like the blossoms of *avalon* growing in the marshes, and there were freckles on it like the freckles on her face, and both were beautiful. Also did Mrs. Limberger wear a new dress. It was black and had a yellow stripe in it, like unto one of those yellow stripes the garter-snake wears on his back.

When I did walk soft upon the porch, they were so busy talking they heard me not. I reached out the eggs. Yet they were so busy talking they saw them not. Then I did edge over to Sadie McKibben. I gave her sleeve a little pull. She looked down at me and smiled. She went on talking. She gave each one of my curls a smooth-out, while she talked on.

When she did get most done with her part of the conversation, Mrs. Limberger did happen to see the eggs I was holding out to her. She reached and took them. I was glad. But my arm was the most glad part of me, because it did have a tired feeling from holding the bucket out so long.

She didn't even notice those satin eggs on top. She did begin to talk about the many ribbons and the many ruffles the new woman wears, that lives up the corduroy road. She talked on and on, and I did wait on for the lard-pail the eggs were in. And I did get fidgety, for she wasn't holding the bucket straight by the middle of its loop, as a bucket ought to be held. I had a little fear she would drop that bucket. That would make a dent in it. And I knew what a spanking I would get if I took that pail home with a dent in it. I did stick my finger in my mouth, to keep from speaking to her about it.

Just when I had feels how that spanking was going to feel, she did take a firm hold on the handle. But she didn't take it in the middle. That did make the bucket to tip. She went on talking. She took a big breath. And two of those satin-feel eggs did roll out. They bounced. They broke. Mrs. Limberger kinked her nose, quick. She put her new black dress to it. Sadie McKibben too did put her new dress to her nose in a quick way. And my apron so did I put to *my* nose. Now this I know, for there I learned: An egg with a satin feel may feel proper, but inside it is not so; and if it gets a fall, it is only a queer odor that one does have longings to run away from.

But Mrs. Limberger made me stay right there, and carry water from the pump and scrub all the bad odors off her back porch. I think some of them odors wasn't from the two eggs with satin feels. When I confided my feelings about the matter to Felix Mendelssohn, Mrs. Limberger did tell me to go on scrubbing. She said whatever smells might have been there, you couldn't get a whiff of, on account of the multiplications of smells that came from the two eggs. Sadie McKibben did help me to scrub. She did ask Mrs. Limberger not to mention the matter to the mamma. Also, she said she was going by that way tomorrow, and would bring the four eggs to make up the dozen.

When I started home, Sadie McKibben did give to me a good-bye kiss on each cheek. She knew how I do long for kisses, and how the mamma hasn't time to give me any.

When I walked by Mrs. Limberger, I did look the

other way. As I passed, she gave me a pat. And when she did, Felix Mendelssohn squeaked. When she gave me the pat, it went through my dress onto the back of the head of Felix Mendelssohn, in a pocket in my underskirt. And he being a mouse of musical tendency does object to being patted on the back of the head — he prefers to have pats on his *throat*. And he won't let anybody give them but me.

I went on in a hurry to home. The mamma came a little ways from the door to meet me. Behind her was a switch — I saw both ends sticking out. I did give my skirt a shake, so Felix Mendelssohn would get out and away. It would be awful for him to get hurt by a whipping. It might hurt his soul.

After the mamma did tend to me as usual, I put some Mentholatum on the places where the whip did hit most hard. Then I did go to take eggs to the folks that live hereabout. I went in a hurry. After that, there were baby clothes to be washed, and wood to be brought in. Then the mamma told me to go find my sun-bonnet, and not to come back until I did find it. I went again to the altar of Good King Edward I, to pray. Then I went to the nursery and the hospital, and came again here, where I print.

Now I do see Elizabeth Barrett Browning at the pasture-bars, and she has got my sun-bonnet on. I knew we would meet again at eventide at the pasture-bars, for often we do. And often on hot days, she wears my sun-bonnet until we meet again. It does so help to keep the sun from hurting her beautiful eyes.

## Thirty-seven

## The Song of Saint Louis, and the Strange Sound in the Woods

Very early in the morning of today, I did go unto the cathedral, for this is the going-away day of Saint Louis, in 1270. I went there to sing a thank song for his goodness, and to say prayers. I did sing the song of Saint Louis that Angel Father did teach me to sing. The little leaves on the bushes growing there under the grand trees — their little leaves did whisper little whispers. I have thinks those little whispers were thank songs for the goodness of Saint Louis. Sometimes I did hear little bird voices, in-between the singing of the songs. I have thinks they were singing the same thank song I did sing, only they were singing it in their way. And when I came again home, the brook was singing the same song.

After other works was done at the house we live in on this morning, the mamma did have me to stand on a box on a chair and give to the windows some washes. Then she did have me to give the steps some scrubs. While I so did, I looked looks about. On the porch-end was a little spider. He made moves in a little, quick way. A *guêpe* came near unto him. She made no stops. She came on to him. She did carry that spider away.

Pretty soon, I did have those steps all clean — nice and clean. Then the mamma did have me to help her to take the children to the house of her mamma. She and they stayed there all day. I so did not do. When they were come to the door of the ranch house, I did go goes in the way that goes to the pasture-bars. I so did go to tell the folks in the pasture what day it was.

It was most warm when I was come to the far end of the pasture. The folks of the pasture were not out in the sun. They were in shade. Elizabeth Barrett Browning was under a big chêne tree. She did look gentle looks at me. And I did put my arm around her neck, and tell her all about whose day it was. Then I went on to tell the gentle Jersey cow. She was near some more chêne trees. I went on. She followed after. She did come with me as far as the brook. I watched her take a long drink.

The day, it was so warm. Elizabeth Barrett Browning did come for a drink. I had thinks of Aphrodite in the pig-pen. I looked looks about for the little bucket I do carry drinks of water in to my friends. I found it where I did hide it, by the willow bush. Then I did go to take a drink of cold water to Aphrodite in the pig-pen. These warm days, she does have longings for a drink of cold water. She did grunt grunts of appreciations. Then she did grunt another grunt. I have thinks that other grunt was to tell me not to have forgets to take a drink of cold water to Cassiopée. I so did. (Cassiopée is a pig that does belong to the man that our lane does belong to.)

After I did tell them all about it being the going-away day of Saint Louis, I did go my way to the garden. The

golden rod did nod, *"It is good that he is born."* The tall
sunflowers in the garden there did say, *"It is his day, it
is his day."* I went adown the carrot-rows. They were all
whispering soft whispers. I have thinks they were saying
little thank prayers for the goodness of Saint Louis. The
cabbage plants were all smiling, as I passed them by. I
think they are right glad for the drink of water I gave
each one of them last night.

From the garden, I did go to tell other folks. I did
sing the little song of Saint Louis as I did go along. The
sun, it was hot down on my head. I took two big maple
leaves, and they did some help to keep its warmness
from my head. I went on.

Once at the edge of the near woods, I met with my
dear Thomas Chatterton Jupiter Zeus. We went on
together. I did carry him in one arm, and I did hold a
maple leaf over him with the other hand. A long way
we went, in about and out about, and many little folks
we did tell about this day being the going-away day of
Saint Louis.

By-and-by, after it was a very long time, there was no
sun. The warmness did have a different feel. There
were gray clouds in the sky — some were darkness. I
did go in hurry steps. I went not from the road. I did
go the way it went around the bend. More dark clouds
did roll across the sky; more grayness was over all.
Thomas Chatterton Jupiter Zeus in my bonnet did
make a move — I did almost drop him. I made a stop to
wrap him more up in the sun-bonnet. Then I did hurry
on.

I climbed the lane gate — it was more quick to so do
than to pull the plug out that swings the gate open. I
went on. There was a great noise. Thomas Chatterton
Jupiter Zeus poked his nose out of the sun-bonnet. He

cuddled up against me. The great noise came again. I whispered to him, *"Il tonne."* ["It thunders."] We went on. In-between times, there was fire in the sky. It made moves in a quick way. After it was the coming of the great noise. Every time, I did whisper to Thomas Chatterton Jupiter Zeus, "Il tonne." I so did so he would not have thinks the great noise was something else.

When we were come near the ending of the lane, there was some very big pats of rain. One fell on my nose, and it did roll off onto the back of Thomas Chatterton Jupiter Zeus. I cuddled him up more close, as more loud noises did come. When we were at the ending of the lane, there was Brave Horatius, waiting for us. I have thinks he had been on looks for us — his looks did look like he had. We went on together.

We was just a-going to start down the path that does lead to our house, when we did hear a calling. It was a mournful sound. I had thinks some little life was much hurt, and did have needs of my help. I felt for the little box of Mentholatum in my pocket. It was there, and some bandages, too.

The sound came again — somewhere in the near woods, a voice was calling. I followed it after. Once I did have thinks it came from a root. And then it was like it did come from a big tree. It was a pain voice, like someone calling someone to come. Then it was like a lost voice, trying to find its way among the ferns. It was not a word voice; it was just a voice without words.

I did have wonders what voice it was. I followed after its queer callings. Brave Horatius followed after me. He would stop, and look queer puzzle-looks at nowhere. We did go on.

The voice sound came again. Then it was like a voice lost from the person it did belong to. It was a clear, low cry, like a ripple of gray ribbon. We were more near to it. We followed it around a big tree. There it was, come from the man on the stump between that tree and the big tree that was beyond it. The man, he did throw back his head, and the voice came out his throat and went to nowhere. It came again like little bits of queer green fire-flame. And then it was low, and again like a ripple of gray ribbon.

As it was so, he did turn his face about — it was the face of the husband of Sadie McKibben. But the look, the look in his eyes, was a queer, wild look that looked looks at nowhere.

# Thirty-eight

## Opal collects her Necessary Things; she visits Dear Love, and learns a Secret

We are going to move to the mill town. For a whole week every morning now after the morning works is done, the mamma does have me to help her make prepares to move. And after I do be helps to the mamma, then I do work at making prepares for moving my belongings, when we go goes to the mill town.

I have made begins a week ago. I have been carrying my belongings to inside an old log, a little way away from the house we do live in. Moving is a big amount of problem. But mostly now, I do have my prepares done. I am going to take with me when we go goes to the mill town just my necessary things. The mamma does say none but my necessary things can go. She said that was my blue calico apron, and my gray calico apron, and the clothes that goes under them, and my two pair of stockings, and the shoes I have on, and my sunbonnet, and my slate, and *Cyr's Reader*.

But I have some more necessary things that the mamma has not knows of. There is my two books that

Angel Mother and Angel Father did write in and I do study in every day, and the pictures of mother and père, and the pictures of grandmère and grandpère, and tante and tante and oncle, and all the others that I do love much every day. And today there was needs to give the dear picture of père a wash in the brook, because last time on yesterday when I did kiss him, a little piece of jam from my bread and butter got on his dear face that does look so like him. And after I did come from the brook, I put them all away in a careful way in the box I do keep them in, and I said a little prayer.

And I went to bring to the old log the willow whistle the shepherd did make for me when it was the borning time of the lambs, and the two flutes he did make of reeds. And now I do have most of my necessaries in the hollow log.

There by it is the lily plant the soul of Peter Paul Rubens has loves for to be near. And I have planted it in a little flower-pot Sadie McKibben has given to me. And when we are moved moves to the mill town, I will put the lily plant under the window of the room I do have sleeps in, so that what the soul of Peter Paul Rubens does love to be near will be near unto where I am.

And in the hollow log, there is the old logging boot of the husband of Dear Love, that he has given me to keep some of my rock collections in. And there is the bath-towel of Thomas Chatterton Jupiter Zeus that Dear Love has made for him. And there is the color pencils that the fairies did bring to the moss-box. And there is many brown papers that Sadie McKibben has given me to print prints on. And there is the cushion Lola did make for Lucian Horace Ovid Virgil to sit on in my desk at school. And there is all the patches I do pin on my underskirt, for my animal friends to ride in. And there is the track of Elizabeth Barrett Browning that I did dig up in the lane. It has so much of poetry in it. And there is one of the gray neckties of the man that wears gray neckties and is kind to mice, that he did give to me for Brave Horatius to wear. And there is the bib of Elsie's baby, that Elsie did give me for Menander Euripides Theocritus Thucydides to wear when he was nursing the bottle.

And there is seven of the tail-feathers of Lars Porsena, that he did lose when he did lose his tail. And there is four old horse-shoes of William Shakespeare, that the blacksmith did have allows for me to have when he was putting new shoes onto William Shakespeare. And there is the thimble of Dear Love, that she has given me to carry drinks of water to the folks in the hospital. And there is the little bell of Peter Paul Rubens, that he did use to wear to service in the cathedral.

And there is Elsie's baby's little old shoe that got worn out and she gave it to me for Nannerl Mozart to sleep in. And there is the lid of Sadie McKibben's coffee-pot that she did give me when it came off. She always did sing over that lid, when cooking-time was come.

And there is the traveling-case of Minerva, that the *pensée* girl with the far-away look in her eyes did make for me to carry all the christening robes of Minerva's children in; and more pieces of white cloth and little ribbons the *pensée* girl did put into Minerva's traveling-case for christening time come next year. And there is the eggshells Ben Jonson and Sir Francis Bacon and Pius VII and Nicolas Boileau and Edmund Spenser and Oliver Goldsmith and John Fletcher and Francis Beaumont and Cardinal Richelieu and Sir Walter Raleigh and the rest of Minerva's children hatched out of. I have thinks there is needs for me to carry those eggshells in my apron when we go moves to the mill town, so they will not have breaks.

And there is the little gray shawl Sadie McKibben so made for Nannerl Mozart. And there is the little cap that Dear Love did make for my Louis II, le Grand Condé. It has got a feather in it. He did nibble the end off the feather, and he had mouse-wants to chew the tassel that she did put on the bag she did make for me to carry him in. And there is the ribbon bow off Elsie's garter she did give me for Felix Mendelssohn to wear. I have heard the women-folks at the farm house say this world would be a nice world, if there weren't any mice in it. I think it would be a most lonesome place.

And there is the big handkerchief of the man of the long step that whistles most all of the time, that he did give to me for Brave Horatius to wear around his neck. And there is Elsie's old lace collar, that Elizabeth Barrett Browning does wear to cathedral service. And there is one of the whiskers of Thomas Chatterton Jupiter Zeus, that he did lose.

And there is all the portraits of my friends on poker-chips. And there is the other white poker-chips that are waiting waits for pictures to be drawed on them. And there is the blue and the red poker-chips that is the breakfast and supper plates of the folks in the nursery and the hospital.

And there is Minerva's white cap that she does wear to cathedral service, with the ruffles on it like are on the morning cap of Jenny Strong. And there is the long green string I pulled my tooth with. And there is the split jacket of Padre Martini that he did last wear before he was become a grown-up *cigale* [grasshopper]. And there is the bottle of Menander Euripides Theocritus Thucydides, the bottle that used to be a brandy bottle. And there is the skins of the caterpillars they did grow too big for when they were growing into *papillons* and *phalènes* [butterflies and moths]. And there is the two tail-feathers of Agamemnon Menelaus Dindon.

And there is Solomon Grundy's christening robe. And there is the little fleur watering-pot the fairies did bring, that I do give my friends shower-baths with. And there is the cocoon that Charlotte Brontë, the big velvet brown phalène, did hatch out of. And there is more cocoons that other phalènes did hatch out of. And there is the ribbon bow Elsie has given me off her other garter, for the pet squirrel Geoffroi Chaucer that the cat did hurt, but is well again.

And there is a whole new box of Mentholatum that Sadie McKibben has given me for the little folks I find with hurts in the mill town. And there is the four Vaseline bottles that got empty after the young husband of Elsie did use all the Vaseline in them to keep his pumpadoor smooth. I have uses for those Vaseline bottles — to keep food in, for the folks of the nursery.

These things I have now in the log. Others of my necessary things I will bring this eventime, and on to-morrow, and the next day, and the day after that.

Some of us go to the mill town, but not all of us so go. Dear Solomon Grundy is sold to a man that does live at one of the edges of the mill town. Aphrodite is going to stay stays here, and so is Mathilde Plantagenet, and Elizabeth Barrett Browning, and Anthonya Mundy, and the gentle Jersey cow, and Savonarola, and Agamemnon Menelaus Dindon. And Plato and Pliny are going to live on in the barn. Brave Horatius is going goes with Aidan of Iona come from Lindisfarne, and too Menander Euripides Theocritus Thucydides is going with the shepherd to the blue hills.

Minerva is going to town with us, and so is Sir Francis Bacon and Ben Jonson and Pius VII and Nicolas Boileau and Sir Walter Raleigh and all the rest of her dear children, and Clementine and Napoleon and Andromeda. And by-and-by, Thomas Chatterton Jupiter Zeus is coming comes to the mill town. And so is Felix Mendelssohn, and Louis II, le Grand Condé, and Nannerl Mozart and some of her children, and Lucian Horace Ovid Virgil, and Geoffroi Chaucer, and the caterpillar-folks in the nursery. All are, when I do have homes fixed for them about the house we are going to live in in the mill town.

Until then, Thomas Chatterton Jupiter Zeus is going to stay with Dear Love and her husband. And too Dear Love does say Lucian Horace Ovid Virgil can live under her doorstep until I do have a place fixed for him under the doorstep of the house we are going to live in in the mill town. And Sadie McKibben is going to take care of Geoffroi Chaucer, and bring him in to me at the house we are going to live in at the mill town. And the man that wears gray neckties and is kind to mice is going to take care of all my mouse friends in his bunk-house, and he is going goes to feed the folks in the nursery and the hospital.

And often it is I am going to come comes back again here to cathedral service and talks with them I know, and to leave letters for the fairies in the moss-box. I have thinks about the mill town. Maybe in the fields over on the other side of the mill town — maybe there there will be *étourneau*, and *ortolan*, and *draine*, and *durbec*, and *loriot*, and *verdier*, and *rossignol*, and *pinson*, and *pivoine*. When I am come to the mill town, I will go explores to see. And I will build altars for Saint Louis. Now I go to see Dear Love.

When I was come near unto her little house, I had seeing of Dear Love. She was sitting on the steps by her door, drying her hair in the sun. It did wave little ripples of light when the wind did go in a gentle way by. She let me have feels of its touches. And she did give me a kiss on each cheek and one on the nose, when she lifted me onto her lap. And then Dear Love did tell me a secret — it's hers and her husband's secret, that the angels did let them know ahead: They are going to have a baby soon.

I felt a big amount of satisfaction. It is about time that prayer was answered. Some prayers you pray a little while, and answers come. Some prayers you pray more times, and answers *don't* come. I have not knows of why. But prayers for babies get answered soon, most always they do. The time is so long I have been praying prayers for Dear Love to have a baby soon. And now the angels have told her it's going to come in about five months. I have thinks that is quite a time long to wait waits.

And Dear Love has showed me the clothes the angels did tell her to make ahead for its coming. And there is two little shirts and bands, and very long underskirts with featherstitches in them. And there's a little cream kimona with a blue ribbon bow on it. I looked looks at it a long time. And Dear Love said she was going to make one just like it for Thomas Chatterton Jupiter Zeus. I am glad.

And there was more little clothes. And while we was looking at them, the husband of Dear Love did come in the door, and he did look adores at Dear Love. It's just our secret; just Dear Love's and her husband's and mine.

Nobody knows it but just us three — and Thomas Chatterton Jupiter Zeus, and Brave Horatius, and Edward I, and lovely Queen Eleanor of Castile, and Michael Angelo Sanzio Raphael, and Aphrodite, and Lucian Horace Ovid Virgil, and Felix Mendelssohn, and Plato and Pliny, and Minerva and her chickens, and Menander Euripides Theocritus Thucydides, and Louis II, le Grand Condé, and the willows that grow by Nonette.

Now Brave Horatius and me and Thomas Chatterton Jupiter Zeus are going to prayers in the cathedral. The great pine tree is saying a poem, and there is a song in the tree-tops.

*Opal,* 1919
(The Bodley Head, Ltd.)

# Postscript — 1920

After this I lived in a great many other lumber camps, and there were new people, and new animal friends, and new nurseries, and other cathedrals. I studied in the woods and wrote down what I saw and heard. In the spring of 1918, I went from Oregon to Southern California to do more research work in natural science, earning my way by teaching nature classes. In the winter of 1918, I published my first nature-book, paying for it by taking orders for it in advance.

In the summer of 1919, I came East, hoping to be able to get another nature-book published. In my going to see publishers, I came to the editor of the *Atlantic*. While I was telling the editor about this book, he asked me if I never kept a diary, and this is the answer.

After the seventh year, and far on into other years, I continued the diary. But perhaps some other time, the story of all these things will be pieced together and made into another book.

# NAPSBURY
# AND
# BEYOND

ON THE MORNING OF January 16, 1985, a train pulled out of London's King's Cross Station, on its way to the city of St. Albans. Even in winter, St. Albans is a popular attraction, because of its cathedral, Roman ruins, and museum. But one traveler on the train — myself — was going there to visit a building of another kind: Napsbury, a brick fortress of a hospital built in the 1890s as a lunatic asylum. I was going to attempt to see one of its patients — a woman registered under the name of Françoise d'Orléans. Years ago, she had been known as Opal Whiteley.

The train moved slowly from the station. Outside the window, grimy buildings seemed to float by in the fog, like a procession of ghosts. In the snow-reflected light, everything appeared unreal. As the train accelerated, the sight of a blurred, whitened London receded from my thoughts as memory after memory arose to haunt my mind. It seemed a long time ago that I'd first read *The Story of Opal* and begun to research the life of its author. Yet only a few months had passed.

Leaning back in the seat, I recalled the late nights I'd spent going over interview notes under dim light bulbs in cheap motels, my eyes out of focus from examining reel upon reel of microfilmed newspaper and magazine articles. I remembered walking unsteadily back to my lodgings at the end of each day, weak from ignored hunger and the persistent effort of searching through cartons of letters, clippings, and photographs.

One by one, the pieces of the puzzle of Opal Whiteley's life had fallen into place. Yet one mystery remained: Had she written her diary as a little girl, or had she forged it as a young woman, as her many critics claimed? Then one day, while looking through one of the boxes in the Opal Whiteley collection at the University of Oregon, I came across a copy of the letter that had provided the cornerstone for the diary's defamation — that from Opal's six-month hostess in Los Angeles to the editor of the Cottage Grove *Sentinel*. As I read it, sunlight seemed to break through the thick walls of the Special Collections room. For within it, I saw unmistakable evidence that the case against Opal Whiteley had been a fabrication. Similar discoveries followed, and soon the investigation became a race against time, in the effort to clear Opal's name and gain some sort of recognition for her while she was still alive.

I drafted a biography of Opal Whiteley and repunctuated her long-out-of-print diary pages, using her name for their setting as the title. I also wrote a screenplay based upon the diary — as a precaution against Hollywood sensationalizing her story — and registered it under the same name. After a while, though, I began to wonder what my efforts were accomplishing. For by the time I left for England, *The Singing Creek Where the Willows Grow* had been rejected by eight major New York publishers and appeared on its way to being turned down by the ninth.

They said it wasn't commercial. Opal wasn't a genius. She had little to offer today's readers. Her diary was sentimental and trite. She couldn't have written it as a child. Neither could the skeptics have engineered its rapid decline in popularity, deliberately or not. Moreover, my biography wasn't necessary. It was too long. It was too short. I was going overboard in my defense of Opal Whiteley. One editor summed up the general attitude toward Opal's diary when she wrote: "I don't see it as literary, as poetic, or as mystical."

I had learned from experience not to accept publishers' judgments without question. In a vague and intuitive way, I'd known I'd come across something extraordinary as soon

as I'd pulled *The Story of Opal* from a shelf at the Multnomah County Library in Portland, and had glanced
through its pages. And the more I'd looked into the events
connected with that book, the stronger the conviction had
become. If I hadn't believed in the drawing power of Opal
Whiteley, I certainly wouldn't have continued on this
grueling journey, one that had already taken me back eighty
years in time, and that was now leading me relentlessly
onward, thousands of miles from home.

Daydreaming to the sound of the rails, I recalled the
morning I'd gone to Walden, Oregon, to search for the
singing creek. I had taken with me a copy of *The Story of
Opal* and duplicates of some photographs taken sometime
after the book's publication had brought temporary fame to
the town of Cottage Grove. The pictures showed the front
of the ranch house, the school, and the bridge over the
"rivière." The latter two structures had been rebuilt before
the time of the photographs — the bridge had been covered,
and the schoolhouse enlarged.

No one I'd asked seemed to remember exactly where the
Whiteleys had lived when Opal was six years old. After
all, it had been a long time ago, and the family had moved
quite often. Some people said their house had been at one
location; some said at another. But I knew where I was
going to start looking. For on the way to one of my first
interviews, I'd driven past an area that had *felt* right — at
the Y-shaped intersection where Layng Road stopped at
Mosby Creek Road, the highway running east from Cottage
Grove. The farther I'd gone from it, the colder the feeling
had grown.

And often it is I go from the willows to the meeting of
the road. That is just in front of the ranch house.
There the road does have divides. It goes three ways.

I saw no house at the intersection. On the north side
were railroad tracks. On the south side, where Layng Road

would have gone had it continued, was a field. The ranch house had probably been torn down years ago, I thought. That left the bridge and the school as landmarks. At first glance, the covered bridge in the photograph could have been any of three similar bridges in the area. And there was at least a slight chance that whoever had photographed it had photographed the wrong one. I'd been told the Walden schoolhouse still existed, and that it had been built at the same location as the one Opal had attended school in. So I decided to start with it, then backtrack.

The road does go the way I go when I go to the school-house where I go to school. . . . As it goes, its way is near unto the way of the rivière that sings as it comes from the blue hills.

I found the schoolhouse about half a mile east of the intersection, on the south side of Mosby Creek Road. It was now someone's home. The belfry had been glassed in and a few other details had been changed, but it was essentially the same as in the photograph, including even the school-yard fence.

Across the road from it ran Mosby Creek, so large it might have been called a river. I walked alongside it, re-membering Opal's words:

Today it is I do sit here at my desk, while the children are out for play at recess-time. I sit here and I do print. I cannot have goings to talk with the trees that I do mostly have talks with at recess-time. I cannot have goings down to the rivière across the road, like I do so go sometimes at recess-time. I sit here in my seat. Teacher says I must stay in all this whole recess-time.

I got in the car, and drove back toward the intersection. A short distance before it, on the north side of the high-way, was a road I hadn't noticed before. I turned onto it. Jenkins Road, the sign said. It ran diagonally from Mosby

Creek Road, crossed Layng Road, then curved a bit and continued in a neglected fashion through the grass by the railroad tracks, heading west toward Cottage Grove. At its junction with Layng Road, I turned north on the latter, and drove toward the "rivière."

The other road does lead to the upper logging camps. It goes only a little way from the ranch house, and it comes to a rivière. Long time ago, this road did have a longing to go across the rivière. Some wise people did have understandings, and they did build it a bridge to go across on. It went across the bridge, and it goes on and on between the hills — the hills where dwell the talking fir trees.

Soon I came to Mosby Creek Bridge. I parked and walked up to it. It seemed to match the one in the photograph, although the surroundings were different. I walked across it, looking down at the water rushing by. Then I returned to the car and drove back to the intersection.

One way, the road does go to the house of Sadie McKibben. It doesn't stop when it gets to her house, but mostly I do. The road just goes on to the mill town, a little way away. In its going, it goes over a hill. Sometimes . . . I do go with Brave Horatius to the top of the hill. We look looks down upon the mill town. Then we do face about, and come again home. Always we make stops at the house of Sadie McKibben. Her house, it is close to the mill by the far woods.

I decided to investigate forgotten-looking Jenkins Road. By the railroad tracks, I turned onto it and followed it in the direction of Cottage Grove. For a little over half a mile, it ran parallel with Mosby Creek, between it and the highway. Then it turned south at a right angle, connected with Mosby Creek Road, and proceeded beyond it under another name. I began to wonder if it had originally continued into town. If so, it would have provided access to the mills that I'd been told had been located along Mosby Creek and Row River, which joined the creek a short distance west. In that case, I thought, the Mosby Creek Road of today wouldn't have existed then. After all, why would there have been two parallel thoroughfares so close together?

I drove back on the highway, looking for a creek somewhere south of the road. Just after I passed the intersection, I noticed a small, curving side road on the south side of the highway, its entrance directly opposite that of Jenkins Road. The sign said Walden Lane. I turned into it, and nearly ran across someone's lawn — for there to my right was the ranch house. It was facing Walden Lane, at an angle to the highway; so when I'd first driven past it, I'd only seen part of its side. It was farther east of the intersection than I'd expected — at least, farther from where the intersection was *now* — but it was unquestionably the right house. It seemed to come right out of the photograph.

Between the ranch house and the house we live in is the singing creek where the willows grow.

I left the car and started circling around, like a bloodhound trying to find a scent. "Excuse me," I called to a woman who had walked out to her mailbox. "Is there a creek around here? Not Mosby Creek — a smaller one, somewhere over there . . ." "There is," she said, pointing in the direction of a modern house beyond the ranch house. "Up that long driveway, across the field." "That's private property, isn't it?" I asked. "My aunt and uncle live there," she replied. I showed her the photographs, and tried to briefly explain what I was doing. "Just ask them," she said. "They'll let you take a look." I thanked her and started up the driveway. In the distance I saw a line of oak trees, and what looked like signs of water.

I walked beside the rapidly flowing creek, listening to its happy, singing sound. There had been willows along it, the

336

man at the house had told me; and beyond the creek, an old house and barn. There hadn't been many other houses in the area, he'd said. He'd passed them as a boy, as he rode into town on horseback. From him I learned that Walden Lane, which the ranch house faced, had been part of the main road years ago, which had continued to Cottage Grove along what is now called Jenkins Road.

I watched the water as it hurried along. The creek must have been bigger, I thought, before the trees in the area were removed. Before crossing the field to see it, I'd asked the man who lived in the ranch house what it was called. "Carolyn Creek, Carolina Creek — something like that," he'd said. He'd seen the name on a map. *Caroling* Creek would fit it better, I thought. It sang on in a high-pitched, silvery voice, like the tinkling of little bells.

I looked at my watch, then consulted the train schedule on the seat beside me. St. Albans was only a few minutes away. Soon I would be at Napsbury. But the closer I came to it, the more I wondered whether I would be able to see the woman I had come so far to meet. As I had done many times before, I thought over the history of my contact with the institution, and with people who had visited Opal Whiteley in the recent past:

In September, 1984, I wrote to the hospital administrators, asking that I be allowed to visit the patient known to them as Françoise d'Orléans, "The Princess." In my letter, I stated that I was researching her life for a biography I was writing of her, and that meeting her would be an extremely valuable experience for me. "I am aware of her mental state," I wrote, "having talked to several people who have visited her . . . so I don't expect much in the way of factual information."

After I'd sent the letter, a few people told me that during their visits, they had been discouraged or prevented from photographing Opal or asking her about her past. One man had recorded an interview with her in 1978, in which he asked many questions about her life history. A duplicate recording was subsequently filed with the Oregon Historical Society, which made a partial transcript of it. Two years later, he told me, he and his wife returned to Napsbury to see Opal. He said that they were told at that time that they could not record the conversation or write any of it down. Such a requirement would not present an obstacle for me, however. Years ago when I investigated alleged criminals, who tended to stop talking at the sight of notebooks and pens, I trained myself to memorize conversations. The critical question was: Would I be *allowed* to have a conversation with "Françoise d'Orléans," recorded or not? While I waited for a response from the hospital, I received a letter from a contact in England who had not found Opal's psychiatrist helpful in the past, "especially if he suspects one is writing about her."

No reply to my letter arrived from Napsbury Hospital.

While I waited for a publisher to accept the manuscript — and send an author's advance for it with which I could finance a journey overseas — I wrote to people in England who were familiar with Opal's situation, one of whom had obtained some of her remaining notebooks and letters. My plan was to spend as many weeks in England as were necessary for interviews and research. That was going to take quite a bit of money, and I was considerably in debt, thanks to ten years of writing book manuscripts while working part time as a tree pruner. But I believed that sooner or later a publisher would see the sales potential of *The Singing Creek*. As the months went by, though, I became increasingly uneasy, for I knew that Opal's time was running out.

While I waited, I received a letter from an acquaintance in England confirming a rumor I had heard — Opal had fallen and broken her hip. Finally, I realized I couldn't wait any longer. With the road to financial ruin looming ahead in my imagination, I managed to borrow some money and buy an economy airline ticket. After hurried communications with contacts in England, I left Oregon ahead of an announced ice-storm, and arrived in London shortly before freezing snow closed Gatwick Airport in the coldest winter in twenty years.

The wind moaned in the ventilator above the window. In the distance, it scattered small puffs of snow across the frozen fields. Now the scenery was changing; more and more houses were coming into view, then other buildings. They streamed by, then slowed and stopped as the train pulled into the city of St. Albans.

From the station, I took a bus to the center of town. There I was told that no buses went to the hospital, so I hired a cab. We traveled on and on, along increasingly lonely roads. Finally we came to the hospital entrance gate, drove down the long road, and arrived at the main building. I paid the driver and the cab pulled away, leaving me with an odd, abandoned feeling. Beyond where I stood, the winding road continued to the rest of the complex. I looked up at the old brick structure in front of me, surmounted by a medieval-looking tower capped with a turret. Then I stepped inside.

I told the man behind the information window that I'd come to visit a patient in Oak Ward named Françoise d'Orléans. He escorted me to an unmarked door. In the office behind it, I sat down and waited for the woman at the only occupied desk to finish her telephone conversation. A man entered the room, sat down at a desk, and asked if he could be of assistance. I told him I'd come to see Françoise d'Orléans. "Oh, yes," he said. "You're the one who sent the letter." He told me to talk to the woman I'd been waiting for.

The woman hung up. I told her I'd come to see Françoise d'Orléans. She asked if I had written. I said I had, and told her my name. She went to a filing cabinet, pulled out the letter, and returned to her desk. "So you're planning to write a book about her," she said. "Most likely," I replied. "You won't get much out of her," she said, looking up.

"From what people have told me," I answered, "I don't *expect* to get much out of her. I've read her two books, and was very impressed by them. I'm trying to make sure that her manuscripts are preserved. I've been talking to people over here about that. I just wanted to meet her, and tell her how much I've enjoyed her writing."

The woman picked up the telephone receiver. "She's been moved to another ward," she said, dialing. After a brief conversation, she hung up. "She's in a restricted category," she told me. "Her condition is deteriorating. There is a list of allowed visitors — family members and friends. Your name is not on it." She gave me the name and telephone number of Opal's psychiatrist in Watford. "Perhaps you could ring him up and explain your situation." I thanked her and went in search of a public telephone.

I found one; but when I tried it, it didn't work. Someone told me there was a telephone by the cafeteria — around the corner, down another hall. As I approached it, a woman wearing a cafeteria worker's uniform came out of the kitchen door and walked in my direction, talking to herself. Then she leaned against the wall and sang a plaintive song. Somehow, she seemed to personify the spirit of the place.

The telephone worked. At the other end of the line, a secretary answered. I asked to speak to the doctor. She said he was out, and asked if she could help. I explained my situation, and she told me the doctor would be back in an hour and a half.

Ninety minutes later, I dialed the psychiatrist's office again. The secretary asked my name, and then asked what patient I was calling about. I told her. "One moment," she said. After what seemed like quite a while, she came back on the line. "The doctor says that she is not allowed visitors unless they are on a special list, and that your name is not on the list. He says that if you want to know more, you must talk to the administration." "I *did*," I replied, "and they referred me to the doctor. I've come a long way to see Miss d'Orléans, and I'd like to explain the situation to her doctor." "I'm afraid there's nothing we can do," said the secretary. "In other words," I said, "the doctor refuses to talk to me." "Yes, at the moment," she replied. "I see," I said, wondering at what moment he might *not* refuse. I thanked her and hung up.

For several minutes I walked around the building, trying to ascertain whether or not it would be possible to get beyond the barriers in my way. I concluded that it would not be wise to try. A forced visit could hardly be productive — or uninterrupted — I thought, even if I were able to manage one. And I sensed that an attempt to do so at that time would weaken my chances of being allowed a comfortable meeting with "the princess" at a later date, if she recovered any of her health. I had doubts she would. On the other hand, I reflected, she had kept herself alive for several weeks since the accident — not to mention the nearly thirty-seven years she'd spent in the hospital *before* it — so who could say?

I called the local taxi company for a return ride. No cabs were available, I was told, and none would be for some time. It was going to be a long walk, and I needed to start soon, for the surroundings were draining my energy. But there was one more part of Napsbury I wanted to see before I left.

I stepped out into the snow, and followed the hospital road to the last building of the complex. On its third floor was the ward that had housed Opal until recently. It rose above me like an elevated dungeon. I looked up at it for a long time. "Is this how the story of Opal Whiteley ends?" I asked myself. "With Opal disgraced, forgotten, condemned to oblivion for something she didn't do?" Suddenly the tiredness left me. *"Not if I can help it,"* I answered.

I turned and walked away, down the long road to the entrance gate. To my left, I saw a grove of trees. In it, birds were singing, sheltered from the snow and icy wind. I stood watching and listening for a moment, tempted to join them for a while and forget the inharmonious world of man. But I had notes to write, people to consult, and papers to go through, and time was running out. As I walked on, the words of a familiar poem seemed to echo in my foot-steps:

> The woods are lovely, dark, and deep,
> But I have promises to keep,
> And miles to go before I sleep. . . .

Light was already beginning to fade from the sky as the train pulled out of the station at St. Albans, on its return trip to London. For a few minutes, I stared out the window, thinking over the events of the day. Then I looked down at the book in my lap: *The Story of Opal.*

It had been published nearly sixty-five years ago, I thought, and had been written fifteen years before that. Two years after I'd been born, its author had been taken to Napsbury. There she had waited, as her book had waited, for someone to come along, someone who understood . . .

I held up the book and started to read it at random, as I had done many times before.

Now are come the days of brown leaves. They fall from the trees; they flutter on the ground. When the brown leaves flutter, they are saying little things. They talk with the wind. I hear them tell of their borning days, when they did come into the world as leaves. And they whisper of the hoods they wore then. I saw them — I used to count them, on the way to school. Today they were talking of the time before their born-ing days of this springtime. They talked on and on, and I did listen on to what they were telling the wind and the earth in their whisperings. They told how they were a part of earth and air, before their tree-borning days. And now they are going back. In gray days of winter, they go back to the earth again. But they do not die.

I recalled what a psychic once told me about schizo-phrenia — that a certain degree of the illness can enable one to "tune in" to other dimensions of existence and other forms of life, and "hear" thoughts as voices, as do people of developed mystical and psychic abilities. But as the disease progresses, it seems, the voices become illusions manufactured or misinterpreted by the malfunctioning mind, as heightened perception deteriorates into hallucination.

Young Opal heard the voices of life around her . . .

All the time it does take to wash the clothes of the baby — it is a long time. And I do stop at in-between times, to listen to the voices. They are always talking. And the brook that does go by our house is always bringing songs from the hills. . . .

I lay my ear close to the earth, where the grasses grew close together. I did listen. The wind made ripples on the grass as it went over. There were voices from out the earth. And the things of their saying were the things of gladness of growing. And there was music. And in the music, there was sky-twinkles and earth-tinkles that was come of the joy of living. . . .

We went on along the dim trail. There by the dim trail grow the honeysuckles. I nod to them as I go that way. In the daytime, I hear them talk with sunbeams and the wind. They talk in shadows with the little people of the sun. And this I have learned: Grownups do not know the language of shadows.

The world Opal passed through was alive with thoughts . . .

When we were gone a little way on from the very tall trees, in the sky, the light of day was going from blue to silver. And thoughts had coming down the road to meet us. They were thoughts from out the mountains where are the mines. They were thoughts from the canyons that come down to meet the road by the rivière. I did feel their coming close about us — very near they were, and all about. We went on a little way, only. We went very slow. We had listens to the thoughts. They were thoughts of blooming-time and coming-time — they were the soul-thoughts of little things that soon will have their borning-time. . . .

Every day now, I do look for thoughts in flowers. Sometimes they are hidden away in the flower-bell, and sometimes I find them on a wild rose, and sometimes they are among the ferns; and sometimes I climb away up in the trees to look looks for them. So many thoughts do abide near unto us. They come from heaven, and live among the flowers and the ferns; and often I find them in the trees. I do so love to go on searches for the thoughts that do dwell near about.

When little Opal said the animals and flowers talked to her, people thought that she was lying. Years later, when she refused to acknowledge that her childhood adoption story was a fantasy, readers and critics concluded she was trying to deceive them. All her life, in one way or another — with spankings or scoldings, criticisms or rejections — she was punished for being schizophrenic. As her illness grew worse, it took her away from the world she loved, and trapped her in a dominion of shadows and ghosts. It robbed her of her once-great energy and ambition, isolated her from other people, and destroyed every chance she had for happiness.

By the time I'd left for Napsbury, I had examined some of the notebooks and other writings found among Opal's possessions in Hampstead. It had been an indescribably depressing experience to read them as they progressed through the years — to see within them the steady deterioration of her abilities and thoughts, as well as of her handwriting; to see the intriguing beginnings of books that *might* have been disintegrate into incoherence.

I turned the pages of *The Story of Opal* and began to read again.

As I did go along, I did have wonders if mothers can see the little song-notes that dance about their babies's cradles when they sing lullaby songs to them.

There were so many questions I wanted to ask, about the contents of practically every page. But I knew "the princess" was not the one to answer them. Too many years had gone by, too many changes had taken place within her mind, for her to be able to tell me precisely what she'd seen and heard at the age of six or seven. Suddenly I realized that there was someone else I wanted to meet, someone quite different from Françoise d'Orléans, the alleged daughter of French royalty. I wanted to meet Opal Whiteley, the little girl who danced in the forest. And I knew I never would.

The months following my return from England were bleak ones for me. By June 1985, fifteen publishers had rejected the manuscript for *The Singing Creek Where the Willows Grow*. Unable to borrow any more money to live on while I wrote, I very reluctantly stopped working on the book and returned to pruning trees for a living. Not only had I failed to find some support for the rerelease of Opal's diary, I had apparently wrecked my future as an author. For I had invested every available bit of time, energy, and money in my research, putting aside other writing projects in the process. Now I had nothing to spend on any of them. While I pruned, publishers rejected. By the end of September, the proposed book had been turned down by twenty publishing houses.

Then came word from my untiring agent that the independent-minded New York publisher Ticknor & Fields and its Boston parent company, Houghton Mifflin, had examined the manuscript and were enthusiastic about its potential. I soon had an encouraging conversation with Ticknor & Fields editor Katrina Kenison, whose fondness for Opal and her writing was obvious. The whole house was behind the book proposal, she said.

On October 21, with contract negotiations under way, I wrote to the medical superintendent of Oak Ward at Napsbury Hospital, inquiring about the health of Françoise d'Orléans and asking whether it would be possible for me to visit her.

A few weeks later, having received no word from the hospital, I wrote to "the princess." I told her of the planned book and briefly described what I and its publisher were trying to do for her. I also told her that I'd tried to see her after her fall, but had been unable to; and that I'd greatly enjoy meeting her. Knowing that my letter might be screened, and not knowing if Opal was capable of responding in writing, I concluded: "I would be very grateful if you could let me know that you've received this letter, and also whether or not you're able to receive visitors."

There was no reply.

Three days after I wrote to her, a letter from her psychiatrist arrived, in response to my October inquiry to the medical superintendent. He wrote that the hospital received a letter similar to my own about once a month, but that "the princess" was old and delicate, and was therefore unable to decide for herself whom she wished to see — so the decision had been made for her in the middle of the previous year to allow visiting only by her closest friends. He assured me that she was being given the best attention. He declined my request.

On December 9, I sent a reply to the doctor, informing him that I was completing a sympathetic biography of Opal, and that I would like to tell her of plans for republishing her diary. "It seems to me," I wrote, "that at this time in her life, she could do with a few words of cheer and appreciation. And it seems clear that this is quite likely the last chance for me to offer them." I assured him that I did not intend to intrude in the touchy areas of her past but merely wished to be allowed "this once in a lifetime opportunity to meet her."

Two days after Christmas, a bluntly worded letter from

Opal's psychiatrist arrived, again denying me permission to visit. After reading it, I no longer had the slightest doubt regarding the attitude of the guardians of Opal Whiteley toward a meeting between her and her biographer.

I thought over my alternatives of action for the weeks ahead: I could go to England and make a fresh attempt to see "the princess," with little chance of succeeding; or I could complete the manuscript. I wanted to do the former, if only to know that once again I'd tried. But if the book was going to be released on schedule, in reality I had no choice. I had a deadline to meet, last-minute research to do, and various manuscript-related chores to perform.

I also had to rebuild my health. For in November, my usually overabundant energy gave way as the result of over two years of pushing myself harder than the human mind and body can be pushed. My nervous system had given me several warnings of what it would do if I didn't slow my pace, but I ignored them. Finally, it shut itself down. On my way to an appointment one morning, I collapsed with vertigo, numbness, and a racing pulse, and was taken to the hospital in an ambulance. Travel was going to have to wait. So, at first with reluctance and then with pleasure, I turned my attention to energy recovery, and the completion of the book.

A few weeks later, I found to my surprise that I was able to turn in the manuscript and photographs several days before the deadline. And . . .

By-and-by, I did have better feels. And today my feels are all right . . . and I am going on an exploration trip.

I decided to go to England.

On the cold, windy morning of March 28, I arrived at Napsbury Hospital. I had with me a letter from my editor, to be hand-delivered to "the princess," and a copy of a letter she had sent to the hospital administrators a few days before, attesting to my good intentions and supporting my request to see Opal. After considering what had happened on my previous attempt, I decided first to try visiting Oak Ward, Opal's long-term quarters at Napsbury. If I got turned away there, I reasoned, I could then go to the administration. But if I was stopped at the beginning by the administration, I couldn't very well go on.

I walked around the last building of the complex until I found an unlocked door. Two flights up, I came to a door labeled OAK WARD. It, too, was unlocked. In what seemed to be the common room, a few sedated-looking elderly patients sat staring at a television set showing a program on traditional Japan. The red and gold kimono worn by the show's hostess contrasted dramatically with the drabness of the hospital room; the sounds of Japanese instruments echoed strangely from the high walls and ceiling. On a bulletin board by the door, a large sign read: THE MONTH IS MARCH. THE DAY IS FRIDAY. THE DATE IS 28.

"May I help you?" someone asked. In a corner of the room sat a group of nurses. I told them I'd come to see Françoise d'Orléans. "She's been moved to Rosemary," one replied, "the building across the way." "Is she allowed visitors?" I asked. "No," said one nurse. "Sometimes she is and sometimes she isn't," said another.

Across the road was Rosemary — a long, low, rather sinister-looking structure set far back on a grassy rise. The wind whined around the corner of the building as I approached. I tried what I thought might be the entrance; it was locked. I went to another door and knocked when I saw some movement behind a curtain. Two nurses appeared at the door's window. "Yes?" one yelled through the glass. "I'm here to see Françoise d'Orléans," I shouted. "You can't see her. I'm not allowed to tell you how she is." "I've come to give her a letter," I yelled, holding it out. "Post it," the nurse yelled back. "This will help to explain." I took out the copy of my editor's letter to the hospital and held it up for her to see. "Have you received a reply?" she yelled. "No. This was only sent a few days ago." She asked my name. I told her. She seemed to consult with the other nurse, then shouted back, "You can't see her." "Can't you just read this letter?" I pleaded, but her reply was lost in the rising wind. "I can't hear you!" She shouted "goodbye," then turned away.

I walked to the administration building. Unsure which of the hall doors led to offices, I asked a security guard who had just stepped out of one of the rooms. "There's no one there," he said. I asked if there was anyone I could talk to about seeing a patient. He told me that there would be no one in the offices until Tuesday. "It's Good Friday, you know. They're gone for the holiday."

A few minutes later, I was just starting lunch at the hospital cafeteria when the guard I'd talked to came up to my table. "You're the one who inquired for the administration, aren't you?" he asked. I said I was. "I've been told that you went to Rosemary Ward just now to see a patient." "That's right," I said. "Can you tell me why you wish to see her?" he asked. "I'm writing a book about her," I replied. He asked my name. I told him. "You're not allowed on the premises," he said. "You'll have to pack up and leave." "I can't finish my lunch?" I asked, incredulous. "You'll have to leave now," he insisted. "This is not a public cafeteria. It's for hospital staff and approved visitors." "All right," I said, putting away my notes of the day. "Thought you'd sneak round on a holiday when the administration was gone, did you?" he asked sarcastically. "I've just come from the States," I answered, "and this is the first day I could get out here." If I wanted to "sneak round," I thought, I wouldn't ask a security guard how to get to the administration offices. It seemed futile to mention that where I'd come from it was not exactly customary for entire hospital administrative staffs to take four-day Easter vacations. "You tried the same thing on Christmas, didn't you?" he went on. "No, I didn't," I replied, beginning to tire of the conversation. "Must have been somebody else, then." I asked if I might finish my juice. "Yes," he said, "finish it, then go." I was glad to.

On Tuesday, the first of April, I returned to Napsbury and asked to speak to someone official about Françoise d'Orléans. I was escorted into an office and introduced to one of the administrators. He showed me a copy of the letter he'd written to my editor on March 24, which stated that Opal was in too delicate a condition to receive visitors. "I can give you a report from her ward if you'd like," he said. "Certainly," I replied, surprised by the offer. He dialed a number and conversed with someone, apparently Opal's nurse. He made notes as he listened. I watched his hand write *deaf*. Then it wrote *going blind*. After he hung up, he told me.

"My publisher sent her an appreciative letter a few days ago," I told him. "Would she have an idea of what it said?" "No," he answered. "I don't think she'd have been told about it. I don't think she'd be able to understand."

"Several people have visited her in the recent past," he said. "Americans, most of them. But we had to put a stop to it because of her health. It's too bad you couldn't have come six months ago." "When I came to see her in January 1985 —" I began. "I said six months," he interrupted, "but it might have been more than that."

I left Napsbury feeling both informed and confused. I'd first written to the hospital a year and a half ago. Surely in all that time there could have been an opportunity for a brief visit . . . Something else was bothering me as well. Although I realized that I had little chance of finding out about it for certain, I decided to try one last source of information.

I went to see Opal's psychiatrist at his office in Watford General Hospital. I asked his secretary if he could talk to me about a patient, then I sat down in the waiting area, where a young man was carrying on a conversation with himself.

The doctor came out and I introduced myself. I told him that I'd been trying to see Françoise d'Orléans at Napsbury since 1984, and that over the past few months I'd gotten the impression that other people had visited her while my requests were being ignored or turned down. "We allow only relatives," he replied, "and close friends who come to see her regularly. That's a policy that we have, and we've had it for two years. She's a very elderly lady, she's in a very poor mental state, she doesn't even seem to know the ward staff, and she's nearly blind. We had to make a policy about visitors." I mentioned someone who had talked to her in September 1984. "That was when she broke her hip and was transferred temporarily to another hospital, out of my care. Another doctor had the responsibility, and he must have let him come in. But now she's grown older . . . We have to make the decisions for her. There are all sorts of consequences that could result from people coming to see her. She gets no benefit from the experience, because she doesn't understand what's going on."

The conversation ended. As I walked to the door, I heard a voice behind me. "Unfair!" it said. I turned around and saw the young man from the waiting area coming up to me. "He should have let you see the lady," he remarked. He expressed some negative opinions of the doctor's therapy. "I wouldn't know about that," I said. "And I'm not sure what to think about the whole situation."

As the train sped back to London, the clacking of the rails seemed to be echoing my thoughts. *Too late, too late, too late*, it seemed to say. If I'd only come sooner . . . What might have happened then? I didn't know, never would know. All I knew was that someone I loved was dying, and that there was nothing I could now do to let her know that her life had not been spent in vain. I felt exhausted. All this, I thought, for *nothing*.

"What would I have said to her?" I wondered. I closed my eyes, imagining. The train and its noises faded away, and I saw myself standing before an old woman in a hospital bed. I leaned over and took her hand.

"*Bonjour*, Princess. I've been an admirer of yours since I first read *The Story of Opal*. I've been doing what I can to prove that your diary was authentic, and to disprove the many false things that have been written about it and you.

"In my search for the truth about you and your writing, I've talked to people you taught when they were little children. They say they haven't forgotten what they learned from you many years ago. They say you changed their lives, by changing their ways of seeing and thinking, and helped them to understand and appreciate the world around them. I'm sure that these people won't be the only ones to benefit. Your ways of teaching are destined to be applied in schools and homes across America, and eventually around the world.

"In a few months, the published portion of your childhood diary will be released again, sixty-five years after it went out of print. And this time the skeptics won't be able to stop it. Now, at last, we'll see what it can do.

"*Bon courage*, Princess. You will be remembered as a

unique interpreter of the earth's wisdom, a perceiver and developer of children's potential, and the bringer of a new awareness to people of all ages. It has been my greatest pleasure to have been associated with you. I know that someday, somehow, we'll meet again."

AFTERWORD

OTHER BOOKS ON
OPAL WHITELEY

ACKNOWLEDGMENTS

# AFTERWORD

Few people in the past have understood Opal Whiteley. But I believe that many in the future will understand her. For she was more than a literary prodigy and educational revolutionary; she was also, consciously or not, a prophet — a forerunner of an age of harmony with the natural world such as ancient legends tell us once existed; an age that prophecies have told us will come again.

As certain people receptive to the earth's communications already know, extraordinary changes in the planet's character are approaching. To a minor extent, they have already begun: The migration of various animals beyond their normal territories; the alteration of weather patterns; the changing of ocean temperatures and currents; the reactivation of long-dormant volcanoes; the shifting of the earth's surface at strategic points — all of these activities are hints or warnings of what will be taking place, and where. At present, mainstream Western science considers them "unexplainable phenomena." But mainstream Western science fails to see the planet as an organism with a life and spirit of its own, a being capable of sending messages; therefore, it does not recognize the pattern of what the earth is saying.

For centuries, the planetary changes taking place and others yet to come have been predicted by seers around the world, some of the most accurate of whom have been found among the native inhabitants of North America. But due to ignorance, bigotry, and insensitivity to their environment, many followers of certain religions have interpreted the prophecies as indications that their own groups will be

357

saved from the coming wrath of an avenging God, and that others will perish. Consequently, the societies upon which these people exert an influence will be ill prepared to deal with the transformations. In reality the predictions, and the wisdom behind them, are not the exclusive property of any one religion or denomination. For the past several years, the earth has been helping all of us to realize what the prophecies refer to, and to understand what we need to do in order to ease the transition between the old age and the new.

It is my understanding of the various predictions, and the signs of the natural world, that over the next few years, our planet will act to eliminate mankind's destructive technologies and the unbalanced social and economic systems that perpetuate their application. Its actions will be taken for its own survival and that of the human race, drastic though some of those actions may appear to many minds. By its signals, it is telling us now that we need to remove the containers of radioactive wastes and industrial chemicals from the oceans, earthquake zones, and groundwater-feeding areas into which they have been placed, before these poisons are released by the earth's activities into the surrounding environment and destroy animal life on earth — including that of our own species — forever. By observing the natural world's clean-up operations — for example, by studying the biodegrading effects of fungus-secreted enzymes — scientists will learn how best to store and neutralize these extremely deadly substances, the proper treatment of which the world's industrial nations have neglected far too long.

If our planet's accelerating rate of change is the warning that many sensitive observers consider it to be, we have little time left in which to rearrange our priorities, and replace the dangerously outdated attitudes that are pushing this nation and its imitators to the brink of environmental, social, and economic collapse. It would be wise, I believe, to spend that time applying the values expressed in the writings of Opal Whiteley.

358

In this adolescents-and-adults-only society of unwanted, neglected, abused, and runaway children, of grammar school–age criminals, drug addicts, and unwed mothers, Opal speaks in behalf of the importance of childhood, the natural foundation of adult wisdom and happiness. In this Puritan-pioneer-cowboy society that has substituted sensationalism and glandular stimulation for emotion — that is deathly *afraid* of emotion — she points to the possibility of a more human way of life, a way of feeling. And in this hypermasculine society so worshipful of earth-pillaging *machismo* that even its *feminists* tend to be male-imitative, she offers a much needed alternative of feminine gentleness, flexibility, and understanding. Without these vital elements, there can be no civilization, and no future for humanity.

Opal Whiteley was doomed to a tragic existence, her destiny shaped by internal and external forces beyond her control. But against the dark background of her lonely life, her youthful writing stands out all the more clearly as a great achievement, the communicative masterwork of an extraordinary human spirit. Its message has outlasted that of other literary works of its time. It will undoubtedly increase in value as years go by.

In my imagination I see young Opal now, a dark-haired little girl in a blue calico dress, standing at the meeting of the roads. The wind is blowing through her hair. In her pocket is a crayon and some folded pieces of scrap paper. She is setting out on an exploration trip. And when she returns she will have stories to tell, in a diary unlike anything ever written, one of the most amazing creations in the history of the English language. And every time I read from it, I celebrate the victory of Opal Whiteley.

*Opal: The Journal of an Understanding Heart*
By Opal Whiteley
Adapted by Jane Boulton
Macmillan Publishing Company, Inc., 1976; Tioga
   Publishing Company, 1984
190 pages

In this adaptation of *The Story of Opal*, selections from Opal's diary are arranged in the form of free-verse poems. The book's afterword gives a brief history of Opal's life and diary, and the controversy surrounding (and obscuring) both. Like the author of the following book, Jane Boulton is one of Opal Whiteley's few supporters in the field of literature. After being out of print for years, *Opal* has recently been rereleased by Tioga Publishing Company, a small publisher in Palo Alto, California.

*Opal Whiteley: The Unsolved Mystery*
By E. S. Bradburne
Together with Opal Whiteley's Diary
Putnam & Co., Ltd. (London), 1962
293 pages

The first section of this two-part book is concerned with what its author calls the "fascinating jigsaw puzzle" of Opal Whiteley's life. Written from a European perspective, it includes quotations from numerous articles and letters not available at present in the United States. The remainder of the book consists of a reprinting of *The Diary of Opal Whiteley*, the British edition of *The Story of Opal*. Unfortunately, Elizabeth Bradburne's book has long been out of print and is very difficult to obtain in the United States, except through the Inter-Library Loan program.

*The Fairyland Around Us*
By Opal Whiteley
Presented by Benjamin Hoff
In preparation

Written in the summer of 1918, Opal's self-published nature book has never before been released by a publisher. Even some fond readers of *The Story of Opal* have turned away after a first glance at it, disappointed by its amateurish printing, inferior binding, makeshift illustrations, hurriedly composed and often excessively wordy text, overabundance of quoted poetry, and general lack of organization. But when I examined it, I saw hidden beneath all that a unique, timeless work that needed only a sympathetic rearranging and refining in order to become the enchanting book its author had intended it to be.

My accompanying essay includes biographical material relating to the creation of *The Fairyland Around Us*, much of it in print for the first time. It also contains an analysis of Opal's enormously successful approach to education, which was practically the opposite of that practiced in traditional American public and private schools, both then and now.

*Fabulous Opal Whiteley*
By Elbert Bede
Binford & Mort Publishing (Portland, Oregon), 1954,
   1978
181 pages

Readers interested in studying an example of the "exposés" of Opal and her diary have been given an excellent opportunity by the republication of *Fabulous Opal Whiteley*. Its author's Cottage Grove *Sentinel* articles, which furnished most of the material in the book, were among the first to dispute the authenticity of the diary.

Elbert Bede was editor and co-owner of the *Sentinel* from 1911 to 1936. He eventually became known as the man who "discovered" Opal Whiteley. But the "discovery" — that is, his first mention of her in print — was a noticeably belated and reluctant one. It took place in 1915, three or four years after he had witnessed one of the locally well-known prodigy's public lectures — at which, as he was later to recall, "a considerable audience . . . listened enraptured." It was not until Opal had been elected state superintendent of the Junior Endeavor program at the annual Oregon Christian Endeavor convention in Eugene that he seems to have realized he was going to have to write something about her, or appear inexcusably ignorant of a phenomenon taking place within his own area. So he put a little article about her in the paper.

A few days later, a story appeared in the Eugene *Daily Guard* describing Opal as a self-educated genius who was astounding the professors at the University of Oregon. Caught by surprise, it seems, Mr. Bede responded with a piece about "Opal Whitely" (*sic*), "the most remarkable little girl [she was then seventeen] the Cottage Grove country has ever produced." This was followed in a couple of months by a short biography, most of which had been written by Opal upon request. It appears to have been the last accurate description of Opal Whiteley printed under the name of Elbert Bede.

In 1920, when Opal became nationally famous, Mr. Bede began a series of "investigative" articles about her and her diary, the pages of which he never bothered to examine. His accounts were reprinted across the country, and fed what quickly became an enormous controversy. As public interest grew, he changed from reporter to cynic to character assassin. Years later, after Opal had been disgraced and institutionalized in Napsbury Hospital — and after it had become evident that no one was going to get her out — he wrote *Fabulous Opal Whiteley*, a book about which it might well be said: Let the uninformed buyer beware.

Elbert Bede's use of the following material can serve to illustrate his method of operation: In the second year of the diary, in what was printed as the thirty-fourth chapter of *The Story of Opal*, Opal described the felling of a large gray fir in the woods at Walden — a tree she called "the great fir tree." After moving to Cottage Grove, according to a letter she wrote in March, 1920, she visited her former home and there witnessed the felling of another of her favorite trees — her beloved Michael Angelo Sanzio Raphael, cut down to make way for a new barn. In the letter, Opal writes:

> His falling, and the blasting of the stump, is recorded in the [later, as yet unpublished pages of the] diary. I was at the ranch the day of the blasting, and got into trouble over the dynamite. The falling of Michael Angelo Sanzio Raphael and the blasting of the stump was one of the tragedies of my childhood.

On page 156 of *Fabulous Opal Whiteley*, we find:

> Several of the incidents described [in *The Story of Opal*] did not occur until after the family had moved to "the mill town" and away from the diary's locale. One of these [the only one specified by Mr. Bede] is the tragedy in which the great fir tree, Michael Angelo Sanzio Raphael, is felled. Opal, in a letter written while the installments of the diary were appearing, explained this inconsistency by saying she happened to be back at the ranch house at the time of the incident. She didn't attempt to explain away the fact that her seventh year, given as the one in which the pub-

lished diary was concluded, was by this time somewhat behind her.

In other words, Elbert Bede turned the gray fir tree in the woods into Michael Angelo Sanzio Raphael, then cited his version of the previously quoted part of Opal's letter (none of which he printed) as an attempt by Opal to "explain away" an untruthful incident in *The Story of Opal.*

After being confronted with column after column of this sort of thing in the newspapers, readers didn't quite know *what* they'd read in *The Story of Opal.* At the very least, they were left with the impression that Elbert Bede had access to a good deal of information unavailable to them. And many considered that information, whatever exactly it was, to be incriminating.

By himself, Mr. Bede might not have been able to cause much damage. But he was hardly alone. Unlike Opal, he cultivated the acquaintance of well-known journalists, authors, and critics, who seem not to have taken a very close look at his "facts" before passing them on in print under their own names. With such reputable backing, his criticisms of Opal had considerable influence. Over the years, they gained him credibility and praise, as they robbed her of the same. Today, the extent to which his claims were believed seems hard to understand, considering their relentlessly smug, patronizing, and vindictive tone; their factual errors and twisted logic; and their shoddy "evidence," which upon examination proves to consist of gossip, speculation, and matters taken out of context. But they were effective.

Particularly disturbing is the fact that Elbert Bede more or less knew who Opal Whiteley was, and was therefore in a position to help a curious public make sense of her. Instead, with the aid of other critics, he wound a Gordian knot of convoluted writings around her until no reader could possibly have understood her, and created a tangle so intimidating that it remained unpenetrated for over sixty years. But the complexities he contrived could not hide forever the simple truth: The published material he denounced as the fraudulent work of a scheming young woman was part of a secret diary printed by a precocious, schizophrenic little girl who read and wrote with great intensity, and dreamed of angel parents.

# ACKNOWLEDGMENTS

Many individuals and organizations provided me with information and assistance invaluable to my research. I would especially like to thank Thomas Vaughan, Glenn Mason, Marty West, Donna Allen, Ken Duckett, Hilary Cummings, Dan Kaye, Joyce Mill, Peter Drummey, Upton Brady, Glennie Scott Lojeski, Walter Scott, Dove Trask, Earl Stewart, Dorothy Chapman Stewart, Kathleen Moody, Ida Schurtz, Lela Ward, Sibyl Veatch, Elsie Patten, Jay Miller, Earl Black, Jan Bush, Howard Jenkins, Jane Boulton, Elizabeth Lawrence (E. S. Bradburne), Dr. Carmen Blacker, W. H. McBryde, Brent Lieberman, and Susan Swecker.

I would also like to thank the Oregon Historical Society; Lane County Historical Museum; Cottage Grove Historical Museum; Massachusetts Historical Society; *Old Oregon*; W. A. Woodard Memorial Library, Cottage Grove; Special Collections Department, University of Oregon; University of Oregon Library; Multnomah County Library, Portland; The British Library; and the Official Solicitor to the Supreme Court, London.

B. H.